Feminist Review is published three times a year by a collective based in London.

The Collective: Avtar Brah, Ann Phoenix, Annie Whitehead, Catherine Hall, Clara Connolly, Dot Griffiths, Gail Lewis, Helen Crowley, Nel Druce, Sue O'Sullivan.

Guest editors this issue: Mary Hickman and Ailbhe Smyth.

Corresponding editors: Kum-Kum Bhavnani (USA); Ann Marie Wolpe (South Africa).

Correspondence and advertising
Contributions, books for review and editorial correspondence should be sent to: Feminist Review, 52 Featherstone Street, Londone EC1Y 8RT.
For advertising please write to:
Journals Advertising, Routledge, 11 New Fetter Lane, London EC4P 4EE.
Tel: 44 (0)171 583 9855; Fax 44 (0)171 583 2298; E-mail jadvertising@routledge.com

Subscriptions
Please contact Routledge Subscriptions Department, Cheriton House, North Way, Andover, Hants SP10 5BE. Tel: 44 (0)1264 342713; Fax 44 (0)1264 342807; sample copy requests, e-mail sample.journals@routledge.com

Notes for Contributors
Authors should submit four copies of their work to: *Feminist Review*, 52 Featherstone Street, London EC1Y 8RT. We assume that you will keep a copy of your work. Submission of work to *Feminist Review* will be taken to imply that it is original, unpublished work, which is not under consideration for publication elsewhere. All work is subject to a system of anonymous peer review. All work is refereed by at least two external (non-Collective) referees.

Bookshop distribution in the USA
Routledge, 29 West 35th Street, New York, NY10001, USA.

Typeset by Type Study, Scarborough
Printed in Great Britain
at the University Press, Cambridge

ISSN 0141-7789

The *Feminist Review* office has moved.
Please send all correspondence to:
Feminist Review
52 Featherstone Street
London EC1Y 8RT

Editorial:

The Irish Issue: the British Question

FEMINIST REVIEW NO 50, SUMMER 1995, pp. 1–4

This is the fiftieth issue of *Feminist Review* and we have turned our attention, not before time, to Ireland. Since 1992 the project of *Feminist Review* has been to explore the interconnexions between the politics of gender, ethnicity and 'race' (see particularly the editorial of *FR* No. 40, Spring 1992) and our belated concern with Ireland comes out of this commitment. The London bombings of 1992 finally focused the attention of a feminist collective based in the 'metropolis' on the curious silence among British feminists on 'the Irish issue and the British question'. Despite the central importance of Ireland and the Irish to British politics, feminists in Britain, along with the left in general, have been exceedingly reluctant to address the ways in which Britain and the British have historically been the central agent in the shaping of Ireland and, currently, the struggles over the North. Crucially, British feminists have neglected the place of the Irish population in Britain. No doubt this reluctance relates primarily to the unresolved issues of the colonial and postcolonial relation – issues which many British people find it hard to confront, whether in the context of the African Caribbean, South Asian, African or Irish presence in the contemporary UK. The British/Irish colonial relation has its own particularities. It has been peculiarly extended – for the Anglo-Norman conquest of Ireland was in the twelfth century; and particularly complex – for Ireland has always been placed differently from other colonies on account of its geographical proximity, its white population and its position as the colony within, incorporated directly into the British state. Ambivalence and binary thinking are always part of the colonizers' relation to colonial Others and are locked into British ways of thinking about Ireland and the Irish. But the Irish have been both racialized and included, constructed as threatening and yet part of the British 'family', because they are white.

This is a joint issue, produced both in Ireland and in Britain. Many of the pieces we are publishing come from Ireland and we have relied heavily on the interest and generosity of women there. For this issue we have had two Irish guest editors, Ailbhe Smyth who lives and works in the Republic, and

Mary Hickman, a second-generation Irish woman living and working in London. The four members of the *FR* collective on the issue group are Clara Connolly, Irish born and living in Britain, Ann Phoenix, Vicentian born, Black British and of African Caribbean descent, Gail Lewis, Black British and of African Caribbean descent, and Catherine Hall who is white English. Such a diverse issue group brought many different voices and ways of thinking into what we hope has been a productive relation. This is the first time that *Feminist Review* has been jointly produced with women outside of Britain and we hope that this may be a pattern which we can develop. It seems particularly important that our attempts to rethink the postcolonial world should be informed from the different places of the erstwhile empire, from both the ex-colonies and the so-called metropolis. This is not to abrogate responsibility but in recognition of the partial understanding which is likely from only one of the different sites of empire. The diasporic identities which seem to hold promise for the future and break with the imagined binaries of the past have to be struggled over and constructed rather than assumed. That struggle focuses on, to name only some of the processes, issues around essentialism, the claim for rights to certain national identities and the tensions internally within diasporic communities about what it means to belong where, and indeed what it means to belong in several places.

As a collective we have certainly faced difficulties with this issue which in part derive from aspects of the postcolonial relation. Historic tensions overlaid with *Feminist Review* practices have been played out in the ways in which we in London have dealt with authors and issues, have caused offence through carelessness, lack of understanding and political differ-ences. The erasure of Irish questions in British political life has meant that, for some of us, working on the issue has been an overdue political education in itself. It has filled in gaps which we should have filled long ago, made us more aware, but only through uncomfortable recognitions of inflections which we have not understood, and cross-currents which we were unprepared for.

Since the eighteenth century the Irish have been the largest migrant group in Britain and the questions which arise around 'race' and ethnicity in that context have been central to our thinking. The construction of a narrative of homogeneity around whiteness in Britain has obscured the full recognition of racialized exclusions and the ways in which they are gendered. The Irish have always had their own kind of 'special relation-ship' in Britain (and 'special relationships' are often fraught with difficulty and power imbalances), a relationship which again most British feminists have been slow to address. Second-generation Irish women and men in Britain have had to construct identities in the face of fierce stereotyping and racist practices – this has effects at every level, on the ways in which Irish people 'here' relate to Irish people 'there', on the ways in which both groups relate to those they construct as representatives of the British state/ nation, in all their diversity, and indeed how diverse populations in Britain relate to the Irish.

The British state has formulated Ireland as a British concern and assumes that it alone has the capacity to solve Ireland's problems. However, in practice, these responsibilities have never been taken on. In British popular discourse there is both a sense of being historically caught in the colonial relation and wanting to be rid of it – contradictory feelings which are common to the postcolonial relation. For it is in the nature of postcolonial relations that the ex-colonizers look back, albeit in peculiarly obfuscating ways, while ex-colonial societies look to a different future. There is a semi-amnesia about colonialism which characterizes British government and popular thinking about Ireland, albeit in different and contradictory ways. The government would now like to be rid of the boil which constantly threatens to burst, and which did indeed burst on the domestic political scene through various bombing campaigns in Britain. Ireland is a part of the colonial heritage, as indeed is the whole of the erstwhile Empire. It is Britain's problem and until that relation is better understood and recognized, it will not be possible for Britain's position to change, and for the British to move to a new kind of figure, a genuinely postcolonial moment.

Since the 1970s the Irish Republic has leapfrogged over Britain and looked to Europe, just as the 'modernizers' in Britain see Europe as the way forward. The Irish presence in Britain casts some questions over that leapfrog. The Irish in the Republic tend to cast the Irish in Britain as the dinosaurs, lost in the old society, while the modern Ireland speeds ahead to a new age. Yet some argue that it was the migrations of the 1950s and 1980s which, in part, paved the way for the reforms and regeneration which have provided the material base for the late twentieth-century republic. Women have, of course, played a critical role in these migrations and in the maintenance of connexions between the two societies.

The British have long constructed Ireland as a backward Other. This has been a staple of anti-Irish jokes for centuries. Britain, meanwhile, represents itself, in the dominant narrative, as a liberal secular state. Anti-Catholicism plays a critical part in this, for popular Protestantism has always been central to English/British nationalism. But the secularization which has been going on in Ireland for the last twenty years is significant here. Indeed, while we have been producing this issue of the journal, the

FEMINIST REVIEW NO 50, SUMMER 1995

Irish government has been toppled on questions relating to sexuality and honesty and the authority of both Church and State have been seriously challenged, events which undermine the dichotomy which Britain makes between itself and Ireland. The dramatic events in relation to the ceasefire and the peace talks, which again have transformed the situation while this issue was being produced, are not disconnected from these events in the Republic.

Feminist Review is now committed to an exploration of ways through the harsh boundaries of racialized identities. Our special issue on nationalisms and national identities (*FR* No. 44) and on ethnicities (*FR* No. 45) are part of that project. In thinking about ways of countering the cruel logic of ethnic absolutism one possibility as, already indicated, may lie in the construction of diasporic identities, which allow people to belong simultaneously in different places and in different ways. Our turn to Ireland is part of that same project, and this can only stand as a beginning. There are many issues not addressed here which we would hope to see addressed in the future – the voices of women from Protestant and Unionist communities are not heard in these pages, questions about the use of the Irish language have only begun to be explored, the tensions which can exist between first- and second-generation migrants, associated with such issues as the moment of migration or with positions on relations between Britain and Ireland are absent. Many more British feminists need to know about these voices and inform themselves on these matters. As our title says, the Irish issue is a British question.

Clara Connolly
Catherine Hall
Mary Hickman
Gail Lewis
Ann Phoenix
Ailbhe Smyth

Deconstructing Whiteness

Irish Women in Britain

Mary J. Hickman and Bronwen Walter

FEMINIST REVIEW NO 50, SUMMER 1995, pp. 5–19

Abstract

The Irish are largely invisible as an ethnic group in Britain but continue to be racialized as inferior and alien Others. Invisibility has been reinforced by academic treatment. Most historians have assumed that a framework of assimilation is appropriate and this outcome is uncritically accepted as desirable. Sociologists on the other hand have excluded the Irish from consideration, providing tacit support for the 'myth of homogeneity' of white people in Britain against the supposedly new phenomenon of threatening (Black) 'immigrants'.

Focus on the paradigm of 'colour' has limited the range of racist ideologies examined and led to denial of anti-Irish racism. But an analysis of nineteenth-century attitudes shows that the 'Irish Catholic' was a significant Other in the construction of the British nationalist myth. Despite contemporary forgetting, hostility towards the Irish continues, over and above immediate reactions to recent IRA campaigns. Verbal abuse and racial harassment are documented in London and elsewhere, but unacknowledged.

The masculine imagery of 'Paddy' hides the existence of Irish women in Britain, although they have outnumbered men since the 1920s. In America, by contrast, there is a strong stereotype of 'Bridget' and her central contribution to Irish upward mobility is recognized. But invisibility does not protect Irish women in Britain from racism. Indeed, they are often more exposed since their productive and reproductive roles connect more firmly to British society. Moreover, women have played a key role in maintaining Catholic adherence, which continues to resonate closely with Irishness and difference.

Keywords

Irish; whiteness; Britishness; racism; invisibility; assimilation

FEMINIST REVIEW NO 50, SUMMER 1995

A myth of homogeneity: the invisibility of the Irish in official discourses

In early 1994 an announcement by the Commission for Racial Equality that it had decided to fund a research project to establish whether discrimination towards the Irish in Britain exists caused considerable interest and surprise in the media, from disbelief in *The Sun* through to attacks in the *Sunday Times* (Irish edition). This article, focusing on evidence about Irish women in Britain, will examine the reasons why such a project should occasion the response it did. We will also suggest why more attention should be given to the experience of the largest migrant group to come to Britain in the past 150 years: Irish women (Walter, 1995).

Part of the explanation for the surprise created by the CRE's announcement, lies in the invisibility of the Irish as an ethnic group in Britain. This article begins by examining the contribution that historians and sociologists have made to rendering the Irish invisible. For example, historians of the Irish in Britain have to date mainly addressed the process of assimilation (the chief exceptions are a number of chapters in Gilley and Swift, 1985, Devine, 1991 and Fielding, 1993). The myth of the assimilation of the Irish is based on the assumption that, whatever the dichotomies of the nineteenth century, religion and national identity no longer distinguish Irish experience and any disadvantage or discrimination Irish migrants may encounter in the twentieth century can be explained by the location of the majority as members of the working class. The assimilation approach has specific contemporary political effects. It is based on the premise that racism is not a paradigm which is appropriate to explain Irish experience. Short of the intractability of skin colour, the assumption is that a major labour migrant group like the Irish can assimilate in Britain.

These historical analyses of the Irish are all dedicated to assessing the degree of assimilation the Irish have achieved and it is rare, indeed, for them to interrogate the concept of assimilation. They assume that the 'whiteness' of the Irish somehow makes the concept suitable. As Peter Jackson has commented about British geographers:

> 'Assimilation' is simplistically defined as the socially desirable converse of 'segregation', an historically inevitable outcome of a unilinear process of ethnic competition and upward social mobility. The advocates of minority group 'assimilation' rarely pause to consider precisely whose interests such a process would serve, casually assuming it to be a universally desirable goal of social policy.
>
> (Jackson, 1987: 5)

An identical critique can be made of many historians of the Irish in Britain. The assimilationists do not dispute the historical evidence that many Irish people in the nineteenth century were disadvantaged, often subject to discrimination and hostility. What is important for the assimilationists is to establish the parallel existence of other experiences which already presage the gradual access of all Irish migrants and their descendants to acceptance within British society. It is therefore critical for the assimilationists to establish diversity as the hall mark of Irish experience (for example, varied residential patterns). They thus assume that they are identifying the processes of and journeys towards assimilation.

Sociology in this country, unlike history, is a discipline that has barely addressed the subject of the Irish in Britain. This is because of the dominance in Britain of a myth of homogeneity which implicitly includes a myth of assimilation. This myth of homogeneity, developed in the 1950–60s, was generated both by the state and by the 'race relations' industry. Racist discourses about migrants from the New Commonwealth and Pakistan seemingly emerged in new expressive forms, sufficiently novel to be designated a 'new' racism (Barker, 1981). This 'new' racism was deemed to be concerned with inclusion and exclusion, with a concern to specify who may legitimately belong to the national community, and simultaneously advanced reasons for the segregation or banishment of those whose 'origin, sentiment or citizenship' assigns them elsewhere – the chief criterion used was skin colour (Gilroy, 1987: 45).

The sociology of 'race relations' rapidly embraced this 'new' perspective. While it is true that the amount of legislation to curb the immigration of specific groups of people was new, the assumption has been that the discourse of cultural differentialism which underpinned this concern with inclusion and exclusion is also new. Only an ahistorical sociology could support such an assumption. Unfortunately, most of the sociological literature proffers analyses of racism only for the period since 1945. The 'race relations' paradigm has rather unquestioningly accepted the myth of British homogeneity prior to the 1940s. The exclusionary practices of the 'race relations' debate have resisted until very recently including any wider consideration of racist discourses and practices other than those whose object are the various Black communities in Britain, with a few honourable exceptions (in particular Anthias and Yuval-Davis, 1992; Miles, 1982, 1993; Cohen, 1988; Brah, 1992).

This is understandable at one level because of the systematic racism and discrimination which has characterized the experience of different collectivities of mainly British citizens who have migrated from the New Commonwealth and Pakistan, and their British-born children. It is also

FEMINIST REVIEW NO 50, SUMMER 1995

explicable in terms of the specific strategies of the state which has channelled ethnic minority demands into a competitive system of proving their disadvantaged place in a league table of oppression. The critiques and struggles these experiences produced have necessarily focused on exposing and resisting a variegated racist discourse and diverse set of discriminatory practices directed at Black people. However, in many ways this has dove-tailed well with the concern of the British state to construct the problem of 'immigrants' and of racism as narrowly constituted and of recent origin.

Noiriel (1990) has shown that ideas of assimilation, uniformity and universality have been crucial in France for masking ethnic, regional and other differences. What discourses and practices of the British state have masked the internal ethnic, regional and national differences which characterize the 'United Kingdom'? Constructions of whiteness are one means. However, the reason for the absence of consideration of the Irish lies not only in the fact of Irish 'whiteness' nor only in the assumption that anti-Catholicism long ago ceased to be a significant phenomenon of differentiation, but, more crucially, in the fact that the issues of nation and nationalism have figured only obliquely in debates on 'race' and ethnic relations in this country. Consequently, 'colour' has become a marker of national belonging and being of the same 'colour' can be equated with 'same nation' implying 'no problem' of discrimination.

It is all too easy for 'whiteness' to be equated with an homogenous way of life. What is necessary is research on the deconstruction of 'whiteness'. This would, for example, entail examining the experience of the Irish in Britain in the context of the problem of constructing the nation in Britain, where colour is not taken as the only marker of exclusion/inclusion. Every nation-state is faced with the problem of how to make the people produce themselves continually as a national community (Balibar, 1991a). It has therefore been a main function of national cultures to represent what is in fact the ethnic mix of modern nationality as the primordial unity of 'one people'. This has been achieved by centralized nation-states with their incorporating cultures and national identities, implanting and securing strong cultural institutions, which tend to subsume all differences and diversity into themselves (Hall, 1992).

The Irish first came in very large numbers to Britain during the period which was most critical for the successful securing of national identity and culture in Britain (and by that means a class alliance), the nineteenth century. In that period the Irish were both the most sizeable and visible minority element in the population. Previous research has focused on the impact of 'strong cultural institutions' upon the history and experience of the Irish in Britain, in particular Catholic state schools (Hickman, 1990).

In this way the articulation of racism, religion, class and nationalism as forming the context for the experience of Irish migrants and their descendants in Britain can be examined.

Processes of racialization are historically specific and different groups have been racialized differently under varying circumstances and on the basis of different signifiers of 'difference' (Brah, 1992). What is lacking are systematic studies of how different racist ideologies have been constructed and made operative under different historical conditions. Balibar (1991b) argues that in France populations of 'Arab-Islamic' origin have been subject to a condensation or superimposition of the colonial and anti-Semitic schemas so that the imageries of cultural and religious rivalry reinforce each other. A similar argument can be made about the Irish in Britain: the colonial racism stemming from Anglo-Irish relations and the construction of the Irish (Catholic) as a historically significant Other of the English/British (Protestant) have framed the experience of the Irish in Britain. Anti-Irish racism in Britain has comprised both elements of racism: colonial and cultural; that is, the Irish have been constructed as inferior and as alien. Historical analysis of the complexity of anti-Irish racism challenges the presumption that there is something novel about the 'new racism'.

The critical period for this was the nineteenth century, the era in which a British national identity became a cross-class reality. One of the significant Others of the nationalist myth generated at that time was the 'Irish Catholic'. The Irish Catholic Other was significant because it intertwined both a discourse of the inferiorized colonial subject, and that of the Other against which English nationalism had pitted itself since the sixteenth century: Roman Catholics. The 'imagined community' of the British was a Protestant community. This remains a resonant formulation in at least three parts of the United Kingdom until this day: Scotland, Wales and Northern Ireland. Both anti-Irish racism and anti-Catholicism contributed to a complex categorizing of the Irish in nineteenth-century Britain and have shaped government and institutional practices regarding the Irish in Britain (Hickman, 1995). Within the Irish population in Britain it was 'Irish Catholics' who, historically, were problematized as a social and political threat. Thus it is important to locate the given significations of the 'Irish' and of 'Catholics' in British national and racist discourses and analyse how they have shaped relations between the state, the Catholic Church and the Irish in Britain.

These points about the nineteenth century are important because it is the history of the place of the Irish in Britain which is ignored by those who construct their notions about what constitutes an ethnic group, or about

FEMINIST REVIEW NO 50, SUMMER 1995

who is likely to experience racism and discrimination, solely with reference to skin colour. Those working within the paradigm of 'colour' have been unable to challenge the myth of British homogeneity constructed in the 1950s which specifically laid claim to the whole of the British Isles as sharing cultural similarities. The myth declared that Scotland, Ireland and Wales shared a common culture with England and consequently the peoples of these countries could be considered the same 'race'. These were the constructions of the state and did not signify the final assimilation of these peoples with the English. The construction of the myth involved pragmatic decisions about the labour market and about the constraints on legislation to control movement between Britain and Ireland because of the continued inclusion of Northern Ireland within the United Kingdom (see Connor, 1987; Hickman, 1995).

This was the myth that came to dominate official discourse. In popular discourse as shown in both parliamentary debates (the assertions of individual MPs), and in evidence from surveys of the period, the Irish continued to be problematized because of dirt, fighting, drink and as social security fraudsters (Hickman, 1995). Holmes (1988), in one of the few attempts to systematically trace Irish experiences in twentieth-century Britain, notes that there has been a tendency to write about the Irish in Whiggish terms (that over time there occurred a progressive assimilation and acceptance of the Irish in Britain) as an increasingly tolerated minority (see, for example, Rose *et al.*, 1969; Jones, 1967). Holmes cautions against such optimism. In a series of examples he argues that there is evidence of continuing hostility towards the Irish on the basis of competition within the labour market, perceived Irish responsibility for various social problems, and Irish politics and Catholicism. What is important about these examples is that they demonstrate that the anti-Irish sentiment evident in Britain today is not solely the product of the situation in Northern Ireland.

British responses to the Irish, if hostile, are often cited as justified given the campaign that has been waged by the IRA in this country. The reliance on a reactive model to explain anti-Irish hostility ignores the evidence of Irish experience in Britain between 1922 and 1968, and ignores the continuing resonance of the Irish as an Other of Britishness. This Otherness coexists with the myth of homogeneity; the specific conjuncture explains which is to the foreground or how they are articulated together. Irish people are simultaneously inside and outside the British 'race'. The designation of the British as an 'island race', which continues to resonate, for example in the Falklands War, helps to bind cultural and biological concepts of the nation. The boundary of the sea makes it necessary to include the whole island of Ireland within the '"British" Isles'.

The invisibility of the Irish in official discourse is one consequence of the construction of this myth of homogeneity. Another reason for invisibility is that the community organizations of Irish areas formed in the 1950s, as with those formed in the nineteenth century, are largely Catholic organizations. To a large extent religion masked ethnicity and hence rendered the Irish in Britain a 'hidden people'. The Catholic Church had developed a strategy in the nineteenth century which involved simultaneously generating insular parish structures and incorporating the Irish to national institutions while exhorting them to adopt a low public profile. The Church was funded by the state for this purpose and incorporatist strategies became part of the ethos and practices of Catholic state education (Hickman, 1995).

The exclusion of the Irish from the tightening-up process in the series of Nationality and Immigration Acts since the Second World War is usually interpreted as representing a tolerance and acceptance of the Irish, because they are white, in comparison with people of the various Black communities in Britain. Control of Irish people takes a very different form, however, and the fact that it does not mirror the strategies adopted by the state towards Black people in no way lessens the fact that the Irish are a problematized, targeted and racialized population. The strategies employed to control the Irish in Britain reflect the specificity of the relationship between Britain and Ireland to this day (for example, the operation of the Prevention of Terrorism Act; see Hillyard, 1993).

The stereotypes of the Irish result in verbal abuse and other forms of racial harassment. In particular in recent years there have been a number of well-documented cases of Irish people living on London council estates being verbally abused and physically attacked, including attacks on property and incidents where inflammatory material and excrement have been deposited through front doors (O'Flynn et al., 1993). As Cohen comments:

> It is worth remembering that most racial harassment involving adults does not take place in the context of public encounter in visible settings, but takes the form of grafitti painted on doors or walls, bricks thrown through windows, hate mail and excrement pushed through letter boxes, threatening phone calls, all of it the anonymous work of invisible hands. These practices not only have the advantage of making it difficult to identify perpetrators. They are designed to dissolve the perceived threat of the alien collectivity by isolating people in their home, to the point where they are sometimes too terrified to go out and seek help.
>
> (Cohen, 1993: 15–16)

Local authorities, such as the London boroughs of Waltham Forest and Tower Hamlets, would not acknowledge these attacks as constituting

FEMINIST REVIEW NO 50, SUMMER 1995

examples of racial harassment of Irish people. Other areas of concern reported by Irish community groups are: the operation of the Criminal Justice system; access to social security benefits; mental health issues and housing problems.

Gendered invisibility and racialized exclusion

Negative British attitudes towards the Irish are applied with the same vigour to both women and men, but the imagery remains masculine. The stereotype of 'Paddy' is strongly gendered and draws on notions of 'navvies', itinerant single male construction workers who lack formal education, and have congenital tendencies to drink excessively and to lash out with their fists in mindless violence. Cartoons depicting the Irish as ape-like, which were common in the later nineteenth century and have been revived in recent political commentaries on Northern Ireland, represent men (Curtis, 1971; Kirkaldy, 1979). Despite contrary evidence, IRA bombers are always 'men of violence'.

Irish women are thus invisible within British constructions of Irishness. In part this mirrors the shadowy place of white English women within national narratives. Mackay and Thane (1987) argue that in the late nineteenth century, when important elements in the English national identity were being fixed, women were believed to possess 'transnational qualities':

> The qualities of the perfect Englishwoman were publicly discussed, but they were not generally perceived as being specifically English. Rather they were those qualities – essentially domestic and maternal – believed to be universal in Woman. The ideal Englishwoman's special quality was that she practised these virtues in a fashion superior to women of other countries.
>
> (Mackay and Thane, 1987: 191)

Irish women were also strongly associated with home and family so did not transgress the central features of this identity, although they could be classed as inferior on the grounds of 'dirt' (Summerfield, 1989: 59) and excessive fecundity. As 'family values' have returned centre stage in late twentieth-century Britain, Irish women appear to conform to the ideal in contrast to the opprobrium heaped on Black women's single parenthood (Carby, 1981: 215) and the image of young Black girls as 'unfeminine and sexually overt' (Mirza, 1992: 15).

The invisibility of Irish women also reflects their marginality in the Irish national myth which emerged during the later nineteenth century, and continues to inform expressions of Irishness in Britain. After the Famine women's economic position was seriously weakened as the spread of pastoral farming removed their key roles in arable agriculture (Lee, 1978). Instead they were offered limited domestic roles, especially as idealized mothers, hidden within the home (Beale, 1986). This placing echoed the feminization of the Irish nation by masculine, controlling Britain, and the characterization of Celts as artistic, impractical and unreliable in contrast to rational, thrusting Anglo-Saxons (Nash, 1993). Suffering, caring 'Mother Ireland' and delicate, chaste 'Hibernia' were its internal and external representations (Wills, 1993).

Many Irish women emigrated as a direct or indirect result of their low status at home. The pattern has continued into the twentieth century and an extraordinarily high proportion of women left Ireland in the post-war period. According to Kelly and Nic Giolla Choille (1990: 12): 'Out of a total population of 769,000 men and 745,000 women in 1946, 1 in 3 had left the country by 1971. During the Depression of the 1950s approximately 409,000 people left Ireland.' The largest number of Irish women now living in Britain emigrated during the 1950s and early 1960s (Walter, 1989a).

By contrast with Britain, Irish women in America had a higher profile and consequently their own stereotype. 'Bridget' appeared alongside 'Paddy' – or more often on her own – as the archetypal servant in an American home or as the 'civilizer' of Irish households (Diner, 1983). Although women are also excluded from full participation in the public realm – Marston (1990) argues that, 'The bourgeois legacy of the gendering of public and private life with respect to government continues' – there were opportunities for Irish women to enter the labour market and become recognized as primary breadwinners in the nineteenth century. High demand for their services as domestic workers gave Irish women a place from which to observe American values and the means to embrace them, which was to lead the Irish community as a whole 'from shanty town to lace curtain' (Miller, 1990).

Striking similarities in Irish women's migration patterns to America and Britain, and their structural position in the economies of the two countries, highlight the specificity of British constructions of Irish women's invisibility. During most census periods since 1871 women outnumbered men in the migration flow from Ireland, a very unusual pattern. In 1900 they comprised 52.9 per cent of the Irish population in the United States, compared with 21.0 per cent of women in the Italian community (Diner, 1983). After 1920 there was an abrupt change in the direction of migration. Whereas 80 per cent of Irish people had crossed the Atlantic in the preceding period, more than 80 per cent now entered Britain (Kennedy, 1973). In 1991 Irish women in Britain comprised 53 per cent of the enumerated Irish-born population of 837,464 and continued to be heavily concentrated in the personal service sector, 34.6 per cent of the total in 1991 (OPCS, 1993), as they had since the mid nineteenth century (for further detail on the socio-economic profile of Irish women see Walter, 1989b; Connor, 1987). As in America, upward mobility of the Irish-born has been strongly associated with Irish mothers (Hornsby-Smith and Lee, 1979).

Irish women play a crucial part in the central paradox of Irishness in Britain, whereby inclusion within a constructed homogeneity coexists with racialized exclusion as Other. Through their productive and reproductive roles Irish women have always had wider contacts beyond the 'community' than have Irish men (Lennon *et al.*, 1988: 16). This has exposed women directly to racism at a personal level, but helped to conceal them as a group. As domestic workers they have been hidden in homes and institutions, often working singly or at most in small groups within a larger body. Mothers have had to act as individuals on behalf of families in dealings with state services, such as education, health and social services. Irish men, by contrast, have often been able to live in more separate group worlds. In 1991, 25.2 per cent were recorded as construction workers, many working in Irish gangs for Irish contractors and subcontractors (OPCS, 1993). British cities still have distinct streets of lodging houses for mobile and settled single men, and there is little choice but to spend leisure time in the pub (Walter, 1986).

Exposure at a personal level has highlighted Irish women's 'accents' – dialects and ways of speaking – the main source of identification of Irish people by the British. Many describe strategies for reducing their audibility, especially at times of heightened anti-Irish expression. One Irish woman, in her sixties, said:

> When a bombing or anything like that happens I say 'Thank God for supermarkets', because you don't have to speak, you don't have to ask for a loaf of bread. I do feel intimidated. I wouldn't want to get into a difficult situation, because I wouldn't know how I'd react. When I buy The Irish Post I fold it over when I am in the shop – and I like to buy it in an Indian shop. I notice myself doing all these things, very much so.
>
> (Lennon *et al.*, 1988: 175–6)

On the other hand the 'lack' of an Irish accent makes it doubly difficult for second-generation Irish people to assert the difference they feel. Yvonne Hayes, who grew up in London in the 1970s, asserts her Irishness strongly despite her English accent:

> Where you happen to be born doesn't make you what you are. Everything about me is Irish, my background, my people, everything, and that's what I am. I'm Irish.
>
> (Lennon *et al.*, 1988: 222)

Catholicism has also functioned both to incorporate and to isolate the Irish in Britain in ways that are strongly gendered. By substituting a religious identity for a national one in the education of the second and subsequent generations, the Church has assisted the construction of the fiction of British homogeneity focused around a common curriculum (Hickman, 1995). Because of their primary concern with children's upbringing, and stronger identification with the Catholic parish, women have had a special role in maintaining Catholic adherence (London Irish Women's Centre, 1984). However, the distinct and hidden social life of the Catholic parish, which provides the older generation of Irish-born women with an intensely significant pivot, removes them from British view.

Two women in their sixties interviewed in Bolton in 1994 described the importance of their religion:

> BW: Do you attend church regularly?
> Mary: We do, yes. The mainstay. It's the mainstay isn't it?
> Margaret: Yes.
> Mary: And the general things that go on around it, you know – outings, social life. We have a good community spirit round here in Astley Bridge, in our parish really.

Yet, for example, in Luton, where 15 per cent of the population was Irish in 1971, newspaper analysis of the *Luton News* in 1961 and 1971 showed no acknowledgement of the large Irish Catholic community in the town, although the activities of more sparsely attended Anglican churches were fully reported (Walter, 1986).

The invisibility of the Irish, therefore, plays an important role in the preservation of white homogeneity in Britain today. This helps to explain the vehemence with which *The Sun* disparaged the announcement of the CRE research initiative into anti-Irish racism. A whole page was devoted to dismissing the survey as a 'load of codswallop' (*The Sun*, 22 January 1994: 9). To give the researchers 'a flying start', forty-one anti-Irish 'jokes' were printed, headlined by one holding Irish male sexuality up to ridicule. Forty of the jokes poured vitriolic scorn on the slow wits, poor language skills and general stupidity of 'Irishmen' – 'Paddy', 'Pat', 'Mick', 'Mike' and 'Murphy'. Ethnicity overrode social class, the linguistic incompetence of an Irish doctor matching that of the tunneller and the labourer. Only one featured a woman, an un-named barmaid, shown displaying similar levels of congenital irrationality.

As Leach points out, the stereotype involved in Irish 'jokes' is 'not so much a figure of fun as an object of contempt merging into deep hostility' (1979: viii). Strong feelings of racist exclusion are being expressed, but these are simultaneously dissolved into joking parody, which deny their reality

FEMINIST REVIEW NO 50, SUMMER 1995

(Cohen, 1988). It is hard to think of any other group in Britain against whom such practices could go unchallenged.

Irish womens' relative invisibility within the stereotype does not protect them from the consequences of this racialized exclusion. Irish nurses have reported being the object of racist attitudes from British people involving assumptions about the stupidity of the Irish and their presumed support for political violence (Walter, 1989b). One Irish woman described her initial experience in England in the 1960s, in the following terms:

> I never knew the English hated us (the Irish!). *I* did not hate *them*! I could not understand the hostility I received – I was not prepared for it. For example, I had to listen to people telling me how thick and stupid the Irish were. I was always told – and made to feel – that I was different. The jokes on the telly and everywhere reinforced this negative attitude. I felt isolated, and seriously thought about going back home.
>
> (London Irish Women's Centre, 1984: 9)

This extract makes clear that despite the official myth of homogeneity, being English was still about not being Irish, and being Irish continued to represent both inferiority and difference within English culture.

Acknowledgement

Bronwen Walter would like to acknowledge support by ESRC Research Grant R000234790.

Notes

Mary J. Hickman is Director of the Irish Studies Centre at the University of North London. She is currently directing a research project for the Commission for Racial Equality about discrimination and the Irish community in Britain. In 1995 her book for Avebury Press, *Religion, Class and Identity*, will be published; this is a study of the British State, the Catholic Church and the Irish in Britain.

Bronwen Walter is Senior Lecturer in Geography at Anglia Polytechnic University, Cambridge. Her main research interest is in Irish women's migration to Britain. She is Senior Research Associate for the Commission for Racial Equality initiative on discrimination and the Irish community in Britain.

References

ANTHIAS, Floya and YUVAL-DAVIS, Nira (1992) *Racialised Boundaries: Race, Nation, Gender, Colour and Class and the Anti-racist Struggle* London: Routledge.

BALIBAR, Etienne (1991a) 'Racism and nationalism' in Balibar, Etienne and Wallerstein, Immanuel, *Race, Nation, Class: Ambiguous Identities* London: Verso.

—— (1991b) 'Racism and politics in Europe today' *New Left Review* No. 186, March/April.

BARKER, Martin (1981) *The New Racism* London: Junction Books.

BEALE, Jenny (1986) *Women in Ireland: Voices of Change* London: Macmillan.

BRAH, Avtah (1992) 'Difference, diversity and differentiation' in **Donald** and **Rattansi** (1992).

CARBY, Hazel (1981) 'White women listen! Black feminism and the boundaries of sisterhood' in Centre for Contemporary Cultural Studies (1981) *The Empire Strikes Back: Race and Racism in '70s Britain* London: Hutchinson: 212–35.

COHEN, Philip (1988) 'The perversions of inheritance: studies in the making of multi-racist Britain' in Cohen, Philip and Bains, Harwant (editors), *Multi-racist Britain* London: Macmillan: 9–118.

—— (1993) *Homes Rules* London: The New Ethnicities Unit, University of East London.

CONNOR, Tom (1987) *The London Irish* London: London Strategic Policy Unit, Greater London Council.

CURTIS, L. Perry (1971) *Apes and Angels: the Irishman in Victorian Caricature* Washington: Smithsonian Institute Press.

DEVINE, T.M. (1991) editor, *Irish Immigrants and Scottish Society in the Nineteenth and Twentieth Centuries* Edinburgh: John Donald.

DINER, Hasia (1983) *Erin's Daughters in America* Baltimore: Johns Hopkins University Press.

DONALD, James and RATTANSI, Ali (1992) editors, *Race, Culture and Difference* London: Sage.

FIELDING, Steven (1993) *Class and Ethnicity. Irish Catholics in England, 1880–1939* Buckingham: Open University Press.

GILLEY, Sheridan and SWIFT, Roger (1985) *The Irish in the Victorian City* Beckenham, Kent: Croom Helm.

GILMAN, Sander (1992) 'Black bodies, White bodies: towards an iconography of female sexuality in late nineteenth-century art, medicine and literature' in Donald and Rattansi (1992): 171–97.

GILROY, Paul (1987) *There Ain't No Black in the Union Jack* London: Hutchinson.

HALL, Stuart (1992) 'Our mongrel selves' *New Stateman and Society* (Borderlands Supplement), 19 June.

HICKMAN, Mary J. (1990) 'A study of the incorporation of the Irish in Britain with special reference to Catholic state education: involving a comparison of the attitudes of pupils and teachers in selected Catholic schools in London and Liverpool' Ph.D. thesis, University of London.

—— (1995 forthcoming) *Religion, Class and Identity* Hampshire: Avebury.

HILLYARD, Paddy (1993) *Suspect Community. People's experience of the Prevention of Terrorism Acts in Britain* London: Pluto Press.

HOLMES, Colin (1988) *John Bull's Island. Immigration and British Society, 1871–1971* Basingstoke, Hampshire and London: Macmillan.

HORNSBY-SMITH, Michael and LEE, Ray (1979) *Roman Catholic Opinion. A Study of Roman Catholics in England and Wales in the 1970s* Guildford: University of Surrey.

JACKSON, Peter (1987) editor, *Race and Racism, Essays in Social Geography* London: Allen & Unwin.

JONES, Philip (1967) 'The segregation of immigrant communities in the city of Birmingham, 1961' *Occasional Papers, No. 7* Hull: Department of Geography, University of Hull.

KELLY, Kate and Nic GIOLLA CHOILLE, Triona (1990) *Emigration Matters for Women* Dublin: Attic Press.

KENNEDY, Robert (1973) *The Irish: Emigration, Marriage and Fertility* Berkeley and Los Angeles: University of California Press.

KIRKALDY, John (1979) 'English newspaper images of Northern Ireland 1968–73: an historical study in stereotypes and prejudices' Ph.D. thesis, University of New South Wales.

LEACH, Edmund (1979) 'The official Irish jokesters' *New Society* 20/27 December: vii–ix.

LEE, Joseph (1978) *Women in Irish Society: the Historical Dimension* Dublin: Arlen House.

LEES, Lynn H. (1979) *Exiles of Erin: Irish Migrants in Victorian London* Manchester: Manchester University Press.

LENNON, Mary, McADAM, Marie and O'BRIEN, Joanne (1988) *Across the Water: Irish Women's Lives in Britain* London: Virago.

LONDON IRISH WOMEN'S CENTRE (1984) 'Our experience of emigration' *Report of first London Irish Women's Conference* London: London Irish Women's Centre.

MACKAY, Jane and THANE, Pat (1986) 'The Englishwoman' in Colls, Robert and Dodd, Philip (1986) editors, *Englishness: Politics and Culture 1880–1920* London: Croom Helm: 191–229.

MARSTON, Sallie (1990) 'Who are "the people"?: gender, citizenship, and the making of the American nation' *Society and Space*, 20: 449–58.

MILES, Robert (1982) *Racism and Migrant Labour* London: Routledge & Kegan Paul.

—— (1993) *Racism after 'Race Relations'* London: Routledge.

MILLER, Kerby (1990) 'Class, culture and immigrant group identity in the United States: the case of Irish-American ethnicity' in Yans-McLaughlin, Virginia (1990) editor, *Immigration Re-considered* Oxford: Oxford University Press: 97–125.

MIRZA, Heidi Safia (1992) *Young, Female and Black* London: Routledge.

NASH, Catherine (1993) 'Remapping and renaming: new cartographies of identity, gender and landscape in Ireland' *Feminist Review* 44: 39–57.

NOIRIEL, G. (1990) *Workers in French Society in the Nineteenth and Twentieth Centuries* Oxford: Berg.

O'FLYNN, Joan, MURPHY, Dave and TUCKER, Martin (1993) *Racial Attacks and Harassment of Irish People* London: Action Group for Irish Youth.

OPCS (1993) *Ethnic Group and Country of Birth Tables* Census, Britain, Table 14.

ROSE, E. and associates (1969) *Colour and Citizenship* Oxford: published for the

Institute of Race Relations by Oxford University Press.

SUMMERFIELD, Penny (1989) *Women Workers in the Second World War* London: Routledge.

WALSHAW, R. (1941) *Migration to and from the British Isles* London: Jonathan Cape.

WALTER, Bronwen (1986) 'Ethnicity and Irish residential segregation' *Trans. Inst. Br. Geogr.* 11(2): 131–46.

—— (1989a) 'Gender and Irish migration to Britain' Anglia Polytechnic University *Geography Working Paper No. 4.*

—— (1989b) *Irish Women in London. The Ealing Dimension* London: Ealing Women's Unit.

—— (1995) 'Irishness, gender and place' *Society and Space*, 35–50.

WILLS, Clair (1993) *Improprieties: Politics and Sexuality in Northern Irish Poetry* Oxford: Oxford University Press.

Coming Home

Cherry Smyth

FEMINIST REVIEW NO 50, SUMMER 1995, pp. 20–3

Coming home is like dying
And coming back from the dead
All at once.
Time stops and time begins again
Where it left off –
Leaving at eighteen.
Here, time isn't pressing to go somewhere,
The last call, the last tube.
Instead it can sit and watch the waves rolling
Behind the raindrops running,
Being blown or flung
Or just clinging to the windowpane.

I see the sea from the house.
The dark blue rim at the edge of the sky
Is the circle round your eyes,
Flecked with yellow like marram grass.

I unpack clothes smelling of London.
Lulled by the tease of familiar voices
I still yearn for the anonymity of city.
Peace to read, think, eat, not eat, to swear,
Clutter, clatter, stay in bed all day
With the one I love
And talk about her openly.
There is no forgiveness
For escaping the rite of match 'n' hatch.
'No sign of a wee wedding ring
slipping on your finger?' they ask.
The spinster is come home with her fancy airs
And graces and new-fangled ideas.

Family engulfs me.
I search their eyes for myself

But see only the nice wee girl they want
Not the proud woman I am.

The tragic banality of my mother's days
Consumes me.
Concern, grim imaginings, laundry worries.
'But she could've been knocked down.'
'Och, sure he won't know where to find a thing.'
'Will you look at the state of this place?'
She demands me to affirm her martyrdom,
Her sacrifices, collude in her anxiety,
Ignore her sadnesses.

I look at my mother's face for the first time
Since I arrived,
As she futters away time in the kitchen.
A tired, sighing mouth, once full-lipped,
Her cheeks have sunk into mid-life hollows
As her children grew up and away.

I steal pieces of her past
When she's off-guard
And hoard them for when
She's no longer there to ask.
Tossing, turning and touching,
I hope that she can't hear in the next room
The sin of my self-pleasure.

I can never sit still in this house.
Never relax; never tuck myself away
Small enough to reflect.
Loneliness waits for someone to call
Longs for the times when small barefeet
Ran through corridors
Trailing sand and damp towels.

My childhood was full of light.
Daz-white fluorescent gleaming on Formica.
Frenchtoast for tea on Saturday nights,
When the whirl of Doctor Who
Sent us flying behind chairs,
Greetin' and gurnin'.
And then we'd queue up to slide down
The smooth, dark wood of the bannisters,
Hands and thighs warmed and squeaking like mice.

'Of course I'm staying in,' she'd say
Through the dark, but her strawberry lips
Gave her away as she bent over for a goodnight kiss.

This house is my memory bank.
Stuffed with tight rolls of goodies.
Photos, pencil-written stories,
Teenage jewellery with broken fasteners,
Rusty hairclips in drawers
Reeking of cheap perfume.
Once I've emptied all the cupboards,
Taken the last box from the attic,
Will there be anything more to come back for?

On the morning of leave-taking,
TV AM announced 'A man was shot dead last night
In Mag-here-a on the shores of Lough Nee.'
Ahoghill, Aghadowey, Magherafelt –
The sticky place names of the North
Get caught in an English throat.
Old meaningless conjectures
Woven out of lost tongues,
Evolving Irish-Anglo non-senses.
They call us British.
Stamp out our language,
Undermine our culture,
Swallow our pride.

Incessant boat people are we.
Forced from Larne to Stranraer,
Belfast to Liverpool,
Dun Loaghaire–Fishguard,
Limerick–Quebec.
Pale with separation
We drag slowly with suitcases and memories
To other lands.

Driving over Slieve Donard,
Emptiness deepened in the night.
Gossip ran out at Ballymena
Thirty miles more to the boat.
My mother desperate to know me
But unable to know how to ask.
Saying goodbye made me want to weep.
I did.

'See you soon,' I lied, guilty and relieved to part.
'If there's anything you need wee pet . . .' he said.
'Be sure and phone to let us know you arrived
safely now,' she said.
Her eyes watered but she never cries in public.

My fear was not of losing them,
Rather how to stop their tears
If they should let them fall.

Memories of Ireland are ice
And sunlight which falls
Down an escalator,
Always in the same place
Yet never still.

Acknowledgement

This poem was first published in *Frankenstein's Daughter*, edited by Sara Boyes, Stride Publications, 1993.

Note

Cherry Smyth was brought up in Northern Ireland and lives in London. She is the author of *Queer Notions*, Scarlet Press, 1992, and a programmer of the London Lesbian and Gay Festival. She reads her poetry regularly on the poetry circuit.

States of Change

Reflections on Ireland in Several Uncertain Parts

Ailbhe Smyth

FEMINIST REVIEW NO 50, SUMMER 1995, pp. 24–43

Abstract

The November 1994 crisis over the extradition to Northern Ireland of a paedophile priest was generally seen in Ireland as marking 'a watershed in the political life of the state'. It provoked unprecedented public interest, raised fundamental questions about democracy and appeared to crystallize the long process of state-church realignment which has been taking place in Ireland for more than two decades. This paper reflects on the repercussions of the crisis, from a personal perspective, and especially with regard to changing gender relations in the Republic and the emergence of peace in Northern Ireland.

Keywords

socio-political change; church-state relations; democracy; feminism; Northern Ireland; gender relations

> All around us, the old moulds are being broken, the old certainties challenged.
>
> (Editorial, *The Irish Times* 25.11.94)

> Long week when the dam burst . . .
>
> (Headline, *The Irish Times* 19.11.94)

> The events of the last week [. . .] mark a watershed in the political life of this State.
>
> (Holland, 1994)

Between two worlds

Where were you when the moulds broke? What were you doing when the watershed came? Do you remember the week when the old Ireland heaved up its soul and (perhaps) died the death?

Ah, which events, which state, and which Ireland? Why such eternally difficult questions? Will they never end in answers we can be living with?

But yes, I do remember.

I was between two worlds, outside my own place, from which rumours of bizarre happenings and momentous upheavals reached me tantalizingly, imperfectly transmitted through the media of a society which has problems understanding itself, never mind the world beyond. How much faith could I place in their reports of a far-away Ireland which seemed entirely to have lost the run of itself? I was beside myself with incredulous frustration. In the event (singular but plural), maybe it was no bad thing to first hear of these disruptions through the haphazard channels of unreliable media. It prevented me, at the very least, from rushing to cover up with orderly explanations what is, precisely, about the un-ordering of Irish society – a place where, it would appear, anything can and does happen. I heard, in chronological disorder, the following:

- The ceasefires (and there are two of them) were threatened, it seemed, by a shooting in Newry. A Post Office worker, Frank Kerr, was killed. Sinn Fein President Gerry Adams expressed 'shock and regret'. Republican leader Martin McGuinness said the killing was 'very wrong'. Nevertheless, it was a deathly and disquieting shot across the tenuous bows of peace.

- A Catholic priest in the west of Ireland was convicted of the crime of sexual assault against a young man. A few days later it was reported that the Gardai were completing an investigation of alleged abuse of a large number of boys by a priest in the south-east.

- A Democratic Left woman candidate won a by-election in Cork, against all expectations, signalling the dissatisfaction of the Southern Irish electorate with the (party) political status quo.

- An elderly Catholic priest sadly died of a heart attack in a gay club in Dublin, in the company of two friends, also priests. The headline of the front-page article in *The Irish Catholic* newspaper read: 'Church Must Not Bury its Head Now'. Hundreds of people, including his parishioners and the Archbishop of Dublin, turned out for the funeral.

- The Attorney-General was appointed President of the High Court, but resigned five days later. The Taoiseach resigned. The government collapsed. A general election or at least a new coalition government seemed imminent. All because of a child sexual abuse scandal involving a priest of the Catholic Church.

As imbroglio followed scandal in surreal sequence, the only certainty was that Ireland was in a state of great volatility. The depth-charges of change embedded in Irish society in the late 1950s were now erupting. For more than two decades, we (feminists) had been alternatively hammering and chipping away at the 'foundations of the state', and suddenly, those foundations were indeed being rocked, as a TD (a member of the Dáil) put it.

How could so much, and so strange, be happening all at once? And why now? Were these events symptoms or causes – and of what? Would life really be so very different after the watershed, and how and for whom? What were the implications for feminists of all this dam-bursting? What did it signify for and about relations between women, men and children in Irish society? Were there connexions between the uncertainties in the two parts of the island? And what might political turmoil in the South imply for the ending of strife in the North? Was the crisis the beginning or the end of a process of change – or somewhere in the middle? Which were the most important aspects of it all – the crisis in the Catholic Church, in the governance of the Irish State, or somewhere in between these all-embracing, interwoven worlds?

Could anyone outside Ireland make any sense at all of these socio-political convolutions? And why would they even want to bother? Or so I wondered, between two worlds. For what does it matter if old certainties are challenged, or by whom or for what reasons, in a small country of uncertain status in the 'new world order' (as like the old one as two new pins)?

The long week: the State

It hasn't all been a bad dream. Just seven days have seen the toppling of a Taoiseach, a Tanaiste, a High Court President and Government.

(Sheridan, 1994: 19)

I remember very well the dreams we had in our revolutionary days, and they were good dreams, not nightmares. Dreams of a world where male-defined and occupied power systems (I called them 'patriarchy' then, unquestioned, and still do, now subject to question) could be overturned and we would change everything, from top to bottom and inside out. Now, of course, such dreams seem naive and I have learnt that it does not do to recount them in public, still less to act as if they might come true. What then are we to do when of a sudden they begin to be realized before our very eyes? Are we now so PR (Past Revolution) that we have lost the desire and the capacity to seize the dream in the moment of its realization and shape it to the betterment of our material world?

So what exactly happened to shake the 'pillars of power' of Irish society? The catalyst for the crisis was a show-down between the leaders of the Coalition Government, Taoiseach Albert Reynolds (Fianna Fail) and

Tanaiste Dick Spring (Labour), over the appointment of the Attorney-General to the Presidency of the High Court. This was the same infamous Attorney-General who had initiated judicial proceedings to prevent the fourteen-year old girl, 'X', from going to Britain to have an abortion in January 1992, culminating in the abortion referendum at the end of that year (Smyth, 1992). He had also been a key player in the long-running tribunal inquiring into fraud and corruption in the beef-processing industry in 1993, when his actions had effectively shielded the Taoiseach from close judicial and public scrutiny.

The Tanaiste's opposition to this key appointment, while originating in the 'X' case débâcle and the Beef Tribunal, arose in this instance from his dissatisfaction with the reasons given by the Attorney-General for the seven-month delay in processing extradition warrants for a paedophile priest, Brendan Smyth, in connexion with child sexual abuse charges in Northern Ireland, and the cause of intense public outrage for over two months.[1] The Taoiseach refused to back down on the appointment and the Tanaiste and the other Labour ministers withdrew from government. The Attorney-General was none the less confirmed as President of the High Court by President Robinson, and a new Attorney-General.

Some days later, the Taoiseach apologized to the Dáil for the delay in processing the Smyth case, which he blamed on 'the system', and defended the Attorney-General's integrity and his elevation. The Progressive Democrat leader, Mary Harney, asked the crucial question – why was the Taoiseach risking so much for one man? – and got no sensible reply. The Taoiseach failed to mention in the Dáil that he and his ministers had been provided with information (by the new Attorney-General) clearly showing that the Smyth report was misleading. The former Attorney-General had explained the delay in processing the case on the basis that it was the first of its kind. However, it emerged that a very similar paedophile extradition case had already been promptly expedited by the Attorney-General's office. Later, an official in the Attorney-General's office was blamed for the delay. It was rumoured that this senior civil servant had been under pressure from the Church to delay Smyth's extradition. This was immediately denied by Cardinal Cahal Daly as an 'absurd' rumour.

Duirt bean liom, go duirt bean lei . . . (A woman told me, that a woman told her . . .)

Wednesday, 16 November 1994 was to go down as 'one of the most dramatic, bizarre, unbelievable and extraordinary days in the [history of] the Dáil' (Sheridan, 1994: 19). Labour signed a new coalition agreement with Fianna Fail – and unsigned it a few hours later; the Minister for Justice offered to resign; the new President of the High Court heard his first and only case; the new Attorney-General told the Tanaiste that the Taoiseach had known about the other extradition case all along; the Taoiseach promised that he would shortly reveal the 'full, full, full facts' of the whole affair; the Dáil was adjourned three times; rumour was chased by counter-rumour; media speculation became wilder by the hour; and the entire country was rivetted to their TV screens as the high drama of 'truth and dare' played out live before them. Coverage of the Dáil debates attracted over three times the number of viewers who tuned in for the IRA ceasefire announcement.

At the end of that extraordinary day, the Taoiseach turned his coat. He announced to the Dáil that he now 'regretted the appointment of the Attorney-General as President of the High Court', and said that had he known of the Attorney-General's 'oversight', he would have forced him to resign. The next morning, the Taoiseach himself resigned. The brand-new President of the High Court resigned. The political parties – minus Fianna Fail, that cornerstone of Irish politics – set about negotiating to form a new 'rainbow' coalition government.

So many 'oversights', 'misleading' statements, omissions, failures to mention and failures of 'systems', half-truths, non-truths, truths known but not told, secrets kept and betrayed, deals made and broken. A blueprint of democratic government at work (behind closed doors). 'There are times when language itself seems inadequate to the reality with which we are confronted' (Stokes, 1994: 11). And times when it is used to cover up realities politicians do not want to reveal.

The severity of the assault on the functioning of the state, at least in its parliamentary and administrative aspects, is clear from the breadth and depth of the fall-out. Key figures within the state apparatus were obliged to give a public account of their actions and their motives; mis-leading leaders had to resign; the decision-making processes of the supposedly democratic state stood revealed as secret, élitist, and of the most doubtful honesty. As the new Fianna Fail leader remarked in a radio interview (apparently without conscious irony): 'There are one hundred and fifty ways of telling a lie, but only one way of telling the truth' (see *D'Side* Dec 1994/Jan 1995). Through the widespread media coverage, Irish people had seen and understood for themselves the murkiness of state processes and the slipperiness of political truth-making. And they did not like it. The on-screen, on-the-page exposure of the 'wheeler-dealer' style of Irish politics was too explicit and immediate to be ignored. The direct insight into the real operation of power broke the undemocratic habits of a state's lifetime of so-called 'confidentiality' and secrecy. In an important article arguing that television was 'not just reflecting [these] events but driving them', Fintan O'Toole observed:

> While we have become used to the idea that television has debased politics, this time it gave real substance to politics. There could be no closed circuits and no private arrangements.
>
> (O'Toole, 1994: 1)

Although repeatedly described as a 'crisis of legitimacy and authority', it would be more accurate to say that the November 1994 upheaval was much more about the meanings and practices of democracy in contemporary Ireland. While there was much grandiloquent (and sometimes smug) bandying-about by politicians of words like 'accountability', 'transparency' and 'openness', one of the strongest public sentiments expressed about the Smyth affair, following so closely on cynicism engendered by the Beef Tribunal, was sheer anger at the discrepancy between the abstract concepts which define democracy and the actual malpractices and unethics of politics.[2]

In a recent discussion of the need for freedom of information initiatives in Ireland, Paddy Smyth suggested that:

> Moves towards freedom of information around the world in the last two decades have been prompted less by the wish to extend democracy than by political crises that have undermined public confidence in the 'impartiality' of the State itself.
>
> (Smyth, 1994: 32)

The Programme for Government of the (collapsed) coalition had in fact already agreed that serious consideration must be given to the introduction of a Freedom of Information Act, as well as to an Ethics Act for the Dáil. The drafting of both Acts was well advanced when the government fell, and will doubtless be pushed through all the more swiftly following the November events. The Beef Tribunal and now the Smyth affair have alerted people, in a quite unprecedented way, to the dangers of allowing politicians, a fortiori governments, to conduct their business out of public sight. As one of the huge number of callers to radio phone-in shows put it: 'A policy of openness is now the only way forward.' Seen from this perspective, the undermining of public confidence in the state and its institutions results in a demand for the strengthening of democracy.

'They are not outside the law': the Church

People have begun to think about the collapse of the Church in this country.
(Caller to phone-in on Pat Kenny Radio Show, 18.11.94)

FEMINIST REVIEW NO 50, SUMMER 1995

If the apparatus of the state was held up to public scrutiny and brought to book by the media and civil society, what of the Catholic Church? Was the Church willing to bow to public anger and media pressure to 'come clean'? Was the Church able to recognize that it no longer occupied its historical position of unquestioned power? To what extent, if at all, did the Church understand that if the Smyth affair had precipitated a crisis of democracy in and for the state, that affair sprang from an equally grave, and perhaps more profound crisis of authority and credibility for the Church? For as Irish people discovered the 'full, full, full facts' and the reality of the 'democratic deficit' within government and its administration, they could hardly fail to note the total absence of democracy within that other pillar of Irish society – the Holy Roman Catholic Church.

An *Irish Times* editorial entitled 'The Church in retreat' commented:

> There is understandable anger that the Church delayed and obfuscated in the Brendan Smyth case, instead of bringing the paedophile priest speedily to the notice of the civil authorities. There is incredulity among the public that the Church could somehow underestimate the horrendous pain and suffering involved in child sexual abuse.
>
> (*The Irish Times* 1.12.94: 9)

Remarkably, during the playing out of the crisis, the Catholic Church offered no account or explanation of anything at all. The hierarchy said as little as possible about the Smyth affair or about the sexual abuse of children by clerics more generally, until Cardinal Cahal Daly ('primate of all-Ireland') issued a lengthy statement in early December in which he absolved himself of responsibility with regard to Brendan Smyth. At no stage did the Cardinal, the Abbot of Smyth's order, or any other member of the Church hierarchy bring Brendan Smyth's (criminal) behaviour to the attention of the Gardai, and no member of the hierarchy explained why this was not done, or why it was not even thought of. 'Cardinal Daly's statements are far from the truth, the whole truth and nothing but the truth, so help me God. We are waiting . . .' (Graham, 1994: 55).

A lone priest publicly denounced 'the hypocrisy, corruption and double standards' of the Church, and its irresponsibility in 'concealing the suffering of innocent victims'. His statement was immediately rejected by a Catholic Press Office spokesman, who said that 'the bishops fully recognise that mistakes have been made and are devising a programme to prevent future paedophile offences (*The Irish Times* 2.12.94: 2). Recognition of a mistake, still less of hundreds of mistakes, is not the same as admitting that a serious crime has been committed. Various church spokesmen asked, incredibly, for 'compassion' and 'forgiveness', while admitting that they could be 'facing 200 charges of child sexual abuse' (Bishop Flynn of

Achonry, quoted in Graham, 1994: 55). In fact, in the few days immediately following an RTE television *Tuesday File* programme on child sexual abuse by priests in Ireland (29.11.94), the Dublin Rape Crisis Centre received about 260 calls from people abused by clerics, and the calls were continuing to come in. The director of the Cork Rape Crisis Centre also reported a 'huge increase in calls from elderly women who were abused by priests in their youth' (*The Irish Times* 2.12.94: 2). While it was carefully acknowledged that 'the child-abusing priests represent no more than a tiny minority' (*The Irish Times* 1.12.94: 9), perhaps '2 to 3 per cent of priests', the media noted almost in the same breath that 'less than 5 per cent of child abuse cases are estimated to reach the courts' (*Tuesday File* 29.11.94).

Eventually, the Cardinal pledged that there would be no church cover-up of child sexual abuse by clerics and promised help for the victims. But, as sociologist Tony Fahey commented:

> Unlike the secular sphere, the Church seems to have little sense that such things, essential though they be, are not enough. They have a mumbling, low-key air about them and lack symbolic resonance.
>
> (Fahey, 1994: 8)

The Cardinal's pledge came all of four years after the setting up of the Irish Bishops' Committee on Child Sexual Abuse. By coincidence (if there are such things in politics, even church politics), the interim report of that committee was presented to the bishops at about the same time the Smyth case became the centre of political attention. Why it took so long for the committee to ponder, and why they presented only an interim report, are not matters which the hierarchy deigned to explain. The Bishops' Committee report and the Cardinal's pledge also 'coincided' with the first financial settlement (for £75,000) paid by the Irish Catholic Church to a victim of child sexual abuse by a priest. In this case, the priest's bishop had publicly apologized, saying that the 'priest was genuinely sorry for the damage he caused, for which he acknowledged responsibility' (quoted in *The Irish Times* 2.12.94). But it was a case of too little apology, far too late.

On the other hand, what difference does 'sorry' make? Maybe, from the twisted depths of its appalling arrogance, the Church got something right. There is no redress which can adequately compensate for the hurt caused by abuse. Although the payment of money and the sanction of the law do signal the seriousness with which both crime and criminal are treated by society.

FEMINIST REVIEW NO 50, SUMMER 1995

'Ordinary people', or the 'laity' as the Church calls that separate species of non-sacred human beings, were angry. They would not tolerate the self-appointed right of the Church to place itself above the common run: 'They are *not* outside the law' (National Parents' Council spokeswoman, RTE *Tuesday File* 29.11.94). Priests had lost their sacred status and would have to pay the price of their criminal actions, like everyone else. The Church was just another institution within the state, and just as accountable.

Coinciding with a massive decline in religious practice (from about 47 per cent attending at least once a month in 1974 to 18 per cent in 1989) (Inglis, 1994: 23), the uncovering of the extent of sexual abuse by clerics comes as the (mighty) straw to break the deferential back of an already questioning and cynical 'laity'. In a sense, of course, there is nothing 'coincidental' about the process – the one is enabled by the other. Following on other scandals and the Church's attempts to prescribe 'acceptable' behaviour (and legislation) in respect of divorce and abortion, this latest scandal has very seriously eroded people's willingness to accept the Church as the prime arbiter of morality:

> The evidence of the opinion polls taken in the months since the 'X' case and its public aftermath show a growing recognition and acceptance of the social need for abortion in limited circumstances, irrespective of Catholic moral teaching. And there can be no doubt that the moral authority of the hierarchy has been undermined by the recent exposure of Bishop Casey as a 'secret' father.
>
> (Smyth, 1992: 144)

As revelations about the moral double standards and sexual crimes of its priests are made public, the traditional role of the Church in policing sexuality is inevitably discredited. It loses authority as the legitimacy of its power bases are revealed as flawed. The viciousness of the more-virtuous-than-thou has been exposed, not once, not twice but many times. It is not at all clear, however, that the Church has recognized the huge shift that has occurred in the kind of allegiance people are now willing to pay it. After the Bishop Casey affair, 'the Church spoke mild words of conciliation and contrition, and realised it couldn't preach so sternly on sexual morality, but gave no ground on the internal matters of celibacy and its authority' (Graham, 1994: 55). Whereas historically it was the Church that dictated how and what people should think (and whether they should think at all), the roles are now being reversed, with people increasingly making their own independent decisions, and refusing to exempt the Church and its priests from the principles of honesty and democracy which apply (in principle) within the state and civil society. And when people change their relation to the Church, the Church itself, qua institution, must of necessity be differently positioned within the power structure. The Church is now in the position of having to defend its ethics and practices, which are no longer taken for granted by the population as a whole.

> The days of the safe, cosy authoritarian Church are clearly drawing to a close. The Catholic Church in Ireland has to begin seriously the painful process of defining for itself a new role in a more secular Ireland.
>
> (Editorial, *The Irish Times* 1.12.94: 9)

I do not mean to suggest, naively, that changes will automatically flow in a secular river of democratic honey, but rather to stress that there is now the potential for a transformation of the socio-political landscape to a degree unknown until very recently. While the Smyth affair somewhat ironically points the way towards a more open and democratic operation of political power, it has equally produced the recognition that the Church is no longer a hegemonic force in Irish society. The Church in Ireland is in the process of being placed in a very similar relation to the state as that in many other Western countries, where it may retain power and influence certainly, but only within clearly defined boundaries, and subject to contest and challenge. In this sense, the crisis has served to identify and explicitly name the significant re-figuring of the complicated triangular relationship between State, Church and Civil Society which has been in process for some time.

But somewhere between these worlds, another voice tells me, something has been lost, forgotten, abandoned. The political implications of the Smyth case rapidly overshadowed its moral and religious dimensions. But then, unlike Dáil Éireann, no television cameras were permitted to record the mid-November meeting of the Hierarchy in Maynooth. Whose doors are most tightly closed?

Someone on one of the talk shows (I can't remember which) said that we were 'dumping Ireland's dream'. The phrase remained in my mind because I think we started doing it a long time ago – and definitely within my memory time. But maybe other things got dumped along with the worthless dream' What is it, I wonder, what really so 'outraged' us about the Smyth affair? The opportunistic dishonesties of politicians, the sanctimonious dissimulations of churchmen, or the fact (quite plain) that Brendan Smyth wrecked the lives of an as-yet-unknown number of children? A victim of clerical paedophilia, interviewed on television, cried bitter adult tears as he remembered his humiliation. Schools, he said, 'are a paedophile's hunting ground' (RTE, Tuesday File 29.11.94). But do we really go on remembering that, or all the other hurt and pain inflicted on our co-citizens, children and adults? 'There has never been any outcry about the children whose non-clerical molesters parade through the courts every day' (O'Faolain, 1994: 14). How really outraged are we, 'ordinary people', legislators, or churchmen, by the daily newspaper reports of violence of all kinds against women of all ages in all kinds of places, including their own homes? What is the real measure of our outrage? That, certainly, is one of the uncertainties.

Crisis, controversy and change

> A woman rang the *Liveline* radio programme last week to say she had nobody to point out to her children. Everyone was letting her down. Taoiseach. Attorney General. Priest. 'My children have no one to look up to except me.'
>
> (O'Faolain, 1994: 14)

It emerges plainly from the Smyth affair that Irish people are no longer prepared to accept without question the diktats of either Church or State. Either, or both, may be right or wrong, and each is equally liable to scrutiny by civil society. The days of blind faith and silent acquiescence are disappearing 'like snow off a ditch'. This is confirmed by the most recent European Values Survey which found that although generalized deference to authority is significantly higher in Ireland than in the European Union generally, it is much closer to the European average among younger people and the more highly educated (Whelan, 1994). Commenting in late November 1994 on the results of a survey of its readers (75 per cent of those surveyed were under 30), the editor of *Hot Press* said that 'a re-evaluation must take place if the major institutions of this state are to regain the respect of young people' (quoted in *Gay Community News*, Dec/Jan 1994: 2).

Of course, the Smyth affair did not suddenly appear as a full-blown crisis on the bright blue horizon of an autumn day to test the authority of the major Irish power blocs. On the contrary, it was but the latest in a long series of crises, scandals and controversies signalling the uneasy depth of the changes taking place in Irish society.

How many crises must there be before the worm turns?

The crisis preoccupying Irish society in different ways over the past dozen years have centred on questions of socio-sexual control. Abortion and divorce have been the most hotly contested (and internationally mediatized) issues, although they are by no means the only ones. Other serious controversies have erupted over the feminist exposure and condemnation of men's violence against women and children, exemplified in the Lavinia Kerwick rape case and the Kilkenny incest tribunal in 1993 (see, for example, Shanahan, 1993). During the 1980s, there had been a series of painfully controversial cases exemplifying the brutal misogyny of Irish culture (the cases of Sheila Hodgers, Joanne Hayes, Anne Lovett, and Eileen Flynn) (see McCafferty, 1984, 1985, 1987).

Virtually all of these crises and controversies have cristallized, and been concretized, around an individual case. It is difficult to say precisely why the expression of crisis in contemporary Ireland should be so intensely personalized. While it may have something to do with smallness of scale, it is intricately bound up with deep-rooted notions of sex-as-sin and sin-as-sex, and the concept of sin as an individual matter which none the less springs from and reflects back on the community as a whole. Sin is thus purged by the sacrifice of named individuals who are made to stand as the bearers of collective shame and guilt. It is highly significant that it is invariably women who perform the penance imposed through this process of public 'confession'.[3] Women are the source of sin (and change), so women must be made to pay the sacrificial price.

> They say we made a sinner
> because we made a sin
> with the evil diction
> of the mutual friction
> of the basest parts
> of our base bodies.
>   (Medbh, 1990)

The most divisive issues (and notorious, given the voyeuristic and often smug tendencies of the international media) have been around the struggle for the legalization of divorce and abortion, and the cruel effects on women's lives of the denial of basic human rights, cristallized in the 'X' case (Smyth, 1992; Ward, 1994).[4] The referenda on abortion (1983 and 1992) and on divorce (1986, and scheduled again for 1995) have been the most bitterly fought of the struggles in and through which the redefinition of Irish society is occurring. These issues bring traditional ideologies and progressive forces of change into headlong collision. In both instances – abortion and divorce – the traditionalists appeared to emerge victorious from the referenda, although with hindsight, their victories seem increasingly like 'holding operations', ultimately incapable of stopping or diverting the momentum towards a more liberal society. Interestingly, however, although the decriminalization of homosexuality was a slow process, beginning with David Norris's constitutional challenge in the mid 1970s, it was eventually achieved (in 1993) without the antagonistic viciousness which has marked the discourse of the extreme right on abortion. The relative ease of decriminalization has been attributed primarily to the new mood of expansive self-confidence of Ireland in the 1990s (Rose, 1994), evidenced by the election of Mary Robinson as President in 1990. However, the traditionalists perceive women's claims for (and partial achievement of) liberation as the principal destabilizing factor in Irish society, and have consistently and singlemindedly targeted *women's* sexuality and reproduction as the major arena of their war against change.

It is not easy to make convincing connexions between the many upheavals which have rivetted and riven Irish society since the 1980s, but that is actually what may be most significant about them. The disruptions we have experienced are precisely about disturbing the order established by history, tradition and habit. In so far as they clear a space for debate, these upheavals are positively healthy in obliging this society to talk to itself, across differences and divisions, about the meanings and values it (variously) considers to be important. These critical turning points have all involved a redefinition of (aspects of) the state, both in its *internal* relations with other institutions (e.g., the Church, business and industry), or with civil society (e.g., emerging interest groups and social movements – feminism most notably), and in its *external* relations (e.g., Britain, the European Union).

The Smyth affair was not so much a classic 'stand-off' between two equal power blocs – the Church and the State – as a critical moment in the realignment by civil society of the place of the Church within the power structure: 'They are not beyond the law'. The state, in the personae of political leaders, government and the administration, was required to give an account of its motives and operations and to concretize its democratic values: those who failed to deliver were unceremoniously removed from office. The Church, in the personae of both the hierarchy and individual priests, was exposed (again) as in breach of its own moral prescriptions, and was accordingly treated with an unprecedented lack of respect: 'Priests told stories of being publicly insulted and mocked [. . .], something that would have been unthinkable even a few short years ago' (Pollak, 1994).

The radical shifts in Irish society have occurred for complex reasons (see Inglis, 1987; Lee, 1989; Hussey, 1993; Whelan, 1994; Hazelkorn, 1994). Inglis observes that the growing dominance of the new urban bourgeoisie and the consequent expansion of the state led to the abandonment of the Church's ideal of 'a self-sufficient, rural society based on small-scale production in which family, community and religious life took precedence over the acquisition of material possessions' (Inglis, 1987: 217). At the same time, this shift produced increasing pressure to break free of the legalistic shackles of the Church. Ellen Hazelkorn, writing about the political implications of the Smyth affair, argues that economic transformation created a deep rift between urban and rural Ireland, shifting the balance of political power from the farming class to an 'articulate and self-confident' urban middle class. She identifies the growing polarization of

Irish society as the major source of the crisis, locating the roots of that process in the socio-economic changes of the early 1980s:

> Rapid transformation of the Republic's economy and its social structure, European Union membership and global media communications have widened the gulf in civil society between 'traditionalists' and 'modernisers' on issues like the North and the 'liberal agenda'.

(Hazelkorn, 1994: 16)

There is wide agreement about the rapidity and depth of the changes that have taken place, which appear all the more significant when set against the context of Ireland's history and contemporary image as an 'inward-looking, rural, deeply conservative, nearly 100 per cent Roman Catholic and impoverished country' (Hussey, 1993: 1). In point of fact, Ireland is currently ranked as the twenty-seventh richest nation in the world (*The Irish Times* 30.12.94). This does not mean, however, that the benefits of change have been equally distributed. High unemployment rates, continuing emigration and persistent widespread poverty bear stark witness to the 'incompleteness' of change (Hornsby-Smith and Whelan, 1994). Just as the rift between the rural and urban populations was a potent dynamic for change in the past, the repercussions of the growing abyss between rich and poor indicate a major trajectory of the late 1990s.

Analyses of modern Irish society generally fail to take account of that other major and on-going dynamic for radical and pervasive change: the shift in gender relations. The transformative impact of feminism and the Women's Movement on the socio-political, economic and cultural structures of contemporary Irish life is rarely explored in depth (but see Hussey, 1993, or Inglis, 1987). The feminist challenge to patriarchal forms of social control, in both their private (domestic) and public (institutional) manifestations has produced massive changes in the ordering of both personal life and collective social arrangements. For over two decades, women have been strenuously contesting the narrow boundaries of their social location(s). No arena is 'sacred' for feminism: family life and structures, personal and sexual relationships, reproduction, safety and security, education, labour market and political participation have all been opened up to critique and in-depth actions for change.

Women in Ireland are making their own decisions and articulating their (collective) demands in matters sexual, 'moral' and social. Despite the absence of divorce, marriage separations are on the increase and significantly initiated by women; the birthrate began to fall dramatically in the early 1980s, long before contraceptives became legally available on a broad basis; at least 4,500 women travel to Britain from Ireland for abortions every year; the numbers of married women remaining in or seeking to re-enter the labour force have more than quadrupled since the late 1960s; women are insisting on state provision of educational, training, health and childcare services. When the state failed to provide vital services in the area of violence against women, women established services themselves and have succeeded in forcing the state to recognize and (at least partly) fund them.

The absence of divorce and abortion and the persistence of poverty mark Ireland as 'backward' and Irish women as leading near-Neanderthal lives. While these continuing denials of human and civil rights constitute real and serious deprivations, the image of Irish women as European 'neo-primitives' is absurd and insulting and feeds into the maintenance of colonialist and racist discourses. Ireland, after all, is still one of the very few countries in the world to have elected a feminist head of state and to positively delight in her adroit leadership on social issues; we have a higher proportion of women in parliament than Britain, France or the USA (Gardiner, 1993) and, somewhat incredibly, employment law prohibiting discrimination on the basis of sexual orientation which puts Ireland at the forefront of homosexual legal rights (Rose, 1994). Most significantly, as exemplified by the Smyth affair, feminism has wrenched sexuality from the control of an authoritarian Church, and placed it firmly on the state agenda. Child sexual abuse is beginning to be taken seriously in Ireland, not because Irish people are particularly 'compassionate' but because feminists have insisted that women and children have individual and collective rights which must be respected in a democratic state.

Ireland is thus nothing if not contradictory and confusing. It is at once a developed industrial society, with increasingly secular tendencies, and a traditionalist 'anachronism' in the Western world. Both dimensions coexist in a state of volatile tension, which creates particular problems for Irish women who refuse the narrow roles allowed them by tradition, law and practice. However – and the paradox is more apparent than substantial – the obstacles placed in the way of women's freedom have meant that Ireland has a continuingly vibrant Women's Movement. Irish women are still subjected to ferocious forms of social control, yet far from reducing us to silent acquiescence, those very controls have served to fuel the dynamics of feminist protest (see Smyth, 1993).

The vitality of the feminist challenge is, at the same time, the very reason why it is subjected to such fierce counter-attack. In this moving realignment of gender relations, it is women who are making the moves and men (or traditional versions of masculinity) who are having to play the game according to new rules – and resisting it. 'Once you destroy the father-figure, the figure of authority, then you haven't got a society' (Jim Sheridan, talking about his film, *In the Name of the Father*). Thus issues of sexual and reproductive control are intensely divisive in the upheavals of a society painfully moving itself towards new values and practices. It was no coincidence that abortion briefly but tellingly surfaced as an issue during the negotiations for a new coalition government in November 1994, for it has become a highly symbolic marker of the power struggle between tradition and modernity, male hegemony and feminist liberation.

All this talk about women, and about sex – for women are 'the sex' – is deeply disruptive in a culture which has never talked openly or seriously, in public or in private, about either. 'Talk big, talk dirty, avoid sincerity and never reveal your heart' (Kevin Casey, 1994: 34). Boyzone Rule Not OK.

> Do you think your background will cause problems later in life?
> I mean sexually.
> Did you ever have it off with a wolf?
> You're too young, I guess.
> I don't mean to be disrespectful
> but, you see, we never heard the full story.
> A lot of people wonder about you boys,
> being brought up by wolves and all that.
> Do you miss them?
> Do you know they're nearly extinct?
> Would you let your daughter marry a wolf?
> How fast can you run?
> Say, what's your favourite food?
> Do you eat raw meat and tear it apart with your teeth?
> Well, I suppose that was quite common in Rome.
> Hey, thanks for your time boys.
> It's been real.
> You gotta learn to talk soon, boys.
> A lotta people are dying to hear about this.
>
> (Byrne, 1991)

Confusions and uncertainties

How could I forget where I was when the dam burst?

In mid-November 1994, I was in Boston with about fifty other Irish women at a conference organized (and financed) by American women. We were a disparate lot, with little connexion between the Northern and Southern women. The Southern group were mainly 'public' and professional women from middle-class, Dublin backgrounds – the 'liberal agenda' incarnate. The Northern women were mostly community activists and working class, from both Protestant and Catholic communities, with a quarter of a century of war behind them, whatever lies ahead.

Entitled 'Reaching Common Ground', the conference aimed to bring together women from the two parts of Ireland to talk about our differences and how we might overcome them. In the event, we did and we didn't. We talked across the dividing lines of class and religion, and even tried, *sotto voce*, to talk about why they keep us apart. What we didn't do was reach the promised land of 'common ground'. We glimpsed it from time to time in moments of discovery, exchange and pleasure, in workshops, midnight bars and Cambridge cafés. But did any of us (Irish women) really think we would do more? Common ground, after all, where it has been cut from under you by the ruthlessness of colonial history, cannot grow again overnight, or even in a week.

The ecology, conservation and exploitation of bogland is complex . . . Boglands can be dangerous; it is unwise to visit them alone or to walk on a bog, as some of the pools are very deep.

It was a difficult week, full of the wariness and tensions stemming from our complex differences, not least our different experiences of war and peace. Where some (mainly American and Southern Irish) insisted on enthusiasm, even euphoria, others (mostly Northern Irish) were more cautious: 'Everybody in Northern Ireland is holding their breath', as one of the Northern women put it. 'Peace is not normal', another young woman said. And it is disturbingly unfamiliar. After twenty-five years of war, a whole generation of young people in Northern Ireland have never lived in a state of peace. But no women in Southern Ireland have lived in a state at war. Peace and war cannot mean the same things to those who have known only the one, but not (yet) the other. Northern women told us so many times, and in so many ways, that it is a fragile thing, this peace. Unlike war, which is tough, durable, unyielding.

But when we listened, what did we make of what we heard?

So who are you to tell us what our peace should mean? What it should live like? How it should feel? Who are you to tell us that it will cost so much, and not more, that the $$$ and £££ must be spent on these things rather than those? How do you know anything about the cost of war and the price of peace? 'This is a peace very bitter to the taste', a Unionist woman said.

Northern women spoke of their anxieties about the 'peace process' and its provenance: 'We have peace by courtesy of the paramilitaries.' And where, they asked, is the process anyway if the brokers behave as if peace were a commodity to be capitalized on the world market? They were angry at women's exclusion from the 'peace talks'. What is democratic and open about a process that shuts women out? 'There is a seam of critical experience and commitment here that, at the very least, should be garnered through consultation. Women have plenty to say' (Rooney, 1994: 28).

In Boston, we made much small talk, but discovered at least (if we didn't know before) that talking about war and the wounds it leaves is both necessary and difficult:

> Two decades later, I listen
> look mostly in vain
> for signs
> that the wounds of the dead
> heal
> that children are not born
> with stigmata
> of those old bullet wounds
> (Smyth, 1990)

In Northern Ireland, the two communities (Protestant and Catholic) rarely talk to one another; Northerners and Southerners don't know how to talk to one another; North or South, the middle class doesn't bother to talk with the working class. In such untalkative circumstances, perhaps we didn't do so badly, after all, in at least trying to find the words to ferry us across the deep divides that have kept us in our separate states of mind and place. The habits of different histories and experiences are not easily put aside, even in a sunny Boston week.

> Many would not talk
> for fear
> of bursting the scars
> or fear of weeping
> or that I
> would put them on tv
> or twist their words
> to prove something.
> (Smyth, 1990)

I am uncertain about what we achieved in a week in Boston. But we did talk, and we didn't (on the whole) twist each other's words. I don't think we proved anything, except that our confusions and uncertainties about ourselves and each other, about the past, the present and the future will take a lot of talking to sort out.

Bogland, they say, takes a long time to regenerate.

Glossary

Dáil (Éireann) The Irish Parliament
Gardai The Police
RTE Radio Telefís Éireann, the National Broadcasting Station
Tanaiste Vice-Prime Minister
Taoiseach Prime Minister
TD Member of Dáil Éireann

Notes

Ailbhe Smyth is a feminist activist and writer, and Director of the Women's Education, Research and Resource Centre (WERRC) at University College Dublin.

1 Brendan Smyth, a Norbertine priest, was jailed for four years by the Belfast Crown Court on 24 June 1994, on charges of sexually abusing children for twenty-four years up to 1988. In early October, a UTV *Counterpoint* programme revealed that serious complaints of child sexual abuse had repeatedly been made against Brendan Smyth; that the head of Smyth's order had known of his abusive activities since the 1960s, but had sent Smyth to work in the USA without informing the relevant church authorities there of this fact. The abbot of the Norbertines subsequently resigned, acknowledging his 'grave errors' in dealing with Smyth's 'wrongdoing'. (See Pollak, 1994: 6)

2 A recent survey found that a massive 82 per cent of respondents believe that a 'sleaze factor' has now entered Irish Politics (*Irish Independent* 30.12.94).

3 Significantly, the only concrete sanction following the Report of the Beef Processing Tribunal was imposed on the woman journalist on the Granada TV *World in Action* programme which led to the tribunal. Ms Susan O'Keefe was charged with contempt for refusing to name her sources to the tribunal.

4 My focus here on issues of socio-sexual control is not meant to diminish the significance of the turmoil generated by the war in Northern Ireland. However, during the 1980s and early 1990s, that turmoil was experienced almost exclusively and most painfully in the North. The war did not generate *crisis* situations in the South, although it contributed powerfully to the sense of uncertainty and confusion underlying the process of change.

References

BYRNE, Mairead (1991) 'Interview with Romulus and Remus' in Dawe, Gerald (1991) editor, *The New Younger Irish Poets* Belfast: Backstaff Press.
CASEY, Kevin (1994) 'Glorious history is not for us' *Irish Reporter* 14: 35–6.
D'SIDE a monthly magazine published in Ireland.
FAHEY, Tony (1994) 'Government made the only atonement' *The Irish Times* 1.12.94: 8.

GARDINER, Frances (1993) 'Political interest and participation of Irish women 1922–1992: the unfinished revolution' in Smyth, Ailbhe (1993) editor, *Irish Women's Studies Reader* Dublin: Attic Press, 45–78.

GRAHAM, Bill (1994) 'Cardinal error' *Hot Press* December: 55–60.

HAZELKORN, Ellen (1994) 'Rotating round the centre' *Fortnight* December, No. 334: 16–17.

HOLLAND, Mary (1994) 'This crisis needs the verdict of the voters' *The Irish Times* 24.11.94: 14.

HORNSBY-SMITH, Michael P. and WHELAN, Christopher T. (1994) 'Marriage and the family' in Whelan (1994) editor, *Values and Social Change in Ireland* Dublin: Gill and Macmillan, 7–44.

HUSSEY, Gemma (1993) *Ireland Today* Dublin: Townhouse.

INGLIS, Tom (1987) *Moral Monopoly: The Catholic Church in Modern Irish Society* Dublin: Gill & Macmillan.

—— (1994) 'A very touchy subject: priests, masturbation and confession' *Irish Reporter* 14: 22–3.

LEE, J. J. (1989) *Ireland 1912–1985: Politics and Society* Cambridge: Cambridge University Press.

McCAFFERTY, Nell (1984) *The Best of Nell* Dublin: Attic Press.

—— (1985) *Goodnight Sisters* Dublin: Attic Press.

—— (1987) *A Woman to Blame: The Kerry Babies Case* Dublin: Attic Press.

MEDBH, Maighread (1990) 'Original Sin' in *The Making of a Pagan*, Belfast: Blackstaff Press, 44–5.

O'FAOLAIN, Nuala (1994) 'We must hear the children in pain in our society' *The Irish Times* 5.12.94: 14.

O'TOOLE, Fintan (1994) 'What a show' *The Irish Times Weekend* 19.11.94: 1.

POLLAK, Andy (1994) 'Moral authority shaken by scandal' *The Irish Times* 31.12.94: 6.

ROONEY, Eilish (1994) 'Excluded voices' *Fortnight* No. 332: 28–9.

ROSE, Kieran (1994) *Diverse Communities: The Evolution of Lesbian and Gay Politics in Ireland* Cork: 'Undercurrents', Cork University Press.

SHANAHAN, Kate (1993) *Crimes Worse than Death* Dublin: Attic Press.

SHERIDAN, Jim Late Late Show (1994) RTE1 television.

SHERIDAN, Kathy (1994) 'Long week when the dam burst and swept Albert away' *The Irish Times* 19.11.94: 19.

SMYTH, Ailbhe (1992) editor, *The Abortion Papers: Ireland* Dublin: Attic Press.

—— (1993) editor, *Irish Women's Studies Reader* Dublin: Attic Press.

SMYTH, Paddy (1994) 'Democracy entails openness' *Irish Reporter* 16: 32–3.

STOKES, Niall (1994) 'The message' *Hot Press* December: 11.

WARD, Peter (1994) *Divorce in Ireland: Who Should Bear the Cost?* Cork: 'Undercurrents', Cork University Press.

WHELAN, Christopher T. (1994) editor, *Values and Social Change in Ireland* Dublin: Gill & Macmillan.

Silences

Irish Women and Abortion

Ruth Fletcher

FEMINIST REVIEW NO 50, SUMMER 1995, pp. 44–66

Abstract

This article considers the forces which act to prevent women in Ireland from speaking about their experiences of abortion. It considers the various forms such silencing can take and the complexity of feelings and circumstance which women who have had abortions are subject to. In so doing it raises important questions about the way public debate about abortion between pro-choice and pro-life arguments – couched in terms of rights – acts to further silence women. Finally, the article calls for the creation of a new public and intellectual space in which the complexities of the issues can be realized. A new public space such as this could then facilitate the enactment of permissive legislation which in turn could enable women to decide the best pregnancy option available for them at any particular moment in their lives.

Keywords

abortion; silence; choice; rights; feminism; public discourse

Introduction

Throughout the lengthy debate on abortion that has twice rocked Ireland since the early 1980's,[1] the lack of participation in this debate by Irish women who have had abortions has been noticeable. Indeed the pro-life movement has sometimes pointed to this lack as evidence of their claim that Irish women do not need access to abortion services. It has sometimes been suggested by pro-choicers that the relation of Irish women's stories about their experiences could work to break down the negative perception of abortion in Ireland. A suggestion that has been met with silence. Aware that this public silence allowed the Irish people to avoid the reality that those women who have abortions are our mothers, our sisters, our friends, I became interested in the questions of how the public image of abortion is distorted by the lack of acknowledgement of the reality of abortion in Irish women's lives and how public discussion of abortion silences women.

What is the relationship between silence of the personal experiences of abortion and the public debate on abortion?

My focus on silence here does not intend to convey a monolithic, oppressive force which renders women speechless. Rather an exploration of how post-abortion silence functions in these women's lives also necessarily engages a focus on the public discourse surrounding abortion. The processes which produce silence at various stages in women's lives also influence the production of the political abortion rhetoric. Also, as I will explain below, factors which contributed to women's post-abortion silence in some contexts motivated speech in others. Ruth Riddick's discussion of her public naming of herself as a woman who had had an abortion provides us with an opportunity to examine one way in which the shifting boundaries between public speech and silence produce images of abortion. While the five other women whom I interviewed, each of whom was known to me personally, had never publicly exposed themselves, each had discussed their experience of abortion to some degree. (I refer to them using false names throughout this paper). Two of the women, Mags and Emma, were especially careful about relating their experiences of abortion and had told only a few close friends. The other three, Tina, Amy and Sue, were fairly open to their peers about their abortions but had preferred not to tell family members, for example. Therefore, while silence in this paper refers in a general way to the apparent public absence of women's voices about abortion experiences, it also refers to the specific ways each woman moves within that public silence in her engagement with and challenge of the public discourse on abortion.

I will focus on four themes which seemed to me to run through the women's discussion of their reasons for keeping or breaking silence about their experiences of abortion. These factors do not pretend to be a complete explanation of post-abortion silence, but rather aim to provide a way of engaging with the complex issues involved in the task of providing a better social climate in Ireland for those women who seek, have sought and will seek access to abortion services. I will briefly outline these themes before going on to explore them in more depth.

Protection is one explanation of post-abortion silence because women often feel the need to avoid the possible negative repercussions of exposing themselves as women who have had abortions.

Ambivalence refers to women's reluctance to talk openly about their abortion experiences because they feel that the expression of mixed feelings would be misconstrued as signifying wrongdoing, for example.

FEMINIST REVIEW NO 50, SUMMER 1995

Concern is another aspect of post-abortion silence since women choose not to expose themselves because they feel that it would upset some of those for whom they care. However, concern may also operate as motivation to break one's silence, because women sometimes open up about their experiences in a gesture of solidarity with other women who have had abortions.

Frustration refers to how women feel about the lack of space in the public forum for the voicing of the complexity of their experiences.

Protection

In this section, I will look at how self-protection serves as a partial explanation of Irish women's silence about their experiences of abortion. I found that the women I interviewed were selective in reporting their experiences of abortion in two ways. First, they were selective of the people with whom they were willing to discuss the experience. Second, they were selective of the aspects of the experience which they were willing to discuss. One of the reasons why women were silent in this way was because they sought to protect themselves from the criticism of others. Some of the women I interviewed voiced the fear that they would be condemned or rejected by others. They felt that the strong disapproval of abortion in Irish society would influence others to think negatively of them for having terminated their pregnancies and they did not want to expose themselves to such criticism.

One of the interviewees, Emma, gave the following reasons for being uncomfortable with the idea of talking to people about her experience of abortion in public:

> Fear, fear of other people's reactions . . . and protection for myself, self-preservation, realizing that I don't want to deal with other people's reactions.

Another woman who was normally fairly open about her experience would not reveal it if she felt it would prejudice her career prospects. Amy had this to say:

> Now I'm thinking of going teaching, well, there's no way, no matter how intimate I get with, say the members of the staffroom, that I am going to discuss the matter of having an abortion there because it would be . . . not a correct move to make, especially if I'm teaching in a religious run secondary school.

Tina felt that she could not tell her old school friends because:

> I would become a different person in their eyes, I would mutate suddenly by the fact that I had had an abortion.

Some of the experiences the women had of being condemned showed that they were acting very rationally when they decided not to risk rejection or blame by keeping quiet. Emma talked about how she now feels about having told her mother when she became pregnant at seventeen:

> I actually wish I'd never told her . . . she was immediately taking over because of my age . . . so I resented that, plus she wasn't supportive at all when I decided that I was going to go ahead and have an abortion, you know, she couldn't . . . she had guilt for me and she was sharing that with me, letting me know how she felt, so that was difficult.

Amy had the experience of being put through an emotional mangle by her pregnancy counsellor at a Dublin clinic fifteen years ago:

> When she discovered that I was adopted she said, well, how would I feel if my mother had aborted me? . . . she also told me I was the hardest faced bitch she had ever seen because I didn't even cry when I was told I was pregnant.

This is how Amy described her feelings after the encounter:

> I felt disempowered, and I felt like I was just a selfish bitch . . . she just pulled the rug completely from under my feet.

Ruth's public disclosure of herself as an Irish woman who has had an abortion, and her subsequent involvement in pro-choice politics, have brought severe repercussions:

> In terms of the male, mainstream world, if you like, I have become anathema, there's no question about that, it's very, very difficult for me to get gainful employment . . . I would not have survived materially, never mind emotionally, but for the support of my partner and my partner's family . . . I've been called for second interview to be told by interview panels that because of my public role in pro-choice politics, that I'm not employable by them.

On other occasions when individual women felt that they could trust a relationship enough to accommodate their experience of abortion, their trust was rewarded. Mags found it difficult to tell her new partner because she still felt very vulnerable about having had the abortion and therefore was hesitant to expose herself to anyone by telling them of her experience. She talked about disclosing it to him:

> I think I was testing our relationship, to see would he go or what he would do, and he said, I had an idea, and I said why? what are you trying to say about me? are you trying to say I'm promiscuous?! he said not every woman who has had an abortion is promiscuous! you have all these ideas, he said, don't be trying to . . . don't be putting them on me, and I said, well, how did you know that I had? and he said, cos there's a lot of hurt.

It would seem that women do not trust others with knowledge of their abortion experiences where they feel that another's anti-abortion sentiments disable them from accepting the woman's experience of abortion. The women I interviewed clearly had a sense that sometimes those who judge the act to be wrong will also condemn the woman who has committed the act. These women believe that a good impression of them, or a relationship with them, might be sacrificed in order to let the other person go on believing that abortion is wrong. However, where they feel that the relevant relationship will accommodate their experience, even if the other person thinks that abortion is wrong, then they will trust that relationship to take the news. Many who condemn the act of abortion say that this does not mean that they condemn the women involved. This principle of maintaining a distinction between the act and the agent is reflected in much of Christian philosophy. Another example is the issue of homosexuality: homosexual acts are condemned, but apparently not lesbians and gay men. However, it is clear that the interviewees did not experience their audience making such a distinction. They fear, and indeed have experienced, personal rejection by persons who believe that abortion is wrong. The problem here lies not in the failure of individual members of the public to make this distinction, but in the untenable nature of the distinction itself. If one condemns the act committed then by definition one is critical of the agent's judgement because one denies that there are circumstances in which execution of the act might be correct. The belief that criticism of the act can be isolated from criticism of the agent is symptomatic of a failure to recognize how social context influences the agent's decision to act.

Another factor in these Irish women's silence about their experiences of abortion is the fact that they felt they would be viewed as irresponsible people if it was known that they had had an abortion, no matter how responsible they felt in making their decision. Tina felt that abortion was seen as an 'immoral cop-out' and that a woman was 'more worthy of respect if you have a baby and give yourself and them a shit life, than if you make a mature decision that is better for both involved, the foetus and yourself.' The interviewees' comments imply that women who have had abortions find themselves judged by the view that because a woman is responsible for getting pregnant, it is not legitimate for her to scapegoat the foetus as a means of escape from a difficult situation. As well as denying men's responsibility for pregnancy, this view fails to address the responsibility involved in making the decision to abort. Women who decide to terminate their pregnancies generally do so because they take the responsibilities of motherhood very seriously, and, for a variety of reasons, feel that they cannot meet those responsibilities in their current circumstances. The comments made about the decision to abort by the women I interviewed reveal how the process of decision-making involved the pregnant woman in consideration of how she could achieve what was best for her, her foetus and her loved ones. For example, Emma said:

> The way I think about it is I respected the life and soul of something by stopping it in time and realizing that I couldn't give it what it deserved and felt that the soul will house itself somewhere else.

Mags said:

> I'll love my baby a lifetime, I've never held it and I'll love it a lifetime . . . but I have to say there are days when I say thank god I never ever had that child, I would never be in the position I'm in now if I had gone ahead with it . . . and I believe that the baby knew that.

These women's words impress on me the seriousness with which they viewed their decisions to terminate a pregnancy. The women saw themselves as acting both for themselves and for the foetus. While they were primarily concerned with the effects on their own lives at the time of decision-making, they also integrated into their thinking a concern for the future they could offer the foetus. It is quite clear that these women did not see the foetus as an independent person but rather as a dependant whose wants and needs were necessarily mediated through each pregnant woman. Each woman's consideration of her own wants and needs was not selfish but pragmatic and balanced with consideration of other factors. Clearly these women's understanding of their behaviour is very different from that suggested by the interpretation of abortion as selfish and irresponsible.

Ambivalence

The women I interviewed were also silent about their abortions because they needed time and space to work out their own feelings about their experiences. All of the women felt that they had made the right decision in having an abortion, but most of them were confused about the significance of their mixed feelings of guilt, shame, regret and relief. By guilt I mean feeling, rather than believing, that one has done something wrong. By shame I mean a sense that one has failed to live up to one's expectations of oneself, as influenced by the opinions of others. By regret I mean the feeling of sorrow at the loss of something. By relief I mean the alleviation of anxiety. Because negative feelings about abortion are often assumed to signify the belief that one has done something wrong, the women felt vulnerable about naming these emotions. For some, silence protected the inner space required for an active process of resolution of their feelings and thoughts. For others, it shielded an area that they didn't want to deal with right now. Those for whom emotional ambivalence was not an issue, felt that silence was not required as a shield to protect vulnerability. The ambivalence that women did confront signified clearly that abortion is a complex and sometimes difficult experience, irrespective of one's political opinions. Dealing with the emotional fall-out of abortion usually meant coming to terms with what was going on in the woman's life at the time. The importance of context, of the particulars unique in a woman's life, demonstrated that abortion can rarely be regarded as a simple, single incident in a woman's life.

Mags finds it difficult to talk to anyone about her abortion because she still feels very guilty and hurt about it. Mags actually would have liked to have had another child but felt that she would have lost her relationship, her home and her business if she had gone ahead with the pregnancy. Her partner at the time would have known that he was not the father because he had had a vasectomy, and, as a mother of two, Mags felt that she could not risk what she thought would be the inevitable break-up of her home. The fact that her home did break up anyway (for different reasons), several months later contributes to her feelings of guilt and loss. She said:

> I still feel guilty about it and there's not a day goes by that I don't think about it and I spend time every day . . . and I mean it's five years and I still cry, but I think that the crying could have stopped if I could have talked and I never could, I just never trusted anybody enough to be able to give so much of myself to them.

The fact that Mags had a strong connexion with her foetus and the fact that she would have liked to have had another baby contributes to her feelings of guilt on having the abortion. Sharon Bishop's analysis of guilt (Bishop, 1987) throws some very useful light on the emotions Mags and the other women express. Bishop maintains that traditionally we have only named one form of guilt as rational, which is the guilt one feels on having breached some moral principle, what Bishop calls 'moral guilt proper'. She goes on to undermine the traditional philosophical assumption that guilt and remorse are irrational if an agent believes she is acting rightly, by showing that choosing a certain resolution of a situation may mean the prioritizing of one set of responsibilities or desires over another set. Therefore, feelings of guilt, remorse and regret often signal sadness at having to let go of one concern in favour of another even where one recognizes that that was the right thing to do. Such emotions may also signify a process of growing through the recognition that this was done as a result of one's own actions.

Other women did not feel guilt or shame but expressed confusion, vulnerability or conflict in their emotional response to abortion. They usually remained silent to others about this because they felt that to speak of such ambivalence signified self-blame and justified the opinion that abortion was wrong because it hurt women. This was a consequence they wished to avoid in their desire to have abortion recognized as the right, if sometimes difficult, option for them and for other women. Another factor in this aspect of silence was that the women themselves were unsure of the significance of their conflicting feelings and did not feel comfortable in exposing their emotional vulnerability because they could not explain it fully. As women explained to me their selectivity in reporting certain aspects of their experiences, references to the above factors were many and varied. Tina commented:

> In a lot of ways I don't know what to say about it, I still haven't really talked enough, you know, I'm really silent to myself, in myself about it [. . .] all across the board your life experiences, no matter how right they are, do have effects on you and sometimes they're traumatic, but . . . and that's allowed, but as regards abortion it's not allowed, because the moment you show a sign of weakness they say, you see! there you go! it's wrong! you're a mess now!

Sue said she wants to speak about the personal side of the experience and about the difficulty of making a decision to abort, to pro-choicers in particular, in order to:

> try and educate them as well, so that they don't think, every time they meet a woman who's very upset about her abortion, that they don't think that she must have been a pro-lifer and that she regrets her decision, that you can still be pro-choice and you can still not regret your decision but that doesn't mean that it can't cause a problem.

It is also interesting to note that although both Tina and Sue decided without much hesitation to have abortions when they became pregnant in difficult circumstances, both also expressed that they did have some romantic curiosity about motherhood when they were pregnant. For example, Sue said:

> When I was pregnant I had some sort of feeling of smugness or security. Even though I didn't want the pregnancy, I still felt proud of myself by being pregnant.

Tina mentioned that sometimes she thinks:

> Isn't it a pity that the way life was at that time that I couldn't have brought her into the world.

As far as Amy was concerned:

> Because I had resolved it and because I felt good about making the decision, there wasn't any need to do an awful lot of talking, you know, it was over and done with and that was fine.

Before Amy first decided to opt for a termination she had spent several weeks trying 'to get my head around it myself and decide what I was doing'. Once she had decided that abortion was the best option for her, she was able to say to the pregnancy counsellor who questioned her decision, 'this was what I wanted and that was it, I did not want to support the child myself and I refused adoption, so I had no other option.' The second time she had an abortion was when she found herself unexpectedly pregnant after a brief sexual encounter while travelling around the world and: 'There was just no way that even continuing the pregnancy was even an issue for that one, you know, I mean that was very, very straightforward.' Amy's ability to accept and own her experiences of abortion was helped along by advice she received from the doctor examining her at the clinic in London:

> You have decided to go ahead with an abortion says he, and I said yes, unfortunately, so he said, what do you mean unfortunately? So I explained my circumstances and sort of was adding but if . . . and he said, but Amy, there's no but ifs, you're making a decision now in the light of your current circumstances and it wouldn't matter if you won the Sweepstakes tomorrow your decision is here and now in the light of the information available; which was brilliant.

Ruth did not voice any ambivalence about her experience of abortion:

> I had decided ideologically, if you like, that I was pro-choice for many years prior to actually being in the position myself. Personally, I had decided very many years previously that I didn't want children at all anyway, and the actuality of this pregnancy didn't challenge either of those assumptions at all.

However, she is very aware that abortion is often a very ambivalent experience for women:

> You can say at the same time, that abortion was the right decision, I made it for the right reasons, I know what those reasons were, my intention at all times was to act for the best even though I was in an unhappy or difficult situation; but having said all of that and feeling all of that and believing all of that, also, I'm sorry that it happened, yes, I feel a sense of loss, maybe I do remember on the anniversary or whenever, and that all of that . . . that none of it is mutually exclusive, rather that it's all inclusive and it's all valid.

The silence about Irish women's experiences of abortion can be explained, in part, by the fact that Irish women do not feel free to voice their emotional ambivalence about the experience without having it remoulded into the expression of remorse. By remorse I mean the feeling that one needs to make reparation for having done something that one believes is wrong (Taylor, 1985). The expression of emotional ambivalence is hindered by a social need to label and categorize every feeling and thought in a clear and precise manner. The fact that women do not easily distinguish or rationalize all their conflicting emotions according to this criterion sometimes has the consequence of causing them to feel insecure about the significance of this ambivalence. However, the problem here lies not in the fact of ambivalence, but rather in the social requirement that these thoughts and emotions *should* be clearly distinguishable. Abortion is a personal, complex and difficult experience in any woman's life. It is not possible to give a simple, universal explanation for each of its many facets.

The dichotomization of mind and body and of reason and emotion has influenced how and what we think about the appropriateness of certain emotions and thoughts. The dominance of the notion in Western philosophy that one needs to remove oneself from emotional and bodily pursuits in order to attain 'reason', has left a legacy which frowns upon 'messy' emotions (Lloyd, 1984). This legacy is evident today in the discomfort many feel when hearing expressions of emotion, and on our apparent need to find the comment that will slot all those feelings back into place. Consequently, emotional work (Calhoun, 1992) has often been devalued. We often think that, as individuals, we should be able to handle our own thoughts and emotions alone and we therefore fail to recognize the need for validation of whatever thought or emotion it is, that is answered by being listened to. The silencing of these women's experiences has often left them feeling vulnerable about the significance of their ambivalent emotions, when often a sharing of their stories would reveal what they need to know: ambivalence reveals complexity, not wrongdoing.

Concern

The concern that others would be hurt or burdened by knowledge of a loved one's abortion was also a factor in women's silence about their experiences of abortion. Some of the women I interviewed felt that they wanted to avoid imparting this information because they knew that it would upset people for whom they cared. The common perception of abortion as an ugly experience meant that women considered carefully whether it was appropriate or not to allow others to connect that experience with them. Sometimes the women felt that others simply would not be able to cope with such knowledge and that enabling them to cope was not appropriate work for the women to do at the moment, if ever.

Tina would like to be able to talk to her twelve-year-old sister, with whom she has a very close relationship, about her experience of abortion. This is partly because Tina knows that she would be sympathetic and would accept the information in a very non-judgemental way. Another reason is that Tina feels that her sister will respect what she has to say now, whereas Tina is afraid that in the future her sister's attitude might be less tolerant if she is subject to anti-abortion influences in school and elsewhere. However, Tina feels that she cannot 'burden her with that because even at her age she knows that abortion is such a wow! big horrible thing.' Tina feels angry that the unpleasant image of abortion in our society has made it difficult

FEMINIST REVIEW NO 50, SUMMER 1995

for her to share her experience in a relationship where exchange over other life experiences is common: 'I get angry about that . . . and it's not because of her, it's because of everybody else and society and everything that I can't say to someone that I really care about.' But because her sister is young and would be upset for Tina, Tina feels she has a responsibility to avoid putting her sister in a situation that could be difficult for her to handle.

Similarly, Emma feels that she will tell her ten-year-old sister about her abortion sometime in the future because she would like her sister to be able to relate to the experience in real, human terms. But Emma doesn't think that it would be appropriate to tell her now because: 'I think that it would disturb her.' However, she has no inclination to share the information with her older brother because: 'I couldn't care what he thinks and I'm not going to put myself through . . . it's none of his business, it's my life, I don't need his approval or his disapproval.' Clearly, a woman's decision not to tell others about her experience of abortion is related to how important or unimportant another person's opinion is to her. However, such a decision may also signify that the woman simply does not feel the need to discuss the experience with anyone else because she is handling it fine herself and feels that it is of no concern to anyone but herself.

Amy's decision not to tell her parents about her abortions involved a combination of the above factors. Her parents 'are probably the only people that are anyway close to me that wouldn't know.' One of her reasons for not telling her mother 'has to do with being adopted.' Amy is aware that her mother's fear that she might come home with an unwanted pregnancy had more to it than the disapproval common to a lot of Irish families:

> For Mum it [the fear] was kinda worse because she felt that if I did that I'd be taking after my natural mother and that all her input as a mother would have gone for nought, right, she would have failed because like mother, like daughter.

Another reason for not telling her parents was because 'it would upset them and there's no point, I mean what's the point? I mean there's no purpose to serve by pointing out I've had two abortions to them.'

Considering whether to tell her family or not was not an issue for Ruth because 'I don't particularly have family'. As far as she was concerned: 'I would have considered that it was none of their business and I didn't feel the need to talk to anybody about it, it was just one of those things that happens.' It is true that because this society makes women's experiences of abortion invisible, many women do need and want to be able to talk about their diverse experiences of abortion in a safe environment. However, this does not mean that every woman who has an abortion 'needs' a sympathetic listening ear, an impression which can in itself cause problems. When Ruth went public about her experience of abortion she found that:

> A number of my other friends expressed their hurt that I hadn't come to them, and at that time because . . . and you know, all I could really say to them was that, in a sense, it wasn't that big a deal, it was something that was happening in my life, I was dealing with it, it was being handled and let's just get on with the rest of it and you come into the rest of it.

Concern for other women who have had abortions has also been a motivation for different women to break their silence. While Ruth's decision to intervene at a meeting and introduce herself as an Irish woman who had had an abortion was spontaneous, her decision to follow it through with radio and television interviews was taken with a lot more consideration:

> The reason I did it was because I wanted to put a face and a name to an experience which, you know, many Irish women were having at the same time, some of whom I had met in London, who themselves were unable to, for whatever reasons, felt that they were unable to speak out of their own experience.

The ways in which concern for others operates as an explanation both for Irish women's silence *and* discussion of their experiences of abortion informs us about their lives in a significant way. It shows us how women are often put in the position of taking responsibility for the reaction of others to a situation which the women themselves do not control. In other words, in an Irish context, the social impression of abortion as, at worst evil, and at best traumatic, creates a situation where women find themselves taking responsibility for the influence this image might have on people they care about (Gilligan, 1982; Kittay and Meyers, 1987; Card, 1991; Cole and McQuin, 1992; Larrabee, 1993). Women know that telling others that they have had an abortion would concern them not because the women have actually had traumatic experiences or have done something wrong, but because others will assume that this is so. The manner in which these women would normally relate to those they care about is, therefore, distorted by the influence of the social taboo on abortion.

Where some of the women expressed that they would like to be able to talk about the experience of abortion with a particular person, but felt that they couldn't, their motivation seems to be that it would be a mutually beneficial experience. For example, Tina wants to talk to her younger sister about the experience partly out of a concern for self: she knows her sister would give her sympathy and support; and partly out of a concern for others: she wants to create a space in which her sister would feel safe in exploring

FEMINIST REVIEW NO 50, SUMMER 1995

issues around sexuality, pregnancy, abortion etc. It seems to me that the process at work here is a balancing of concern for self and concern for others, but that this process gets distorted by the social taboo on abortion (Blum, Homiak, Housman and Scheman, 1976). The effect of this distortion is that women often sacrifice their desire to discuss a personal experience with someone for whom they care, in the interests of sparing that person hurt and pain. In other words, the negative social appraisal of abortion requires Irish women to give more emphasis than usual to their consideration of others when deciding how open they should be about their experiences. If Irish society viewed abortion more favourably, then concern for others would not be so strong a factor in Irish women's silence about their experiences of abortion.

Frustration

Another aspect of post-abortion silence was these women's frustration and anger that the public discussion of abortion does not make space for the voicing of personal experiences of abortion. Emma talked about her annoyance that: 'If I was to talk about it [abortion] as a political issue that's okay, but if I talk about it as a personal experience it's not okay.' Sue described how she felt about the public debate of the issues surrounding the 'X' case and the subsequent referendum: 'It just really frustrated me because I felt people on both sides were debating the issue in a very impersonal way.' This is what Mags had to say about the same debate: 'I was so annoyed that the debate and everything that seemed to be going on was done by men, everything was done by men.' As far as Tina was concerned: 'The debate that goes on in Ireland, it's not about feelings, the feelings of the women concerned, it's just, it's just simply right or wrong.'

There are a number of issues involved in these women's impression that there is no public space for the expression of their personal experiences. The first one that I will address is how the polarization of the public discussion of abortion has inhibited women from naming the complexity of their experiences. As Ruth said:

> I would see that women would feel that it's very difficult to explore the richness of their experience in an arena where the debate is conducted in slogans . . . the abortion debate is conducted very much in soundbites, one side gets to say that abortion is murder and the other side say we have to be pro-choice and there's no middle ground for the two soundbites to meet because it just isn't there, whereas the middle ground, as it's being called, is actually where women live.

It is likely that elements within both the pro-choice and the pro-life movements have a more complex understanding of abortion than is popularly perceived. However, polarization of the political debate and the fear on both sides that a recognition of diverse experiences will cede ground to the other side, has meant that the public is generally presented with an entrenched debate that revolves around two very distinct and oppositional images of abortion. The pro-choice movement has been associated with a perception of abortion as a straightforward procedure which a woman undertakes in pursuit of control of her reproductive capacity with little or no consideration of the foetus. The image of abortion that is connected with the pro-life movement is one of an evil act where the woman is responsible for the killing of an innocent unborn child, resulting in her feeling guilt and remorse. It has become clear that members of the public are alienated and confused by these polarized images of abortion and often place themselves somewhere between the two extremities. Many feel sympathy with women in crisis pregnancy but are uncomfortable with the idea of abortion. Here, it is important to recognize that none of the women I interviewed identified with either of the two oppositional depictions of abortion either. As Ruth said, 'these situations are very much more complex than a polarized position one way or the other allows for.' The public debate's failure to recognize that women's experiences of abortion do not fit neatly into either of the two dominant portrayals of abortion has left women feeling alienated from a political discussion that devalues, depersonalizes and often erroneously renames their experiences.

While the dichotomization of attitudes towards abortion has misrepresented many aspects of women's experiences, two of the main issues which figured prominently in the interviews as having a very different significance than is commonly portrayed were women's evaluation of foetal life and women's emotional experience of abortion. Tina is afraid that if she addresses the subject of her abortion in a way that acknowledges it as a difficult experience, the pro-life movement would use such information as validation of their argument that abortion hurts women: 'They'll all jump on the bandwagon and go you see! you see! there you go, abortion is wrong, look you're all upset about it.' She feels that such a reaction would be unfair and inappropriate because it remoulds an expression of her feelings about her experience into an expression of remorse: 'I mean with so many things in life, I mean it's the right thing for you to do but it messes you up, I mean even like a divorce.' Yet, because she feels that an honest depiction of her experience of abortion could be used as fuel for the pro-life arguments against abortion, she avoids discussion of her experience with those whom she does not know well. Emma's story about the reaction of two pro-choice people to her reference to her experience when all three were discussing abortion is also relevant here:

Their reaction immediately made me regret opening my mouth at all . . . I thought that they were afraid that I was going to pour my heart out to them or, you know, totally personalize it and I didn't, I just merely made a comment and really wanted for myself to say it without feeling ashamed . . . I really felt angry at the fact that, oh, you can be so politically right on.

Some of the women talked about how they avoided thinking about the foetus while they were pregnant and considering abortion. Tina's comment was, 'I was afraid to think that there was a child growing inside . . . what would become a child growing inside me.' In a similar vein Amy said, 'To a great extent you have to think of . . . in terms of the foetus as something in your body as such, you can't personalize the foetus, at least not when you're planning an abortion, I found.' In their initial coming to terms with their decisions women often suppress any recognition they have of the foetus's right to life or of it's human qualities, because they associate such recognition with the opinion of abortion as wrong. As Amy put it: 'There would have been a conflict of interest, you know I would have to sort of consider the right to life.' Irish women have heard so often that abortion is wrong because it is the murder of an unborn child, that any identification of the foetus as more than just a bunch of cells can be confusing for them.

On the other hand, a woman's feelings for her foetus may be negated by those who are under the impression that it would be better for her not to relate to the foetus at all. This point is illustrated by Mag's description of a conversation she had with a nurse in the clinic when she awoke after the abortion operation:

> I said I want to see my baby, and she said, Mags, you could spit bigger than what we took from you, and I said, I don't care, I really need to see, and she said, but Mags it's gone, you know; and they couldn't understand my whole fascination with wanting to see.

Here we can see how the polarized depictions of abortion – if the foetus is not a baby, then it must be a bunch of cells – have failed women. For many women, having an abortion does not mean that one devalues foetal life and valuing foetal life does not mean that abortion is wrong. However, the prevailing assumptions to the contrary make it very difficult for women to work through their complex emotions and thoughts without feeling contradicted and undermined.

All of the women I interviewed considered that they had made the right decision in having an abortion, even though coming to terms with the experience had been particularly difficult for two of them. At the same time, considering the humanity of the foetus and taking responsibility for the ending of some form of life were processes in which most of the women were engaged at some level. For example, throughout our conversation

Mags referred to her aborted foetus as her baby and spoke of her personal connection with what she thinks would have been her baby girl. Her desire for and identification with her foetus contributed to her feelings of guilt on having aborted it, but now her recognition that she made the right decision is facilitated by her belief that her baby understood that she had to have an abortion. For Amy, the 1983 referendum was a difficult time: 'The referendum with all its right to life and unborn babies and children and personalizing the foetuses, just really sorta made me feel like a murderer for a while.' It took her about two years to resolve this conflict and come to the following point of view: 'That it was my body, my right to life and then, of course, well, if my life was going to be so miserable and limited, well, what kind of quality would my . . . would I be giving the potential child anyway?' Emma had this to say: 'At the time, being so young, I tried to think that it wasn't a life, but I realize now that it was the beginning of a life that I decided to stop and that the soul of it would go off somewhere else.' As far as Tina was concerned: 'I think that when I'm going to explore the emotional side is actually when I do have a child, I think that's when it's going to be hard.'

Sue's reference to the possibility of her infertility is also pertinent here:

> There's a chance you know, that I might not be able to have kids, I think that . . . if that ever comes about for sure, that would probably be the most hurtful part of the abortion for me, the thought that I had the chance once . . . even though it wasn't right then, you know, so it's kinda ridiculous, but it's just an irrational feeling.

The fact that these conflicting emotions towards the foetus are usually not publicly voiced signifies that the public forum has failed to provide a safe environment in which women can work out their complex emotions and thoughts without fear of their distortion in the interest of scoring cheap political points.

While both the pro-choice and pro-life movements have misrepresented how women feel about the foetus – the former by suggesting that abortion is akin to having a tooth pulled and the latter by referring to abortion as the murder of an unborn child – I think there is another aspect to the pro-choice movement's failure to represent itself as valuing foetal life. A cursory glance at what the six interviewees had to say demonstrates that women's conceptualization of the foetus may vary between a piece of tissue and a named, gendered baby. The fact that women relate to the foetus in so many different ways has led to a reluctance to recognize this relationship in any way at all because of a fear that to name one experience of foetal life would be to marginalize another. The irony is that the consequent public silence within the pro-choice movement on the issue of respect for foetal life has

FEMINIST REVIEW NO 50, SUMMER 1995

actually betrayed women's experiences by creating the false impression that pro-lifers are the only ones concerned about the foetus.

The reduction of the public discussion of abortion to a focus on rights discourse – the right to life v. the right to choose – is another reason why Irish women who have had abortions feel alienated from the public debate. There was a lot more going on for these women than the exercise of their rights. As Tina said, 'I wasn't exercising a right or a choice or anything, I was just in a desperate situation.' Sue was also frustrated with the application of rights discourse to her experience: 'it's not just a political right, it's not just a civil right.' Also, the manner in which they integrated into their decision-making a concern for the foetus means that they did not necessarily see their abortion decisions as the prioritizing of a woman's rights over those of the foetus. Rather, it was a case of looking for the best solution to a difficult problem. Ruth's comments are pertinent here:

> Certainly it has been my experience that Irish women asking for my help in organizing an abortion do not speak in terms of their rights, they don't talk about – I have a right to have you tell me what I need to know . . . and equally where women are expressing concerns about foetal life, for example, one of the questions that can be asked is whether the procedure of abortion will hurt a foetus, whether a foetus will feel pain or whatever, that's . . . those aren't questions which are conducted in terms of a rights discourse either . . . they're expressing a compassion that unnecessary suffering be avoided and, in fact, I think that what they're focusing in on more is what is necessary or unnecessary in this situation.

While all of the women I interviewed wanted to see abortion available in Ireland, it would seem that they found the political emphasis on locating that aspiration within the concept of a right problematic (Himmelweit, 1988; Smart, 1989). One of the reasons why this may be is because defining human needs and wants in terms of rights seems to necessitate the formation of a hierarchy in order to decide between conflicting rights, whereas the concepts of opposing rights and of a hierarchy of rights do not appear to be ones which women find useful in their decision-making in the context of abortion. Also, naming a woman's decision to have an abortion as 'her right' locates all responsibility for the decision within the individual woman and inhibits an appreciation of the context which informed and influenced that decision. The context of their pregnancies was an all-important factor for the women I interviewed as it often determined their priorities.

Rights are interests which are so important that they warrant holding others duty-bound to respect them; even though majority opinion may differ. If such interests, e.g., a woman's control of reproduction, were already respected by the public and its institutions, there would not be the need for women to fall back on rights discourse in arguing for political protection of their interests. It seems to me, therefore, that these women's expressed dissatisfaction with rights discourse is not necessarily meant to suggest a rejection of rights rhetoric altogether, but rather seeks to challenge the political use of rights language in a manner which de-emphasizes the need to challenge the socio-political climate which continuously puts women in the defensive position of having to assert their rights. It may be impossible and even undesirable to avoid the use of rights in the current political climate, but that should not necessarily mean that we have to lose sight of the other aspects of women's experiences of abortion. Perhaps one of the ways we could begin to remedy this imbalance is by developing discourse around the concept of trust (Baier, 1986, 1991, 1993; Govier, 1992, 1993). Such a discourse might be used profitably to help create a social environment where women would feel that their decisions are respected and where the public would believe that women's reproductive decisions are responsible and worthy of respect. In this context it is interesting to note the popularity during the 1992 referendum campaign of a pro-choice slogan: 'If you can't trust me with choice, how can you trust me with a child?'. In order for women to feel more comfortable about discussing their experiences of abortion, they need to feel that they are trusted to make good decisions. Trusting women to make good reproductive decisions means acknowledging that they act responsibly while recognizing the need to address the obstacles – such as family or financial pressure – which often hinder women making what they regard as the best decisions.

Exploring how social circumstances influence women's decision-making in these situations involves addressing another popular concept in the discussion of abortion: the concept of choice. One of the issues that stood out particularly for me in the interviews was the fact that most of the women expressed that they felt they didn't have a choice with regard to their abortion decisions. For the women I interviewed, not having a choice meant that they did not believe that they had any viable option apart from abortion in their particular circumstances. Reference to some of their comments will illustrate the point. For example, Sue said:

> I didn't really have the option of having the child, cos I didn't have the financial security, so that's not a full . . . it's not an actual choice in the true sense of the word, so maybe that's why . . . the whole pregnancy thing, maybe there is in some sense, there is some possible way that it wasn't a decision that you really, really wanted to make.

Tina's words were: 'I wasn't a woman with a choice at the time, I was . . . there was only one thing for me to do and I had to do that, I couldn't . . . I mean there was no other way.'

This is what Mags had to say about her choice to have an abortion:

> I blame everybody else because I would have gone ahead with the pregnancy –
> I know a lot of women say that – if the circumstances were right, but they
> weren't right . . . I'd have lost everything, my relationship, my home . . . I lost it
> all anyway and then I felt really hard done by.

Listening to these women explain to me that they perceived that they had no other option but to go for an abortion, it struck me that part of what was at issue here was, as Sue suggested, the 'true sense' of choice and what the women understood by that concept. Despite the fact that these women considered their circumstances, made decisions and 'chose' abortion as the best resolution of the crisis with which they were faced, they were telling me that they didn't feel or think that they had made a 'choice'. As feminist writers have pointed out (McDonnell, 1984; Rapp, 1984; Rothman, 1986: Chapter 7; Rowbotham, 1990), it is important to recognize and work to alleviate the constraints placed on women's reproductive choices by social factors such as the lack of financial resources. However, another part of the problem here seems to be the expectation that choice can be exercised in a decontextualized way. By this I mean that one of the reasons why the women expressed themselves as not having a choice is because choice is commonly understood as the expression of individual freedom, rather than as being influenced by the circumstances of the chooser's life. But, if women are to come to terms with and take responsibility for their abortion decisions, we must recognize that *all* choices are informed by their context.

The women's lack of identification with the concept of choice can also be explained by the influence of the notion that one chooses to do something because one wants to do it. However, while I may choose to do something because I want to do it, it is equally likely that I choose to do it because I prefer it over my other option. In other words, women do not choose to terminate their pregnancies because they want to have an abortion, but because termination of the pregnancy is the preferred option over its continuation. The distinction between *choosing* to do something and *wanting* to do something has been further blurred by the positive sense (i.e., the sense that this is a good thing) in which choice is used in the discussion of abortion rights. The right to choose does have positive connotations for women because it means giving women more control over their reproductive lives. However, this positive sense of choice is often a source of confusion for those women who have felt constrained rather than liberated in their exercise of the right to choose.

Conclusion

Exploring the reasons for Irish women's post-abortion silence reveals a cycle whereby a political discourse which has evolved without acknowledging women's experiences then becomes instrumental in silencing those experiences. More specifically, Irish society's negative view of abortion, which has developed without listening to women's words, now inhibits Irish women voicing their experiences of abortion. The public discussion of abortion focuses on how the legal and social institutions should address the question of reproductive rights while the emotional and personal experience of abortion is deemed relevant only to the private realm. Feminist theory and practice has long recognized the need to challenge the public/private divide if we are to undermine gender stereotyping (Pateman, 1987). What has become clearer over the last few years is that the interaction between the personal and the political is not achievable by restricting ourselves to the use of concepts, arguments and discourses as they have evolved alongside the dichotomy. I deliberately use the term 'interaction' here because I want to avoid any inference that breaking down the public/private divide is achievable by collapsing the distinction. While the feminist slogan 'the personal is political' has great power in alerting our attention to the influence that the personal and the political exert on each other, it can become problematic if it is understood to mean that the personal and the political are synonymous, or that the political answers lie in personal identity.

In the context of the experience of abortion, the public forum should be encouraged to react to the private experiences of abortion by passing permissive legislation which would help create the conditions for each woman to decide privately what the best pregnancy option is for her. In other words, the way to validate various personal experiences of abortion is to create the public space for all of them. A woman's bad experience of abortion should not mean that she has the right to limit other women's access to abortion. To believe that she does have such a right is to view the political as a personal instrument and denies validation of other experiences.

Some of the women I interviewed expressed themselves as feeling caught in a vicious circle: they felt that they would not be free to voice their experiences of abortion until the public perception of abortion changed, and yet they felt that the public perception of abortion would not change until women's voices were heard. Clearly breaking the cycle is not easy and setting the process in motion will require the adoption of many different strategies. Feminist intellectuals could take up the challenge of developing concepts and discourses which acknowledge the variety of women's experiences. Feminist activists and women who have had abortions could try to create a safe space for women to discuss and share their personal experiences of abortion in all their complexity. Perhaps instead of increasing the burden on these women by 'requiring' them to make the first move in breaking their silences, together we can try to create an environment which will allow us all to learn from the richness of their experiences. Certainly we can learn from the sadly ironic fact that it was an anonymous fourteen-year-old rape survivor that forced the Irish people to wake up to the reality of abortion in their midst.

Notes

Ruth Fletcher is currently doing an LLM at Osgoode Hall Law School, York University, Canada.

1 In the 1983 referendum, the Irish public voted to accept a constitutional amendment which would protect the life of the unborn by regarding it as equal to the life of the mother. Article 40. 3. 3. of the Irish Constitution. In *A.G. v X. and others*, 1 I.R. [1992] 1, the Supreme Court overturned a High Court injunction stopping a pregnant fourteen-year-old rape survivor from travelling abroad for an abortion. Although the Supreme Court decided that Article 40. 3. 3. of the Irish Constitution allowed women to avail of abortion when their lives were in danger, including the case of a suicide threat, it gave the non-binding opinion that Irish women (who were not in imminent danger of death) did not have the right to travel abroad to avail of foreign abortion services. In the November 1992 referendum, the Irish public passed two constitutional amendments affirming the right to travel and the right to information on abortion services. The third constitutional amendment restricting the right to abortion to cases where the pregnant woman's life, as distinct from her health, was in danger and not including the risk of suicide, was defeated (see Smyth, 1992).

References

ANONYMOUS (1983) 'The right to grieve: two women talk about their abortions' *Healthsharing* 5: 19–21.

ARDITTI, Rita, KLEIN, Renate Duelli and MINDEN, Shelley (1984) editors, *Test-Tube Women: What Future for Motherhood?* London: Pandora.

BAIER, Annette (1986) 'Trust and antitrust' *Ethics* 96: 231–60.

—— (1991) 'Whom can women trust?' in CARD (1991).

—— (1993) 'What do women want in a moral theory?', in LARRABEE, Mary Jeanne (1993) editor, *An Ethic of Care: Feminist and Interdisciplinary Perspectives* London: Routledge.

BISHOP, Sharon (1987) 'Connections and guilt' *Hypatia* 2(1): 7–23.

BLUM, Lawrence, HOMIAK, Marcia, HOUSMAN, Judy and SCHEMAN, Naomi (1976) 'Altruism and women's oppression' in GOULD, Carol and WARTOFSKY, Marx (1976) editors, *Women and Philosophy: Toward a Theory of Liberation* New York: Capricorn Books.

CALHOUN, Chesire (1992) 'Emotional work' in COLE and McQUIN (1992).

CARD, Claudia (1991) editor, *Feminist Ethics* Lawrence, Kansas: University Press of Kansas.

COLE, Eve Browning and McQUIN, Susan Coultrap (1992) editors, *Explorations in Feminist Ethics: Theory and Practice* Indianapolis: Indiana University Press.

DUGGAN, Maria (1988) 'Whose right to life? A roundtable discussion' *Marxism Today* January: 14–19.

DWORKIN, Ronald (1993) *Life's Dominion* London: HarperCollins.

FAIRWEATHER, Eileen (1979) 'Abortion: the feelings behind the slogans' *Spare Rib* 87: 26–30; reprinted in M. ROWE (1982) editor, *Spare Rib Reader* Harmondsworth: Penguin.

FISHER, Berenice (1984) 'Guilt and shame in the women's movement: the radical idea of action and its meaning for feminist intellectuals' *Feminist Studies* 10(2): 185–212.

FLETCHER, Ruth (1993) 'The significance of Irish women's silence about their experiences of abortion' MA thesis, Cork: University College.

FRANCKE, Linda Bird (1978) *The Ambivalence of Abortion* New York: Random House.

GILLIGAN, Carol (1982) *In a Different Voice: Psychological Theory and Women's Development* Cambridge, Mass: Harvard University Press.

GOVIER, Trudy (1992) 'Trust, distrust and feminist theory' *Hypatia* 7(1): 16–33.
—— (1993) 'Self-trust, autonomy and self-esteem' *Hypatia* 8(1): 99–120.

HIMMELWEIT, Susan (1988) 'More than a woman's right to choose? . . .' in *Feminist Review* 29.

KITTAY, Eva Feder and MEYERS, Diana T. (1987) editors, *Women and Moral Theory* Totowa, New Jersey: Rowman & Littlefield.

LARRABEE, Mary Jeanne (1993) editor, *An Ethic of Care, Feminist and Interdisciplinary Perspectives* London: Routledge.

LLOYD, Genevieve (1984) *The Man of Reason – 'Male' and 'Female' in Western Philosophy* London: Methuen.

LUKER, Kristen (1984) *Abortion and the Politics of Motherhood* Los Angeles: University of California Press.

McDONNELL, Kathleen (1984) *Not an Easy Choice: A Feminist Re-examines Abortion* Toronto: The Women's Press.

MALOY, Kate and PATTERSON, Maggie Jones (1992) *Birth or Abortion? – Private Struggles in a Political World* New York: Plenum Press.

PATEMAN, Carole (1987) 'Feminist critiques of the public/private dichotomy' in PHILLIPS, Anne (1987) editor, *Feminism and Equality* Oxford: Blackwell.

PETCHESKY, Rosalind (1984) *Abortion and Woman's Choice – The State, Sexuality and Reproductive Freedom* London: Verso.

Philosophy and Social Policy (1993) 'Altruism' 10(1).

FEMINIST REVIEW NO 50, SUMMER 1995

RAPP, Rayna (1984) 'The ethics of choice' *Ms.* April: 97–100; reprinted in ARDITTI *et al.* (1984).

RIDDICK, Ruth (1993) *Profile Report – The First 100 Clients* Dublin: Irish Family Planning Association.

ROTHMAN, Barbara Katz (1986) *The Tentative Pregnancy – Prenatal Diagnosis and the Future of Motherhood* New York: Viking.

ROWBOTHAM, Sheila (1990) *The Past is Before Us: Feminism in Action Since the 1960s* London: Penguin.

RYNNE, Andrew (1982) *Abortion – The Irish Question* Dublin: Ward River Press.

SMART, Carol (1989) *Feminism and the Power of the Law* London: Routledge.

SMYTH, Ailbhe (1992) editor, *The Abortion Papers* Dublin: Attic Press.

SOLOMONS, Michael (1992) *Pro-life? – The Irish Question* Dublin: Lilliput Press.

TAYLOR, Gabriele (1985) *Pride, Shame and Guilt: Emotions of Self-Assessment* Oxford: Clarendon Press.

THOMSON, Judith Jarvis (1971) 'A defence of abortion' *Philosophy and Public Affairs* 1(1): 47–66.

VAN GELDER, Lindsy (1978) 'Cracking the women's movement protection game' *Ms.* December: 66–8.

WARREN, Mary Anne (1989) 'The moral significance of birth' *Hypatia* (Special issue on 'Ethics and reproduction'), 4(3): 46–65.

Mothercare

Rita Ann Higgins

The girls came over
to see the new buggy,
the rainbow buggy
the sunshine stripes.

O.K. it was expensive
but it was the best
and welfare pitched in.

It had everything –
she listed its finer points
under belly things we hadn't seen.

A little touch here
and it collapses
a little touch there
and it's up like a shot,
you barely touch this –
and you're in another street
another town.

A mind of its own
a body like a rocket
its yours to control –
just like that.

She swears she'll keep it well
immaculate she says
immaculate.

When she's nearly eighteen
it will still be new,
Tomma-Lee will be two and a half

FEMINIST REVIEW NO 50, SUMMER 1995, PP. 67–8

FEMINIST REVIEW NO 50, SUMMER 1995

she can sell it then
and fetch a high price,
almost as much as she paid.

© Rita Ann Higgins

Note

Rita Ann Higgins is Writer-in-Residence at University College, Galway. Her last collection of poetry was *Philomena's Revenge*, Salmon Press, Galway, 1992. Her next collection will be called *Higher Purchase*.

'I Won't Go Back To It'[1]

Irish Women Poets and the Iconic Feminine

Lia Mills

FEMINIST REVIEW NO 50, SUMMER 1995, pp. 69–88

Abstract

This paper explores the dynamic interaction between contemporary Irish women poets and the notion of tradition in Irish poetry. Looking at the work of Eavan Boland, Susan Connolly, Paula Donlon, Mary Dorcey, Paula Meehan and Nuala Ní Dhomhnaill, the paper suggests that women poets today are subverting tradition and destabilizing a conventionally accepted fusion of the feminine with the national. This is achieved through direct challenge, through dislocation and through establishing a dialogue between the mythical and the real in the context of the lived experience of women in Ireland. Finally, the paper suggests the potential for civil and social effect of the work of women who engage consciously in the process of giving women an active voice.

Keywords

Irish; women; poets; iconic feminine; national; tradition

This article looks at the often uneasy relationship between Irish women poets and the notion of the iconic feminine which is strong in Irish cultural traditions. The 'iconic' referred to here includes three apparently disparate figures: the poetic muse, the 'virgin mother' and Mother Ireland/Cathleen Ní Houlihan. The context of my discussion is the dominant iconography and rhetoric of the Republic, whose symbolism idealizes women while its policies, on the whole, ignore us.

I focus on the poetry of Eavan Boland, Susan Connolly, Paula Donlon, Mary Dorcey, Paula Meehan and Nuala Ní Dhomhnaill, relating their work to the civil and political aspect of poetry, its potential for subversion and radical change. I suggest that these poets are actively engaged in destabilizing the very notion of feminine icons. This process is discernible in women's writing in both English and Irish. Although it is not usual to

FEMINIST REVIEW NO 50, SUMMER 1995

conflate the literature of the two languages in a discussion like this, I found I could not avoid it. Such an integration is problematic because of the gap between the traditions, a gap which I suggest may be narrowed through a poetic discourse which is also engaged in collapsing the space between women and poetry, giving women a discernible presence in the cultural life of the country, which is, in its turn, distinct from the 'nation'.

Early in 1984, not long after the people of Ireland had voted in favour of an amendment to the Constitution in which the state acknowledged the right to life of a foetus,[2] a fifteen-year-old girl named Ann Lovett died while giving birth in the small Irish town of Granard, County Longford. Her death and the death of her baby were made all the more poignant because the place where she chose to give birth and where she died was one of the many shrines to Mary, the 'virgin mother', which are familiar in the Irish landscape (McCafferty, 1984). The shrines serve as reminders, impossible images, models of inhuman perfection. Although these figures have particular relevance to women who are Catholic, their presence is obvious to all of us, while the ideology that sustains them also sustains our Constitution.

What does this juxtaposition mean? The image of a child giving birth at the feet of an implacable icon, a monument to female chastity, monstrous image of the unattainable which has alternately crippled and empowered women in Catholic countries in her various incarnations over the centuries, is difficult to accept (Warner, 1976; Condren, 1989). Did Ann Lovett believe that she might find help from this maternal image? How can our icons fail us to such a horrifying extent?

But how are those icons constituted? Who (and what) do they represent? In her poem, 'The Statue of the Virgin at Granard Speaks,' Paula Meehan gives the iconic figure a voice. Empowered to speak, she complains of isolation as if she has little choice in the matter:

> The whole town tucked up safe and dreaming,
> even wild things gone to earth, and I
> stuck up here in this grotto, without as much as
> star or planet to ease my vigil.
>
> (1991: 40)

From her shrine the statue is witness alike to faith and hope and human grief. Her sense of distance from the role assigned to her is clear:

> They call me Mary – Blessed, Holy, Virgin.
> They fit me to a myth of a man crucified.
>
> (40)

Figure 1 'Serpent Halo' by Carmel Benson. Reproduced with permission of the artist.

Further:

> They name me Mother of all this grief
> though mated to no mortal man.

(41)

But there are moments of relief, of loveliness, the beauty of girls in communion frocks in the spring, of flowers:

Or the grace of a midsummer wedding
when the earth herself calls out for coupling
and I would break loose of my stony robes,
pure blue, pure white, as if they had robbed
a child's sky for their colour. My being
cries out to be incarnate, incarnate,
maculate and tousled in a honeyed bed.

(41)

Meehan's choice of imagery here is powerful: the plundered sky of a child, the yearning of a plaster image to be embodied. A desire for touch, for the sexual, is tangible in the statue's longing to break free of the stone mould in which she has been cast. 'Maculate', a word no longer in use, of necessity summons its opposite, 'immaculate', part of the familiar phraseology of the virgin. Mary Immaculate, the immaculate conception: it is the immaculate nature of this image that sets her apart from ordinary women, you and me, the rest of us, tainted. The statue remembers:

On a night like this I remember the child
who came with fifteen summers to her name
and she lay down alone at my feet
without midwife or doctor or friend to hold her hand
and she pushed her secret out into the night,
far from the town tucked up in little scandals,
bargains struck, words broken, prayers, promises,
and though she cried out to me in extremis
I did not move
I didn't lift a finger to help her,
I didn't intercede with heaven,
nor whisper the charmed word in God's ear.

(42)

This is a play on the popular conception of the virgin's function as intermediary, intercessor on behalf of sinful humanity. There is a prayer beloved of her devotees, the rhythms and cadences of which are embedded in the pulse of many women raised as Catholics in this country. It goes like this:

Remember, O most gracious Virgin Mary, that never was it known that anyone who fled to thy protection, implored thine aid or sought thine intercession, was left unaided . . .

Meehan's poem demonstrates how far removed our hollow images are from the realities of life as it is lived by women on this island. The extraordinary power of this poem lies in its subversion of our familiar sense of the mythical. The icon, made to speak, voices ordinary human urges, loneliness, a desire for expression, hunger for contact, touch, experience. The voice with which Meehan endows the statue is out of character. These are not the words we would expect to hear from the virgin as she is cast in traditional iconography.

This process of ventriloquism and consequent subversion of traditional images is an intriguing and dynamic force at work in women's poetry in Ireland today. Eavan Boland, who is arguably our most influential poet writing in English, has written extensively about the difficult and constraining intersections between the idea of a nation, the influence of 'a specific poetic inheritance' and the facts of being a woman and a poet[3] (1989a). In Ireland, the familiar concept of the Muse as 'feminine' is further complicated by the symbolism of Mother Ireland, a relatively modern ideological construction of a Celtic figure.

The figure of sovereignty, the triple goddess who assumes the form of a crone, transformed by sexual union with the hero into a radiant young woman, a trope for the land and fertility, is common to many cultures. But in Ireland, during the period of colonization, this mythical female figure became transformed into the dream woman (*spéirbhean* or *aisling*) who inspired Gaelic poets and patriots, the woman who appeared to the poet demanding justice, restitution, a symbol of dispossession and of loss. When the Romantic Nationalist movement got under way in the context of the Irish literary revival during the nineteenth century, the *aisling* figure was given renewed significance. Her range was extended to embrace the Anglo-Irish. The image of the *Shean Bhean Bhoct* (Poor Old Woman)/Mother Ireland/Cathleen Ní Houlihan became a source of inspiration, a call-to-arms for patriots.

There was an explosion of literary activity in the country at this time. Much of the poetry was written by women and with a primarily political agenda. Since this was the ideology/imagery espoused by the group that eventually emerged as the leaders and architects of the new state, it became sanctified in the genesis of the new republic. Elsewhere, more specifically feminist struggles were underway such as the battle for suffrage and education (Ward, 1983; Owens, 1984). But there was a predictable tension between feminism and nationalism. The poetry written by the turn of the century nationalist women was framed in and by a political agenda and stayed within the canon of imagery allowed by the leaders of the movement.

But the new republic was not especially sympathetic to women. Or, indeed, to alternative versions of the mythology. (For a discussion of the erasure of alternative identities by nationalist ideology see, for example, Longley, 1990.) The resulting, composite, image of Cathleen almost erased all others. Celtic mythology holds a number of distinctive legendary female figures, many of them strong, overtly sexual, active and independent. None fitted comfortably within a modern agenda that defined the family rather than the individual as the unit of society and recorded in its constitution that a woman's place should be in the home. This arrest of the 'feminine', freezing it into a programmed political form, stilted, 'pure', lifeless, is being challenged and reversed by contemporary Irish women, most notably the poets who pose cultural and aesthetic challenges to a stultifying tradition.

The conventions and expectations of the iconic feminine in Irish poetry are well defined and well documented (Boland, 1989; Meaney, 1991; Longley, 1990; Ní Dhomhnaill, 1993). As these writers have argued, it has also been constraining to women, making it difficult for Irish women writers to engage with the national canon.

Boland's assertion that it is only recently that 'women have moved from being the subjects and objects of Irish poems to being the authors of them' (1989a) is one with which I would take issue. At the turn of the last century, for example, women were among the most enthusiastic practitioners of a form of cultural nationalism/nationalist culture which reinforced the image of Mother Ireland/Cathleen Ní Houlihan. Boland's (1989a) later qualification of her statement, pointing to the lack of role models, of the artistic life consciously lived, is more difficult to contradict. In this, she has been supported by her contemporaries (Ní Dhomhnaill, 1993). It is undeniably difficult for women to enter a creative arena dominated by the sense of the poem as feminine, the poet as masculine. It is doubly difficult when that image is compounded by what Boland has called the 'fusion of the national and the feminine' (1989a: 7).

The nature of the challenge has undoubtedly also changed because women are writing poetry today with a sense that they have a right to do so. Largely, it must be added, through the work of poets like Boland, who has contributed hugely to the development of women's poetry (and indeed, to the intellectual life of women in Ireland) through her public speaking, her writing and her commitment to workshops throughout the country (Boland, 1991), affirming women's right to enter the poetic arena.

Boland has written and spoken extensively about the dangers, for women, of a reflex fusion of the national and the feminine:

> Once the idea of a nation influences the perception of a woman then that woman is suddenly and inevitably simplified. She can no longer have complex feelings and aspirations. She becomes the passive projection of a national idea.
>
> (1989a: 12–13)

But this is exactly the point where the work of the women under discussion in this article poses a direct challenge to the traditional values of the establishment.[4] These poets resist the passive assumption of an idealized 'mythical' voice. They reject the standard relation of women to art, both in their work and in the arena of public debate.

Boland herself, for example, has an early and angry encounter with the 'mimic' muse in her 1980 collection *In Her Own Image*, a volume which followed a five-year period of apparent absence from the discourse.[5]

> I know you for the ruthless bitch you are:
> Our criminal, our tricoteuse, our Muse –
> Our Muse of Mimic Art.
>> ('Tirade for the Mimic Muse' 1980: 9)

This, being the opening poem of the collection, carries particular weight. In the poem, Boland berates the Muse for her betrayal of reality, the specific details of a woman's life. She demands that the muse 'look' as she shows a series of epiphanic experiences, instances of reality, a challenge that predates Meehan's very different articulation. Boland confronts the muse with her failures:

> How you fled
>
> The kitchen screw and the rack of labour,
> The wash thumbed and the dish cracked,
> The scream of beaten women,
> The crime of babies battered,
> The hubbub and the shriek of daily grief
> That seeks asylum behind suburb walls –
> A world you could have sheltered in your skirts –
> And well I know and how I see it now,
> The way you latched your belt and itched your hem
> And shook it off like dirt.
>> (1980: 10–11)

But 'Your luck ran out' (11), because now Boland's words take hold of the Muse, charge her with her own falsity. The poet warns:

> I will wake you from your sluttish sleep.
> I will show you true reflections, terrors.
> You are the Muse of all our mirrors.
> Look in them and weep.
>> (1980: 11)

The 'mirrors' Boland holds up reveal stark, uncompromising reflections: a woman battered, a woman post-mastectomy, an anorectic. The whole is framed in a play on appearance, reflection, cosmetics, artifice (as opposed to art). The image of the 'ideal', the 'desirable' woman.

In contrast to these idealized images are the crude stone carvings known as sheela-na-gigs (Sheila na gCíoch/Sheila of the Paps) to be found on the

FEMINIST REVIEW NO 50, SUMMER 1995

walls of early Irish churches and later castles. These female figures display exaggerated genitalia. They can be interpreted as representative of negative attitudes to women prevalent in the early Irish Christian church (Hickey, 1985). Recently, however, the role and meaning of the sheelas is being re-evaluated. Susan Connolly is one of many women who have come to reject the conventional interpretation of the figure. To Connolly, the sheela is a positive figure, representative of female sexuality and fertility. Because of the distortion of meaning associated with it, the sheela has also come to represent something wordless and hidden, and the repression of this specifically female energy, rendered grotesque and fearful through distortion. In *Áit Bhríd*, a collection of poems privately published by a collective of women poets which features many 'sheela' poems, Connolly writes:

> Caught in stone
> I celebrate
> all who tell
> the truth –
> over centuries
> of darkness.
> ('Female Figure' 1991)

The sheela poems in this volume represent a reclamation of a sense of female sexuality, going beyond the merely national to something older, deeper, more primitive.

Elsewhere, Connolly's invocation of legendary women represents a search for a tradition within which to locate herself. For Connolly, the reclamation of the spirit within each legend (Boann, the Banshee, Fedelm) is what is important. Of all our contemporary young poets writing in English, she is probably the one who has most consistently and thoroughly engaged with specific folkloric and mythological figures in the Celtic tradition. But her engagement is not a passive regurgitation of stale images. Nor is it wistful or backward looking.

In Connolly's work, the persona of the poet is always present while invoking the mythical figure: the two are not fused. In the process, the specific female figure contained within each legend is named and reclaimed, with the effect of overcoming the stifling homogeneity of the overarching Mother Ireland image. The figure remains emblematic, but represents a spirit to work with, invoke, define oneself in relation to, often making demands for speech or commitment which the poet is as yet unwilling or unready to make, although ultimately she knows that she must. Silence is perhaps an easier option, but in the end the poet's role is to break it, because truth has its own imperative.

**Figure 2 'Crouching Sheela', lithograph by Carmel Benson.
Reproduced with permission of the artist.**

Connolly's use of particular figures from legend is the start, for her, of a quest for expression. In 'Fedelm', for example, the eponymous poet of death begins foretelling the outcome of battle in a ritualized manner:

FEMINIST REVIEW NO 50, SUMMER 1995

'. . . I See it
crimson
I see it red
always crimson
always red . . .'
        (1991: 18)

But she has an urge to break free of prescribed forms:

'Away with myth
and metaphor –
I want to tell
things
as they are . . .

I want to tell
things falling apart –
to the death'.
            (19–20)

Ultimately, the struggle for expression is life-affirming. Death is the inevitable other face of life, and in facing up to its reality, these poets restore mortality and humanity to our poetry. For too long, our evasions have been fundamentally anti-life. Sometimes death, too, can be life-affirming, for example in the legend of Boann.

Boann broke a spell of prohibition that surrounded a magical well and was drowned for looking into the forbidden water (Smyth, 1989). Her spirit is associated with the river Boyne, which runs close to the necropolis of Newgrange, Knowth and Dowth, the region where Connolly lives and writes. For Connolly, specifically, the figure of Boann represents a flowing 'against the tide', a need to express something unspoken and dark which the poet is resisting. She manages to resist conflating the woman and the river, is clear that Boann is not the river, but the woman who was drowned by the river. Yet her spirit lingers at its source, where Connolly seeks it out and calls for release of a burden of words she cannot bear to shed.

those things
I want to say
I cannot say

so I say your name
instead Boann
and speak to you
            (1991: 5)

The tension between silence and utterance, between stylized images and living voices is nowhere more insidious in Irish literature than in the area of

Figure 3 'Leaping Sheela', lithograph by Carmel Benson. Reproduced with permission of the artist.

language itself. There is a distinct division between the literature in Irish and the literature in English, a gulf which is difficult to cross.

Boland has written in 'Mise Eire' that

> a new language
> is a kind of scar

and heals after a while
into a passable imitation
of what went before.
                    (1989b: 72)

But the critical silence between the two languages of this island is an open wound in Irish literature. Two separate and distinct traditions exist, each with its own crucial issues. It is not usual to approach the two in the same context. In doing so there is a great risk of distortion, conflation and assumption. However, it is impossible (and would be meaningless) to discuss the work of contemporary Irish women poets, especially in the context of the subversion of national icons, without referring to the work of Nuala Ní Dhomhnaill.[6]

Ní Dhomhnaill writes from the heart of the Irish language and the Gaelic tradition. She grafts the mythical/magical and the real together and destabilizes both in a playful, energetic, and powerful style that is doing as much to keep the Irish language alive as any other force on this island. She is exuberantly iconoclastic, playful and irreverent, more than a match for any fairy woman she might encounter.

Ní Dhomhnaill's poem 'Fuadach' ('The Abduction') illustrates the easy confusion of the mythical and the real:

Do shiúl bean an leasa
isteach im dhán.
Níor dhún sí doras ann.
Níor iarr sí cead.
                    (1991: 60)

The fairy-woman walked
into my poem.
She closed no door
She asked no by-your-leave.
(1991: 61; *Trans. Michael Hartnett*)

When the poet's husband comes home, he is unaware that a switch has been made and that the poet has been displaced:

Ach táimse i bpáirc an leasa
i ndoircheacht bhuan.
Táim leata leis an bhfuacht ann,
níl orm ach gúna fionnacheoigh.
                    (1991: 60)

For I am in the fairy field
in lasting darkness

and frozen with the cold there
dressed only in white mist.
(1991: 61; *Trans. Michael Hartnett*)

From her place of exile, the poet reveals the magic required for her
husband to banish the succubus and win the poet back.

It is difficult, perhaps presumptuous, to include Ní Dhomhnaill here
because she is operating within a different tradition which she has
consciously and deliberately chosen. But the thematic parallels are there,
and the fact remains that Irish poetry continues to develop in both
languages. In fact, it could even be argued that it is in poetry that we come
closest to breaking the language barrier. The traditions may be separate,
but they do not necessarily have to be in conflict.

Many contemporary and emerging poets writing in English find themselves
increasingly drawn to the use of Irish words and phrases in what the poet
Joan MacBreen has described as a process of osmosis between the two
languages. There are times when the precision (or, indeed, the fluidity) of
poetry demands expression in Irish, when no English substitute will do.
Ní Dhomhnaill, on the other hand, has used English words in her work, to
amusing effect.

Besides nuances of sound, association and meaning, there is a vast political
dimension to this issue which is outside the scope of this article. Not the
surface or obvious politics either, but more profound questions of power
relations, of loss and dispossession. Irish is a language which has been
suppressed, devalued and almost destroyed and as such is a particularly
interesting and valuable site for exploration of feminist issues. Similarly,
there are peculiar nuances and advantages to being Irish and working with
the English language, which Paula Meehan has described as her 'step-
mother tongue'.

Women working within both traditions have a great deal of shared interest
in these issues, and they often work, read and speak together. Poets writing
in Irish attract a wide audience, even from among people who do not
speak Irish easily or at all, but who want to hear the sound, the cadences
of it. The format of Ní Dhomhnaill's (and other) collections in translation,
with the Irish and English versions presented on facing pages, make the
Irish rendition more accessible to those readers who may be hesitant or
tentative in Irish. Bi-lingual readings, such as those staged by Poetry
Ireland to celebrate International Women's Day in 1992 and 1993, are well
attended.

In Ireland, poetry is still a living and to a large extent an oral tradition,
remnants of our poetic tradition in the past. Some poets (notably Ann Le

FEMINIST REVIEW NO 50, SUMMER 1995

Marquand Hartigan) perform as much as they read their poems. Poetry readings are popular social occasions and the launch of new collections are half-reading, half-party. The effect of this is to give the printed poem an echo of the tones and rhythms of the poet's voice, enriching our sense of the poem. Irish women poets today form a living tradition, visible, audible, exuberant. We demand more from our poets than art, as if their presence, their voice, their vitality is an essential part of the process.

Mary Dorcey, a poet with a powerful voice, has used the notion of readings as the site of her direct challenge to the comfortable, established notions of what poetry is or might be. In her poem 'Deliberately Personal', she describes the desperation of a woman who commits suicide after cleaning the house, the misery of a child raped by her uncle, the self-protective distancing from responsibility which the community achieves afterwards. The poet then turns the focus neatly on to her audience:

> And who are you
> come to that?
> All of you
> out there
> out of the spotlight –
> out for a night's entertainment,
> smiles upturned so politely;
> asking me
> why I have to be –
> so raw
> and deliberately
> personal?
>
> (1991: 23)

In this way Dorcey destabilizes the cosy intimacy between poem and reader, while challenging hierarchies of meaning. Many other poets, such as Rita Ann Higgins and Medbh McGuckian also engage in this process.

There is a civil as well as an aesthetic aspect to the role of the poet within a community, which is well recognized. In Ireland, women poets are actively engaged in articulating new challenges to our most comfortable assumptions, even when it seems most heretical to do so (Dorgan, 1994; Mills, 1992).

In 'The Journey', a powerful poem where Boland articulates a sense of reconciliation and affiliation with poetry and with human experience, she writes:

> 'Depend on it, somewhere a poet is wasting
> his sweet uncluttered metres on the obvious

emblem instead of the real thing.
Instead of sulpha we shall have hyssop dipped
in the wild blood of the unblemished lamb,
so every day the language gets less

for the task and we are less with the language.'
(1989b: 97)

But Boland's own poetic practice is very different. In a later poem, 'Outside History', she moves towards resolution of the problem and makes her choice:

I have chosen:

out of myth and into history I move to be
part of that ordeal
whose darkness is
only now reaching me . . .
(1990: 45)

Part of humanity is mortality, an inescapable part of life is death. By restoring the dark side of experience and mortality to her poetic range, Boland achieves a balance, a reconciliation, not only for herself but for the many voices she represents in the process of exposing an alienating rhetoric of imagery (1989a: 7).

In her poem 'Ard Fheis' Paula Meehan writes of the numbing effect on individual consciousness of this national rhetoric. Listening to a speaker at a political meeting,

I wind up in the ghost place
the language rocks me to,
a cobwebby state, chilled vault
littered with our totems.
(1991: 21)

This 'ghost place' is the site inhabited by our iconic figures, our 'totems'. It is the cold fairyland to which the poet was banished (Ní Dhomhnaill, 'Fuadach/Abduction'); it is the land of prohibition, of unacceptable law, for Connolly ('BoAnn'); it is the site from which Meehan's own plaster-figure observes human distress and does nothing to intervene ('The Statue of the Virgin at Granard Speaks').

In Boland's most recent collection, *In a Time of Violence*, the figures appeal to the poet for release from this barren state of exile:

This is what language did to us. Here
is the wound, the silence, the wretchedness
of tides and hillsides and stars where

FEMINIST REVIEW NO 50, SUMMER 1995

we languish in a grammar of sighs,
in the high-minded search for euphony,
in the midnight rhetoric of poesie.

We cannot sweat here. Our skin is icy.
We cannot breed here. Our wombs are empty.
Help us to escape youth and beauty.

Write us out of the poem. Make us human
in cadences of change and mortal pain
and words we can grow old and die in.
('Time and Violence' 1994: 49–50)

A primary focus of Boland's latter development as a poet has been in bringing living women to occupy the space formerly occupied by mythic figures, empty icons. In 'Anna Liffey', she introduces both trope and woman in the same poem, but is clear, as Connolly is, as to the distinction between the two:

A river is not a woman.
(1994: 43)

In this poem she clearly articulates and defines her artistic project in relation to the iconic:

Make of a nation what you will
Make of the past
What you can –

There is now
A woman in a doorway.

It has taken me
All my strength to do this.

Becoming a figure in a poem.
Usurping a name and a theme.
(1994: 43)

The difficulty of the process of gaining purchase in a discourse which is usually carried on over the heads of women while ignoring reality and pain, is notorious. The ventriloquism practised by our women poets at least makes the struggle conscious and confronts the state and its iconography with its failures.

In 1992, while the country raged once more over the effects of the 1983 Amendment, this time when the travel rights of a fourteen-year-old girl, raped and pregnant, who had gone to England for an abortion, were restricted,[7] Paula Donlon wrote, in 'The State Acknowledges the Right to Life of the Unborn':

Figure 4 'Floating Sheela', lithograph by Carmel Benson. Reproduced with permission of the artist.

We are driven to carry
images that will not be aborted.
                    (1992: 6)

This is a clear indictment of the failure of the various images of women permissible in this country to sustain and empower living, breathing, mortal, human women. In the middle of the storm of national debate, accusation and counter-accusation, Donlon called attention to the real, the simple issue at the heart of the matter.

> She is saying;
> *This is my body*
> Listen.
> (Original emphasis; 1992: 6)

The italicized phrase is an echo of Catholic liturgy, a sacrament enacted daily around the country, of communion. Donlon's use of the declaration 'This is my body' in the mouth of the female child who is not allowed choice, is a powerful reversal, exposing the ludicrous imbalance and asymmetry of power. Its use in this context underlines the complicity of the government and the Catholic Church, Catholic attitudes, in the subjection of women (including women of other, or no particular, religious beliefs) to unwanted pregnancy, even following unwanted sex. Again we have a poet who uses a particular displacement of voice to destabilize our icons and bring them into a closer relation with truth.

Eavan Boland has argued that 'once the image is distorted the truth is demeaned' (1989a). Irish women poets are actively seeking to express and make visible those aspects of experience previously ignored, obscured and falsely represented by two-dimensional, lifeless, inhuman icons. In the process they are restoring vitality to our culture and claiming a right to full participation in the civil and political life of this island.

Notes

I would like to thank Susan Connolly, Fidelma Farley, Gerardine Meaney and Ailbhe Smyth for their comments on earlier drafts of this article.

Lia Mills is the research and teaching Fellow at the Women's Education Research and Resource Centre (WERRC) in University College, Dublin, where she is a doctoral candidate. Her research is focused on Irish women writers at the turn of the last century.

1 Opening line of 'Mise Eire' ('I am Ireland'), a poem by Eavan Boland (1989b: 71).

2 The 8th Amendment to the 1937 Irish Constitution reads: 'The state acknowledges the right to life of the unborn and, with due regard to the equal right to life of the mother, guarantees in its laws to respect, and as far as practicable, by its

laws to defend and vindicate that right.' Women in Northern Ireland are also restricted in their right to reproductive choice. See McWilliams, 1993 and Northern Ireland Law Reform Association (1992).

3 Terms that are often held to be mutually exclusive. Sean O'Riordain, for example, has famously written 'Ní file ach filíochta, bhean' ('Woman is not poet, but poetry').

4 Catherine Byron's (1992) challenge to Seamus Heaney also directly confronts this tradition.

5 'I didn't disappear. Of course not. What really happened was that, as far as poets were concerned, I went off the radar screen. I went to the suburbs. I married. I had two small children.' Interview with Jody Allen-Randolph (1993).

6 For an introduction to the work of Ní Dhomhnaill, see Nic Dhiarmada (1988). It is interesting to note that the issues of power/language and of tradition/ mythology are changed within the context of the Irish language. See also Ní Dhomhnaill's own essay, 'What foremothers?' (1992), itself a warning to those who would make careless assumptions in this area.

7 A subsequent referendum in 1992 following this case reversed the previous decision of the people. However, the promised legislation regulating the practice of abortion has not yet materialized.

References

ALLEN-RANDOLPH, Jody (1993) 'An interview with Eavan Boland' *Irish University Review: A Journal of Irish Studies Spring/Summer 1993*: 117–30.

BOLAND, Eavan (1980) *In Her Own Image* Dublin: Arlen House.

—— (1989a) *A Kind of Scar: The Woman Poet in a National Tradition* Dublin: Attic Press.

—— (1989b) *Selected Poems* Manchester: Carcanet.

—— (1990) *Outside History* Manchester: Carcanet.

—— (1991) 'In defense of workshops' *Poetry Ireland Review* Vol. 31: 40–8.

—— (1994) *In a Time of Violence* Manchester: Carcanet.

BYRON, Catherine (1992) *Out of Step: Pursuing Seamus Heaney to Purgatory* Bristol: Loxwood Stoneleigh.

CONDREN, Mary (1989) *The Serpent and the Goddess: Women, Religion and Power in Celtic Ireland* San Francisco: Harper & Row.

CONNOLLY, Susan and MacCARTHY, Catherine Phil (1991) *How High the Moon* Dublin: Poetry Ireland.

DONLON, Paula (1992) 'The state acknowledges the right to life of the unborn' in *MsChief* 1: 2.

DORCEY, Mary (1991) *Moving Into the Space Cleared by Our Mothers* Galway: Salmon.

DORGAN, Theo (1994) 'Interview with Eavan Boland' *Inprint* RTE Radio 1: 9 January 1994.

HICKEY, Helen (1985) *Images of Stone: Figure Sculpture of the Lough Erne Basin* Fermanagh District Council.

FEMINIST REVIEW NO 50, SUMMER 1995

LONGLEY, Edna (1990) *From Cathleen to Anorexia: The Breakdown of Irelands* Dublin: Attic Press.

McCAFFERTY, Nell (1984) 'The death of Ann Lovett' in *The Best of Nell* Dublin: Attic Press.

McWILLIAMS, Monica (1993) 'The Church, the State and the Women's Movement in Northern Ireland' in **SMYTH, A.** (1993) editor, *Irish Women's Studies Reader* Dublin: Attic Press.

MEANEY, Gerardine (1991) *Sex and Nation* Dublin: Attic Press.

MEEHAN, Paula (1991) *The Man Who Was Marked by Winter* Oldcastle: Gallery Press.

MILLS, Lia (1992) 'Interview with Paula Meehan' *MsChief* 1: 1.

NÍ DHOMHNAILL, Nuala (1991) *Selected Poems: Rogha Danta* Dublin: Raven Arts Press.

—— (1993) 'What foremothers?' in *Poetry Ireland Review* Vol. 36: 18–31.

NIC DHIARMADA, Bríona (1988) 'Tradition and the female voice in contemporary Gaelic poetry' in *Women's Studies International Forum* Vol. 11(4): 387–93.

NORTHERN IRELAND ABORTION LAW REFORM ASSOCIATION (1992) 'Abortion: the case for legal reform in Northern Ireland', in **SMYTH,** (1992).

OWENS, Rosemary Cullen (1984) *Smashing Times: A History of The Irish Women's Suffrage Movement 1889–1922* Dublin: Attic Press.

SMYTH, Ailbhe (1989) 'Introduction', in **SMYTH, A.** (1989) editor, *Wildish Things: An Anthology of New Irish Women's Writing* Dublin: Attic Press.

—— (1992) editor, *The Abortion Papers: Ireland* Dublin: Attic Press.

WARD, Margaret (1983) *Unmanageable Revolutionaries: Women and Irish Nationalism* Dingle: Brandon.

WARNER, Marina (1976) *Alone of All Her Sex: The Myth and Cult of the Virgin Mary* New York: Knopf.

Irish/woman/artwork

Selective readings

Hilary Robinson

FEMINIST REVIEW NO 50, SUMMER 1995, pp. 89–110

Abstract

This paper concentrates upon particular artworks from Irish women artists. It demonstrates that there are certain themes which recur in their artwork. These include dislocation, particularities about place and contestation around language, all of which are rooted in the lived experience of being Irish, being female and being an artist. At the same time the paper provides readings of this artwork which demonstrate that these experiences are diverse, and that the areas of representation within which the artists are working are socially produced constructs. There is therefore no romantic essentialist category of 'Irish woman artist', but rather the richly interplaying histories, readings and contexts of Irish/woman/artwork.

Keywords

Irish; woman; artist; artwork; selective readings; representation

This paper has two main aims: to introduce selected but diverse fine art work currently being produced by Irish women artists to an audience who may not be familiar with it; and secondly, to begin a demystification of that very category 'Irish woman artist'. It will achieve the former by concentrating on particular works by a range of artists; and will achieve the latter by juxtaposing these works to the specifics of place, of culture, and of language as experienced by – and as producers of – women artists in Ireland, in Northern Ireland, and in the first generation Irish diaspora.

To write an article about Irish women artists begs a number of questions. Not the least of these are: what is Irishness?', 'is there a commonality of women?', and 'how do you define artist?'. In turn, combinations of these categories could be questioned ('what is so particular about being an Irish artist? – or an Irish woman? – or a woman artist?'). The full discussion of the context and work of Irish women artists could either become a book or head towards a narrow definition.

This article will not try to fulfil either role. I have no wish to attempt a definition of the Irish woman artist or her work; nor do I wish to mention as many Irish women artists as possible. Neither would be feasible – the first would be proscriptive, and the second would end as a list of names and spurious categories. Instead there are various parameters which this article will work within, and aims which it will have, which should be made explicit. First, *Feminist Review* is an academic feminist journal, and its readership is primarily British; however, a 'special' issue on Irish women and their contexts will bring in an additional readership. The bulk of the audience for this will therefore not be Irish, nor will it be a specialist visual arts audience. But the readers will be diverse, and the diversity of their interests will be further widened by the diversity of the subjects discussed in the issue. Second, I am not Irish: although I now live and work in Northern Ireland, in Belfast, I was born in England and brought up English. This raises another set of questions around representation – who speaks for whom, who represents whom, and how.

As a writer on art and an art college lecturer, by choosing to live in Northern Ireland I have made a number of commitments, not the least of which is to the women artists on both sides of the border. I would question the essentialism that sometimes goes hand in hand with an insistence upon the 'authentic voice'; but at the same time I have to negotiate a position which is neither representing (or speaking on behalf of), nor rendering invisible the actual women whose work I shall discuss. Yet there is a fundamental paradox here, which many feminist artwriters attempt to unravel: ultimately, a viewer of artwork is left with the artwork, not the artist, and to collapse artwriting back into biographical description or anecdote can either reinforce reactionary and patriarchal notions of the artist as 'gifted' individual, whose talents are beyond social construction, or it can portray the artworks as merely an illustration of the life. The other side of the paradox is that feminism rightly insists that the personal is political, and that only by exposing details of lived experience can their underlying political structure become clear. This is a paradox which comes into even sharper focus in this context: on the one hand, the reactionary construction of 'genius' can map quite closely onto the more romantic and sentimental (but still racist) British constructions of 'Irishness' – a certain wildness, instinctiveness, lack of concern for social niceties, irresponsibility and unpredictability; and in both cases the lure of difference is exoticized. On the other hand, anecdote and autobiography can be used to re-enforce those notions, to construct notions of victimhood, or to place Irish culture and artworks as symptom, emblem or illustration.

There is a distance that is inevitably found in the gap between the audience and the artist – the gap that resides in the literal space and bodily relation between the audience and the artwork as well as the gap between their experiences. This physical gap is where meanings are created by the audience – and in this case that distance will have a certain added and significant layer of difference. Aware of this, I do not aim to represent Irish women artists, as individuals or as a category, but rather to negotiate a reading of a selected number of artworks. I have selected artists whose work demonstrates a strong sense of their Irishness and of their womanliness, but also for whom these identities and definitions are questionable constructions. One of my aims, as I have indicated, is to demythologize the very category 'Irish woman artist' which can be so easily stereotyped and romanticized by the outsider, and replace it with a series of readings of artworks, readings which have to be presented within particular contexts. These contexts (feminist analyses of particular social structures in the island of Ireland) I hope will not be seen as producers of the artworks as symptoms, but rather will elucidate the strategies and choices of the artists.

Two of the artists (Fran Hegarty and Anne Tallentire) are of the Irish diaspora. Both spent their early lives in the island of Ireland and have emerged as artists while living in England. The position of the diasporic woman artist, who identifies as Irish not only through her personal life but also overtly through her work, is particular. The work has not yet been done on the cultural negotiations they have to go through and the strategies which are available to them to make work indicating location or positioning, but which does not reaffirm the colonial and patriarchal view of them as the eternal and ahistorical 'other'. It is indicative of their situation that the work of these two artists attends to dislocation, particularities of place, and loss of language.

**Figure 1 Monument to the Low-paid Women Workers,
Louise Walsh, 1993 (cast bronze).**

Monument to the Low-paid Women Workers, Louise Walsh, 1993 (figure 1):
In the tradition of Western civic sculpture, the piece is made of cast bronze
and stands in a busy city street. Unusually, the two sculpted figures do not
stand on a plinth, but occupy the same space as us, although they are slightly
larger than life-size. Also unusually, they are female: a mature woman and
her younger, adult daughter. The city is Belfast: in common with most nineteenth-century industrial Western cities its public sculptures show figures of
historical men (leaders, soldiers, politicians) and allegorical women (virtues, personifications of colonialized countries, the muses). (See Warner,
1985 for a full discussion of this, particularly the first chapter.) In one respect

this sculpture is not unusual, as these figures are not representative of individual women. Instead it seeks to make visible a deconstruction of a class or categorization of women – the low-paid women workers of the title – and the contexts of their lives. Each figure is sculpted in a realistic fashion, augmented by objects which make up their lives – for instance the older woman has a shopping basket for a belly; the younger has a typewriter. Their bodies literally carry the traces of their working lives: the accoutrements of low-paid and unpaid female labour such as scrubbing brushes help form a shoulder here, a breast or an arm there. Additionally, inscribed upon them are the facts and statistics of work for these women – listings of the lowest-paid jobs, which are traditionally women's occupations; the rates of pay for particular jobs; and so on. But in order to read these, to know the circumstances of life for these women, you have to get close, become intimately acquainted with them, as the type is small. It becomes a wider political metaphor in a public place: only those who care enough to get close will ever know. Maybe this is why local journalists, sectarian in more ways than one, still refer to the sculpture as 'the two bimbos'. Maybe that is why the city fathers, having commissioned the work, later refused to accept it. Maybe knowing they are supposed to represent these voters the sculpture shames them into knowing they represent far different concerns. The piece was given space by a private company, which placed it on its land: the entrance to a small shopping mall which leads to the main Belfast Bus station – ironically a far more 'public' situation than their original destination.

The press (particularly the Protestant press) and TV in Northern Ireland are fond of giving statistical details of what it means to live in this particular part of the island of Ireland. Thus we are told variously that Belfast has one of the lowest crime rates of any city in the UK; that the cost of living is the cheapest; that the middle classes have the highest disposable income rate; that the highest rate of new car ownership in the UK is here. Sometimes they may also let on that some of the UK's highest unemployment is also here, up to 80 per cent male unemployment in some areas. What the visitor to Belfast sees is a vast and obvious class divide, a pretence of 'normalness' on the part of the middle classes, and a working class divided against itself.

Figure 2   The Great War Continues (After René Magritte), Mary MacIntyre, 1992 (detail; colour reversal print).

The Great War Continues (After René Magritte), Mary MacIntyre, 1992 (figure 2): A series of four colour reversal photographic prints, each 36 × 24 inches, these images make reference not only to *The Great War* by Magritte, but also to traditions of portraiture within fine art. More insistent than the fine art references, however, are the critiques of representations of women. MacIntyre is from Northern Ireland, and this series forms an ironic critique of certain types of Northern bourgeois femininity. This is achieved through iconographic simplification and stylizing, so that the constructions of that femininity become clearly indicated. In each print, a woman is seen frontally, half or three-quarter length, formally posed. They are imaged in garden settings, which become a reference to a cumulative number of fine art iconographies of women. In the early Renaissance, the Madonna would often be painted against a landscape of recognizable type, to add veracity to the main narrative. From the mid Renaissance a naked woman would be represented against a landscape, conflating notions of femaleness, nature, fecundity and eroticism (this still continues with artists such as Jeff Koons and in pornography). In the eighteenth century society portraitists such as Gainsborough would paint their patrons in the landscape they – or their husbands – owned. MacIntyre ironizes this tradition. Her women are posed wearing the formal, expensively tailored clothes that are the twentieth-century equivalent of those worn by the nineteenth-century bourgeois women painted by Ingres. They enact states of denial, to use the word in its psychoanalytic sense. The poses are rigid, arms held across the body, barring access; knees beneath a pleated skirt held firmly together. In the most extreme image of sexual denial a woman stands before a greenhouse, a place where the talk is of seeds and propagation; in her hand, held down across her genital area, she holds a three-pronged gardening fork. The women's faces are obliterated by masks of flowers, those constant clichés of femininity and metaphors for female sexuality. They mask individuality or expression, and prevent personal access. This iconographic denial, coupled with the title, may also cause the viewer to reflect upon the state of denial in which much of the middle class of Northern Ireland lives, whether Catholic or Protestant, evidenced through the lavish spending upon cars, clothing, restaurants and so forth in order to maintain a visible normalcy.

Images of women in the press become powerful reproducers of ideologies of femininity. In the Republic a large number of gratuitous images of women at social events are used by the newspapers (Miss so-and-so pictured at the reception held for . . . etc, etc) – also being part of the pool of references evoked by MacIntyre's work.

To Kill an Impulse, Sandra Johnston, 1994 (work in progress) (figures 3a, 3b): A package of dozens of slides arrive, images which are the work in progress of this young Northern woman. Her previous work has included video and photographic installation. There are two long series of images: one is of photographs taken of women at political funerals, women who have lost through violence the men they loved – husbands, sons, lovers, fathers; women grieving and bereft. Some of the images are familiar to me from newspaper or TV reports; many seem to be taken with a motor-drive on the camera. Juxtaposed with these, in pairs, are images of the artist; abjecting herself, stripping herself of self-consciousness and even (it appears) of conscious expression, traces of grief, loss and bereavement mark her face and body. The sets of images could be provocatively voyeuristic, but instead are emotionally challenging and moving. An older woman artist, recently returned from 'Irish Days II', a group exhibition in Poland, which Johnston

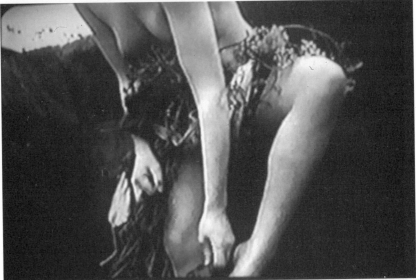

Figures 3a, 3b *To Kill an Impulse*, Sandra Johnston, 1994 (work in progress) (detail; slide transparencies)

also took part in, tells me she thinks the work of this young woman is the most important coming out of Ireland at the moment.

Part of the stimulus for the work was trying to puncture or 'freeze' significant moments inside media coverage, excavating the moment when people touch or cry or stifle their feelings through an awareness of the camera . . . By contrast the second sets of imagery are taken from performances done with full acceptance and directness into the face of the camera, responding through the body like a random-fitting discourse to the burial 'spectacle' which is at once both banal yet voyeuristic, familiar but prohibited territory. The alliance between the media and performance imagery is . . . uneasy . . . it rests on exploiting a certain vulnerability within the media pictures, stilled into sequences separate from . . . their original broadcast. If you look into the images stilled in time they are deeply moving, they contain sparks of recognition in the pain silenced. I decided not to address this material in a rationalizing vein but to unearth the disquiet in me, and explore the sense of being switched off, or hardened, so my intrusion into other people's grief is equally a violation of my own security and distance.

(Sandra Johnston, letter to the author, 1994)

Johnston later tells me that the images have been used in a projected installation in Berlin, where the audience reaction was either empathetic, immediate and personal, or silent, as if not knowing what to say. Projected images have particular qualities: dematerialized, formed by light alone, needing darkness; the audience has to take up particular positions in order to see the images, or risk disrupting or blocking them. These qualities resonate with the representations Johnston had made.

In contrast to the South, in the North, newspapers and TV are marked by an iconographic litany, images of weeping women. Even after the cessation of military violence from the paramilitaries, these images continue to be re-shown as prisoners are released, cases come to court, anniversaries occur, other deaths happen. In the Protestant press images of young girls sometimes appear, made-up and dressed as if ten years older, taking part in ballroom dancing competitions. In the Catholic press images of young girls sometimes appear, in the 'traditional' dresses developed after the 1921 partition, taking part in Irish dancing competitions.

Do You Know this Place, Anne Tallentire, 1990 (figure 4): This installation and performance work draws attention to the particularities of the occupation of place, and the construction through language of the legitimacies of location. Brought up near the border between the Republic and the North, now living in London, Tallentire redirects us to consider all places as contested, not only as physical sites but within language. In a central park in Rochdale, overlooked by the city hall and the police station, Tallentire removed a square of turf. The topsoil was removed to the gallery and placed in an equivalently-sized square; the park site had wire link fencing laid over it. Suspended over the soil in the gallery was a square of perspex with letters and symbols inscribed into it. Tallentire had transposed the dictionary definitions of the words 'do you know this place', removing the words themselves to leave only the etymological and phonetic

Figure 4 _Do You Know this Place_, Anne Tallentire, 1990 (detail; mixed media).

details. The concept of 'place' was thus demonstrated to be maintained through the construct of language. During the exhibition, the topsoil in the gallery dried and cracked, and in the park, weed grew through the wire mesh. In a performance, Tallentire took some of the bedrock of Rochdale, ground down, and 'wrote' with it in the square in the park again 'do you know this place'. The turf was then replaced, leaving a woman's questioning written in stone beneath it.

The whole of Northern Ireland is a border between concepts of legitimate occupation, concepts of Irishness and Britishness. Like all borders, identity is crucial, flags are waved, ambiguity ridiculed; all of the land is spoken for, colour-coded – green/white/gold – red/white/blue – on the kerbstones, postboxes and on young men's clothing. It is often women who insist on maintaining the in-between (a no man's land?) as a legitimate space – privately, keeping the links in families which are both Catholic and Protestant; publicly, in the peace movements.

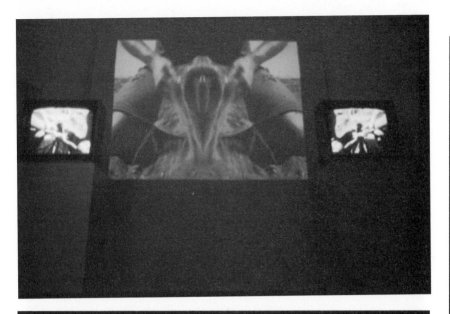

Figure 5 *Gold*, Frances Hegarty, 1993 (detail; video still)

Gold, Frances Hegarty, 1993 (figure 5): Against one wall of the gallery, a triptych: three spaces for video. In the centre, as with a traditional triptych, the largest: a video projection screen. To either side, smaller images, on TV-sized video monitors echoing and complementing the centre. The images are taken in rural Donegal, in the city of Derry and in the Australian outback, reflecting patterns of migration and emigration in Hegarty's own family. The sounds include a single female voice singing in Gaelic; insect and bird noises of Australia; the incomprehensibly mutated voices of soldiers in Derry and the sullen, slowed-down clang of their checkpoint barrier falling with finality. The camera-work in the Donegal sequences is roving and confident; in Derry it is furtive, a transgressive, illegal watching of the checkpoint barrier past the elbow and automatic weapon of a British soldier. In Australia we see the artist in front of the camera, standing survey-ing the seemingly empty land. But if the sequences from Ireland speak of colonization, aided by the woman's clear Gaelic voice and the listener's bafflement at the soldier's senseless growl, then the Australian images are equally problematized. The camera no longer mimics the artist's eyes; instead it sees her; and in one sequence it sees out from inside a cave or rock-built shelter. The curve of the rock echoes the curve of the gate in the city walls of Derry, and tied reeds echo the army barrier. We are left wonder-ing whose eyes we see through here, and at their relationship with the distant Irishwoman. In the final sequence, in rhythmic and compulsive movements, we see the artist repeatedly lifting dry sand into the lap of her skirt, the sand always slipping back to the ground. The camera is in close-up; we see her thighs as she kneels, her hands, and her lower torso. The film is split vertically and mirrored; it is run backwards as well as forwards. The symmetrical imagery is at times reminiscent of female genitals. The artist is both identified with the colonized soil, but unable and unwilling to contain it herself; in a never-ending taking and giving she is both similar to and different from it.

The identities of an individual are multi-layered and changeable; the contestations an individual has to face shift as she moves from place to place. I have been told that Ireland is unique among countries with high emigration in that more women than men leave. Feelings of separation, dislocation, and the need to maintain links are frequently found in the work of Irish women.

Folt, Alice Maher, 1993 (figure 6): 'Folt' is a slightly archaic Irish word which can mean tresses, foliage, abundance, or forests of hair. Three deep wooden frames each house nine smaller paintings on paper in black, white and grey. The images are recognizable to anyone who was once a little girl fantasizing about having long hair, or who drew princesses who had to have elaborate hairstyles: they are girlish, simple (but not simplistic) renderings of female hairstyles as seen from the back. The committed, involving, girlhood fantasies of evolving femininity are immediately evoked, and the pleasure in remembering them forms a disjuncture with all-too-present womanly realities of dealing with hair in a way which is at one and the same time socially, emotionally and professionally appropriate. A further deep frame holds a rope of hair, gatherings from hairdressers, bound together in terrifying intimacy. The sensuality of hair growing on the head immediately tarnishes when it falls or is cut; it has the quality of something excreted or otherwise discarded by the body. The two forms of representation – actual hair, and paintings of hair – highlight the way that the binary opposites of nature and culture meet in hair. Hair is frighteningly of nature – it grows, dies, falls, changes colour, develops texture, all beyond our control; yet what it does and what we do with it are surrounded by cultural taboos and significations.

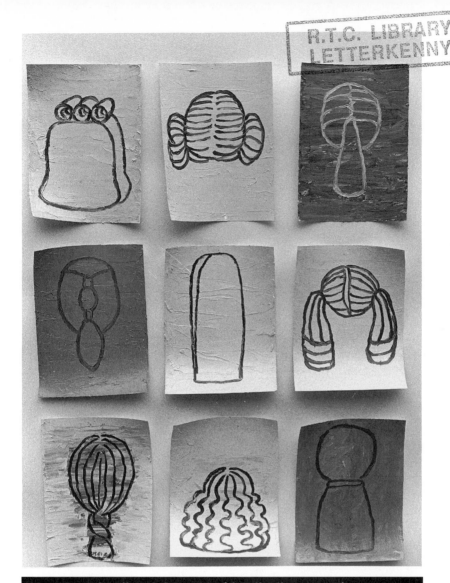

Figure 6 *Folt*, Alice Maher, 1993 (detail; oil on paper)

Among the artists in Ireland dealing with broadly political concerns overtly in their work, it is the men who are more likely to deal with the up-front politics of nationality, history and political violence (see Willie Doherty's photoworks and video installations, shortlisted for the 1994 Turner prize; Ken Hardy's work deconstructing colonialism; Micky Donnelly's painterly recreation of republican symbolism; Paul Seawright's documentation of the Orange Order). Women artists are more likely to deal with the politics of identities and cultural changes as they manifest on place and body.

FEMINIST REVIEW NO 50, SUMMER 1995

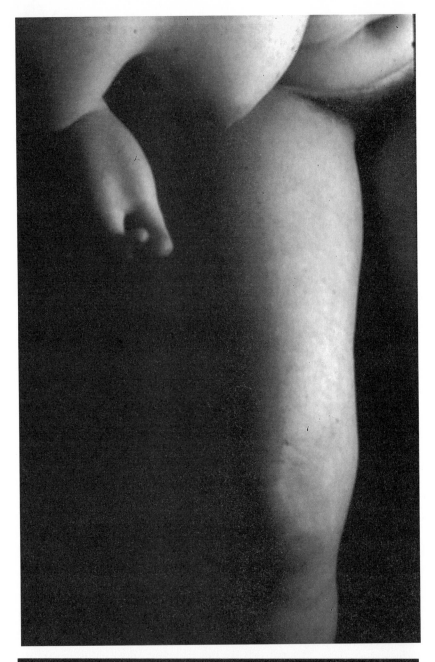

Figure 7   *Untitled*, Mary Duffy, 1985 (detail; tape/slide).

Untitled, Mary Duffy, 1985 (figure 7): A tape-slide presentation: the images are of the body of the artist, in warm colours and (in a common glamour or portrait tradition) side lit in an otherwise darkened environment. Where our expectations are disrupted is that Duffy has only tiny arms due to Thalido-mide; in photographing her body in a traditionally glamorous fashion, Duffy forces us to reconsider our own preconceptions of feminine beauty, what constitutes the aesthetic, and what constitutes wholeness. Far from being a cause for victimhood, Duffy's wholeness is palpably celebrated in the piece; any feelings of threat or disgust are thereby placed in the realm of the viewer as her problem to deal with.

> Through my work I try and find a balance in relation to my feelings towards my body. My work has been both subjective and objective. It is based on contradiction. It is not a comfortable or definitive statement about images of women or images of disability. My political experiences have taught me that contradiction can be confrontational or creative.
>
> I have been surrounded all my life by images of a culture which values highly physical beauty and wholeness, a culture which denied difference. My identity as a woman with a disability is one that is strong, sensual, sexual, fluid, flexible and political. Reclaiming and redefining my body and its politics continues to be an extraordinary learning experience. I am just beginning to define for myself, my difference, my sense of wholeness and to welcome it deeply and intensely.
>
> (Duffy, 1987)

Many Irish women return again and again to the body as the place from which – and the medium through which – they must speak. Not as an unproblematic, pre-verbal or pre-patriarchal place of retreat, but as a site of struggle – struggle for control, struggle for meaning – from which it is important not to become alienated. The desires of the body are not simple

Figure 8 *Cranium*, Kate Malone, 1991 (cibachrome).

pleasures, from a biologically pure place, but become inscribed in the body through experience. Irish women have demonstrated this through their critiques of the controlling of women's bodies and sexuality through the ties between Catholic morality and state legislation on abortion, contraception and divorce.

Cranium, Kate Malone, 1991 (figure 8): A series of photographs, in luscious cibachrome colour, each 2 ft square, some grouped to form a 4 ft square. Crimson is the dominant colour, crimson velvet filling the image. It appears to be stretched over a limb or part of a body: a woman's hands appear at unlikely angles and wrestle with the velvet, twisting and pulling at it. The tension the fabric is under forms a startling contrast with the luxury of its surface and the surface of the print: the fingernails of the taught hands are bitten back to the quick. The struggle for – or battle against – sensual pleasure that is being enacted is reinforced by the jolts to the viewer's visual pleasure in the image, eased and seduced by the sensual surface of the print reinforced by the imagined feel of the velvet; disturbed by the tension of the twists (is this anguish? sexual tension? anger?); shocked by the distressed nails and fingertips.

As particular places are, so too the bodies of women are contested sites throughout the world: Ireland should not be picked out as particularly retrograde in this respect. But the Republic is almost alone in Western Europe in maintaining overt legal control over women's bodies through legislation on divorce and abortion – in most European countries such control is covert.

Most clearly, women's critiques of this have emerged through literature, journalism and political activism. Visual artists have mainly avoided the literal or narrative in their work, in order to avoid becoming simplistically illustrational, but also because the poetics of bodily experience lie in a place that is not mediated by the verbal, and understandings of bodily experience can be reached by means other than the literary. Artworks can be particularly effective in mediating this experience. They are experienced first through the body, in space, walking around them, through the eyes, through their scale, through recognition of textures and materials: it is at the point of analysis, discussion and reflection that words about artworks, and words about words about artworks, are developed. If Irish women have turned to the poetics of the politics of the body, rather than the body politic, which is more the domain of male artists, then the impetus is not to be found in a lack of political activism. Instead, it is to be found in the occupation of the site of some of the fiercest of Ireland's political battles: the female body, an occupation enforced by the Church and policed by the state to

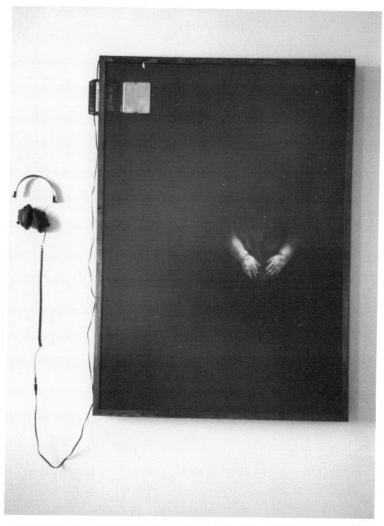

Figure 9 *Hand to Mouth*, Sharon Kelly, 1993 (drawing and tape recorder).

be disempowered and silent. Many artworks by Irish women make visible, un-silence, the experience of occupying that body, and are in turn experienced by their audience in a highly bodily, sensual and visceral way.

Hand to Mouth, Sharon Kelly, 1993 (figure 9): A densely black charcoal drawing, about 4 ft high, is in a simple frame. In the soft surface to one side are the hands and forearms of a baby, about life-size and at breast-height. Is it emerging from the softness of the charcoal, or sinking gently back into it? In the top left corner, set into the drawing, is a tape recorder; its headphones are hanging on a hook next to the frame. Putting them on, you hear the sound of a baby suckling. As the headphones make the sound resonate inside your head, you vacillate positions: at one and the same time you are the mother feeding and listening to her baby, and you are also that baby feeding from her mother. The work is both very simple and intensely moving.

The representation of 'Mother Ireland' is complex in its uses and multi-faceted in nature – far more so than Britannia in Britain or Marianne in France. She has been Hibernia in the same vein as Britannia; she has been linked to the concept of the Virgin Mary found in Irish Catholicism; she aided the metaphor of Dark Rosaleen when the mention of Ireland was suppressed; in one version she is represented as a Celtic warrior and Celtic goddess; for Loyalists she has been used to represent Ulster. As concept, as ideological representation, she has varied histories and contexts (see Loftus, 1990). This all-encompassing and fluid metaphor must surely be one reason why womanliness as an attribute is so powerfully recurrent in artworks by women – and one reason why the patriarchies of Church and State have conspired so long and hard to maintain absolute control of women.

Figure 10 *Amazon*, Dorothy Cross, 1992 (tailor's dummy and cow-skin).

Amazon, Dorothy Cross, 1992 (figure 10): An old dressmaker's dummy stands upright and alone. Fitted tightly over it is a cow-skin. The skin came from a cow who had only one large teat on her udder, rather than the usual four; the udder and its single teat are formed into one vast breast across the chest of the dummy. This is a complex work to encounter. On the one hand, it would seem to be wide open to the charge of essentialism. Indeed, we have here the potential universal woman. But the actuality of encountering this piece produces something quite different. The height of the dummy, the size of the breast, the size and position of the teat/nipple, the actuality of the skin and the teat, all return the viewer to infant anxieties and pleasures, unsure as to whether this is indeed the phallic mother, or the bringer of sustenance and pleasure. The phallic nature of the teat – it is in fact more or less penis-sized – further complicates the reading of the work by sexualizing our relationship to our mothers and relating oral sexual pleasures directly to other initial oral pleasures.

Mother Ireland is reflected conceptually in the Irish use of language. The Irish use in language of the definitive mother – 'the mother' – is precise and particular as it can be interchangeably used instead of the possessive – 'my mother', 'his or her mother'. (People can say 'she took the mother with her' rather than 'she took her mother'). It is a construction therefore which is rooted not only in fable and iconography, but in the Irish use of language in commonplace situations today. It is a concept of 'mother' which has altered the construction of the English language as it is used in the island of Ireland.

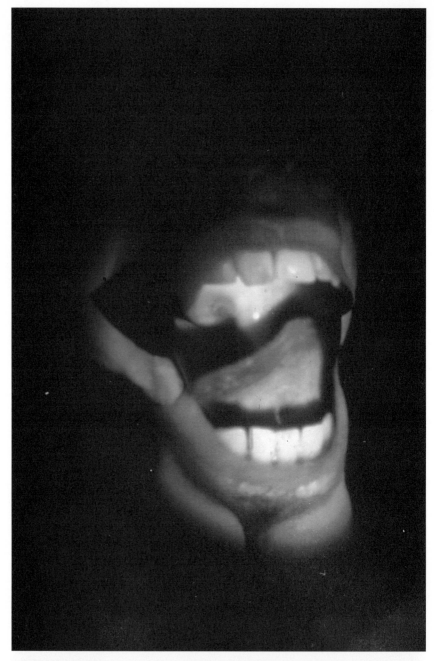

Figure 11 *Sounding the Depths*, Pauline Cummins and Louise Walsh, 1992 (detail; photograph).

Sounding the Depths, Pauline Cummins and Louise Walsh, 1992 (figure 11):
A video shows images of a woman's mouth, tightly pursed, the lips gripping
together. Hands clench, wringing each other, knuckles white. The two sides

of a clam shell are pressed against each other, grating uncomfortably. Something is being held in, unexpressed anger, disapproval, grief maybe. The images intersperse, building tension. Finally the tightness breaks, the shells grate past each other, the hands slip and loosen, the mouth relaxes, opens, ready to give and receive, to take its own space. Next door, the room is darkened, the walls black; in the warmth there is the gentle sound of a woman's quiet laughter – a contented laugh coming from deep within the body. On the walls are large photographs: the naked torso of a mature woman emerges into warm colour from the darkness. A transparency of a mouth has been projected upon each torso, and the photograph has then been taken. The open mouths give the women's bodies a hugely deep interior space and also the ability to enunciate. The laughter rolls around the room. The body has found voice, both highly disturbing and beautiful.

The particular concept and use of 'the mother' in Ireland has significance for women artists as it contributes in a subtle but strong fashion to the cultural construction of mothering, the body of the mother, and the mother herself. It provides for a concept of the mother where the abstract or universal can constantly be drawn across to the particular or personal, and vice versa. It elides mothers and potential mothers – i.e., women. For the woman artist, this has two main effects: first, it avoids the trap of essentialism and demands a redefinition of that word; and second it allows for a space where shifts and changes can be made within the ideologies and representations of womanliness. In the full variety of its potential imagery, this is the conceptual and representational space where many contemporary artists choose to work.

In concentrating upon particular artworks in this paper, I have demonstrated that there are certain themes which recur – themes which are rooted in the lived experience of being Irish, being female and being an artist. At the same time, by providing readings which layer one upon the other, I have demonstrated that these experiences are diverse, that they are socially produced constructs, areas of representation within which the artists are working. There is therefore no romantic essentialist category of 'Irish Woman Artist', but rather the richly interplaying histories readings and contexts of Irish/woman/artwork.

Notes

Hilary Robinson lectures in the theory and practice of fine art at the University of Ulster, Belfast. She has written widely on contemporary feminist art and edited *Visibly Female: Feminist Art Today* (London: Camden Press 1987; New York: Universe Books 1988).

FEMINIST REVIEW NO 50, SUMMER 1995

References

Available Resources (1992) Derry: Orchard Gallery.

Circa Art Magazine, passim.

DUFFY, Mary (1987) 'Statement' in *Irish Art: Pauline Cummins, Mary Duffy, Alanna O'Kelly* New York: WAAG Publications.

In a State: An Exhibition in Kilmainham Gaol on National Identity (1991) Dublin: Project Press.

LOFTUS, Belinda (1990) *Mirrors: William III & Mother Ireland* Dundrum: Picture Press.

Presentense (1993) Belfast: Arts Council of Northern Ireland.

Relocating History: An Exhibition of Work by 7 Irish Women Artists (1993) Belfast: The Fenderesky Gallery.

Sounding the Depths: Pauline Cummins and Louise Walsh (1992) Dublin: Irish Museum of Modern Art.

Strongholds: New Art from Ireland (1991) Liverpool: Tate Gallery.

WARNER, Marina (1985) *Monuments and Maidens: The Allegory of the Female Form* London: Weidenfeld & Nicholson.

Self-determination
The Republican Feminist Agenda

Claire Hackett

Abstract

This article defines a republican feminist agenda by reference to the key term 'self-determination', in its nationalist and its feminist meanings. It describes the activities of a republican feminist group, Clár na mBan, including a conference organized in March 1994, and initiatives taken since then.

Keywords

Northern Ireland; Irish republicanism; feminism; self-determination; Clár na mBan; peace process

I believe that a republican feminist agenda presents a tangible and powerful vision of a future Ireland which brings equality to all of its citizens. The concept of self-determination is what best defines republican feminism for me. This concept is perhaps better known for its nationalist than its feminist connotations. Yet it must be clear that it has meaning for feminist discourse – self-determination as the right and ability to make real choices about our lives: our fertility, our sexuality, childcare, the means to be independent and all the areas in which we are currently denied autonomy and dignity in our various identities as women.

In its republican meaning, national self-determination is not simply the question of Irish nationhood – a question which incidentally has never been put to all the people of this island. It is more. It includes the questions about the kind of society we want as a people and most crucially our ability to decide this ourselves. Self-determination in both feminist and republican meanings is a simple concept but a revolutionary one. It carries with it implications for great change in Ireland.

The republican feminist agenda is a thorn in the flesh of both the republican and feminist movements in Ireland. It is an agenda with a long and still-developing history. Women in Ireland have always been faced

FEMINIST REVIEW NO 50, SUMMER 1995, pp. 111–16

with the dilemma of where to place their formidable energies. Do we organize around an exclusively feminist struggle for true equality in society or do we join the Republican struggle for national self-determination? This problem has faced women in colonial societies down the ages and is no easier in 1994 than it was in the early years of this century when women were striving for full suffrage. For many of us the answer has been that neither struggle is complete if it ignores the claims of the other. However, we still have to fight for the legitimacy of our priorities not only in Irish society generally but also within the women's movement and the broad republican movement.

Clár na mBan began with a series of informal meetings of women who wanted to discuss issues facing women within an anti-imperialist context. Many of us have a history of activism at a political and community level. There is currently a Derry group and a Belfast group. The political developments in 1993, including the Hume/Adams talks and the Downing Street Declaration, prompted concern at the marginalization of women's voices in the debate. As a result we began to take a more active role. In the last year, we have attempted to create opportunities for debate about the future for women in Ireland. We have organized a women's conference in Belfast entitled 'Women's Agenda for Peace', produced a conference report, participated in a follow-up conference in Dublin, made a submission to the Sinn Fein Peace Commission, held a discussion as part of the West Belfast festival, and hosted a seminar with a delegation of women from Nicaragua. We have just completed a submission to the Forum for Peace and Reconciliation which was set up by the Irish government to forward the peace process.

The climate of censorship in the North has not made it easy for republican feminists to voice our opinions or develop our thinking. The politics of reconciliation have been an insidious doctrine within the women's movement in Ireland and particularly in the North where such politics have been promoted by the state. For women the attempt to reach an area where we can all agree and unite is understandable as an effort to find a strong voice in an oppressive society. But it is ultimately destructive because it leads to the suppression of difference.

It is certainly true that there are areas where women can find a united front – for example, in single-issue campaigns on health and domestic violence. Sometimes solidarity is achieved with great courage as in the instance of the support of the Shankill Women's Centre in Belfast for the Falls Women's Centre in the latter's fight against grant cuts from Belfast City Council. I believe we must continue to find ways of supporting each other and defining the areas on which we can fight together.

Too often, however, the concentration on common ground, reconciliation, and the lowest common denominator leads to the politics of avoidance – an attempt to maintain unity even at the cost of covering up injustice and inequalities. The reluctance of many feminists North and South, to see state violence against women prisoners and activists as a legitimate feminist issue is an example of this.

In March, 1994, Clár na mBan organized a conference, the 'Women's Agenda for Peace' for women who saw the future of Ireland lying within the context of national unity. The conference aimed to enable women to contribute to the current debate around a lasting settlement and an end to the war. Clár na mBan faced criticism from both feminist women and republican men.

Some feminists felt that the declared context of Irish national unity made the conference exclusive and divisive, making it difficult for women who did not share that objective to attend. This is a perplexing notion. Women with shared political objectives *need* to meet together to discuss their aims and clarify their ideas. It is this very process which enables them to name their own experience and identities. In such settings, Black women, disabled women and lesbian women have grown in strength and articulated their goals. This in turn has allowed the women's movement to become more representative of all women.

There is still much to be done to make feminism truly inclusive. But I believe that we can only create the basis for strong alliances by acknowledging the different identities of women rather than striving for a common ground that may only be an illusion. Clár na mBan believes strongly that a multiplicity of women's voices in Ireland need to be heard. We welcome the creation of opportunities for other women to define their own agendas. In doing this we move forward acknowledging our differences rather than suppressing them. It is often assumed that there are only two communities in the North: the nationalist and the unionist. This inaccurate notion misrepresents unionist as much as nationalist people and lessens the opportunity for the expression of our differences. What we need now are the politics of negotiation not of reconciliation.

The pressure to conform also exists within the republican movement. Feminists challenging the republican movement from within are often seen to be disloyal, to be breaking ranks which need to be solid in order to be strong. It is easy to see why this is so. The British and Irish establishments seize on evidence of disunity to try and undermine the republican movement. The other factor in suppressing dissent is the sexism within the movement. Sinn Fein is still a male-dominated party and as such cannot always be trusted to make women's interests a priority. There is a need for

FEMINIST REVIEW NO 50, SUMMER 1995

a strong and independent republican feminist voice to bring our agenda to the fore.

The Clár na mBan conference also faced criticism from some men within Sinn Fein who felt that a women's conference was unnecessary and exclusive. Others felt that it was letting the side down. But a movement that cannot face criticism from its supporters is already weak. Sinn Fein and the broad republican movement is stronger today because of challenges in the past. The feminist challenge to the whole republican movement must continue if we are to make real and radical changes to Irish society.

One of the major themes to emerge from the Clár na mBan conference was the exclusion of women from male-dominated political structures, republican/nationalist or more mainstream ones. In Clár na mBan we are concerned that women's voices will not be heard or will be ignored in the current debate about the future of Ireland. If women of all shades of opinion are excluded from the deliberations on a new constitution for Ireland then it will be no more representative of Irish society than the 1937 constitution which shaped the narrow and repressive society from which we are now emerging.

I envisage a future for Ireland as the whole island nation but I am not unaware of the difficulties this entails. Not least of these is the relationship between the North and the South. I was reminded of the effects of seventy-four years of partition on our dialogue and communication when I participated in the Dublin conference in September 1994, organized as a follow-up to the conference in Belfast. For many of the women in Dublin, nationalism meant the Ireland of de Valera – the architect of the 1937 Constitution of Ireland which was narrow, conservative, Catholic, inward-looking and deeply oppressive of women. However, the nationalism or republicanism of the North represents something very different to me. It is a hunger for democracy and justice in Ireland. It is neither a romantic obsession nor an historical anachronism. It is the daily struggle against the injustice of British and Unionist rule and the fight for equality and control over our lives. There were other women from the South who shared this idea of national self-determination and these women spoke of the pre-vailing censorship which made open discussion of republican aspirations impossible.

One of the major effects of this silencing of debate has been the absence of a realistic vision of a future united Ireland. There has been a tendency when this is envisaged to think glibly of the North merging into the South. This is of course a very limited notion – one might just as easily speak of the South joining the North. There is a great need for feminists in the North and the

South to have much more dialogue, to think creatively about the possibilities of the future, to imagine what a new Ireland could mean for us and to build on the many gains for women that we have achieved North and South.

Women both North and South have emerged as leaders at a community level. The growth of women's groups and single issue campaigns in the past decade has demonstrated the ability of women to organize not only in their own interests but in those of the general community. This level of activity is not reflected in mainstream political and social life. The existing structures effectively prevent women from contributing to the larger political debate and have denied us access to power.

Alternative structures and processes need to be established to bring this politic to the centre stage. The experience of other countries can be drawn on to achieve this. The ANC consulted extensively with women's groups and community organizations while conducting peace negotiations and deciding the future agenda of South Africa.

Clár na mBan are working on defining for ourselves what a republican feminist agenda might mean in concrete terms. This work took a specific form when we decided to make a submission to the Forum for Peace and Reconciliation. The Forum was set up, in its own words, 'to consult on and examine ways in which lasting peace, stability and reconciliation can be established by agreement among all the people of Ireland.' The Clár na mBan submission calls for a new constitution in Ireland, one which reflects the diversity of all the people on this island and represents us equally. We have spelt out the rights we wish to see guaranteed and have described the concrete steps that an Irish state could take to make these rights a reality. These steps range from new democratic structures ensuring equal participation, to the guarantee of a home and a social security system aimed at eliminating poverty. The document is intended as a focus for debate rather than a completed blueprint and we plan to publish it for further discussion.

The emphasis I have placed in this article on a vision of a future Ireland is perhaps misleading in the note of optimism it strikes about the current so-called peace process. The reality is that I don't feel this optimism about any outcomes of the process we are now engaged in. Doubt about the peace process and where it is leading was a major theme to emerge in the March conference. This doubt has not receded in the months that have followed. It has if anything increased. This is a time when many republicans fear a repetition of history's record of failed British policy in Ireland and many republican women foresee another occasion when our agenda is swept aside by other more powerful interests.

FEMINIST REVIEW NO 50, SUMMER 1995

I believe, however, that what has been gained in the last two years is the space for the airing of new ideas and possibilities. There are many different groups and individuals who are exploring options, engaged in national and international exchanges, imagining a new future and way forward. It is not yet possible to say if these hopes will be realized.

Notes

This is an expanded version of an article written by Mary Quiery and Claire Hackett for the *Irish Reporter* and published in Issue 16, Fourth Quarter 1994.

Claire Hackett is a member of Clár na mBan and Lesbian Line. She has been active in the women's movement in Belfast for fifteen years. She works in the voluntary sector, has an MSc in Women's Studies, and an MA in Irish Political History.

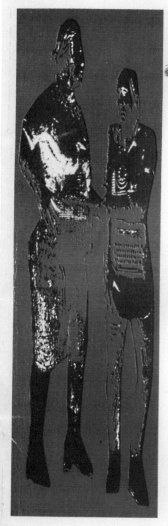

A WOMEN'S AGENDA FOR PEACE

CONFERENCE REPORT

A CLAR NA MBAN PUBLICATION

Ourselves Alone?

Clár na mBan Conference Report

Clara Connolly

FEMINIST REVIEW NO 50, SUMMER 1995, pp. 118–26

Abstract

This article is a review of a report of a republican feminist conference, published by its organizers, Clár na mBan. The conference took place in Belfast in March 1994. The article supports the conference's criticisms of the 'peace process' as exclusive and undemocratic. It also takes issue with a number of republican and nationalist assumptions about historical and contemporary Ireland.

Keywords

Irish republicanism; nationalism; democracy; feminism; peace process; Irish Republic

For many years, republican and Southern Irish feminists have been involved in a war of mutual recrimination. Northern Irish republicans, and their allies in the South, have accused mainstream feminists of ignoring the conflict in Northern Ireland, and the effects of the British occupation on Northern Irish Catholic women. Southern feminists, in conflict not only with the Church but with Irish nationalist representations of women, have been hostile to what they see as the hijacking of feminism for nationalist ends. This lack of mutual understanding was encapsulated in feminist reactions to the slogan 'Armagh is a feminist issue.' (For an account of the campaign on behalf of women prisoners in Armagh, see McNab, 1984). The divisive effects were felt not only at women's events in Ireland, but also among Irish women in Britain. (For an account of the first London Irish women's conference in June 1984, see Dowds, 1984). Not the least significant outcome of recent developments in Ireland may be the possibility of healing such splits, or at least of conducting a lively and productive discussion which is no longer a dialogue of the deaf.

It is in that spirit that I write this review. It is not a report of the 'Women's Agenda for Peace' conference, held in Belfast in March 1994, since I was not present. It is a response to the Conference Report,[1] a remarkably clear and full account of the proceedings, published by the organizers, Clár na mBan.[2] I write as an Irish feminist, reared in the South to become implacably hostile to the twin pillars of reaction as I experienced them in the 1960s – the Catholic Church and official nationalist ideology. I have written an account of two years spent in Northern Ireland at the beginning of the 1970s, which was coloured by my experience of the South (Connolly, 1991). For the last twenty years I have lived in London; despite my involvement with Irish women's events and organizations here, I have not revised my opposition to nationalist solutions, whatever their source. But in the last year – the lifetime of the Downing Street Declaration, and of the preparation of this issue of *Feminist Review* – I have been overwhelmed by the speed of events in Ireland North and South. Whatever the eventual outcome, I cannot help feeling that a process has begun which (I hardly dare hope) is irreversible – something which has little to do with talks between the British and Irish governments, and which will burst the strait-jacket of the official 'peace process'.

The Clár na mBan conference is a tentative and brave contribution to just such a broad and meaningful process. First, because it happened at all, in a context of uncertainty about the meaning of 'peace'; the temptation to preserve a show of nationalist unity must have been strong. And second, because of the decision to publish such a full report, with its expressions of difference and doubt, as well as of hope; the temptation to preserve a show of women's unity must have been strong. But precisely because it is not a bureaucratic report, giving the 'line' (whatever that might be in such a fluid situation), it allows for the possibility of dialogue with others who are critical of some of its fundamental premises.

The conference was organized by a group of women with a 'history of activism at a political and community level, who came together in 1992 for discussion around the future of women in the context of Irish national unity' (Report: 3). Clár na mBan members from Belfast and Derry made the decision to issue invitations to a conference, which 150 women attended. Groups came from Belfast, Dublin, Cork, Derry and Galway, and from all over Northern Ireland; 'women from over 25 voluntary and community organisations and eight women's centres were present'. All the women attended in a personal capacity, which probably contributed to the relative openness of discussion.

The text of the preliminary speeches is given in full; there were two speakers from each part of the island. Although I cannot comment on everything that was said, I would like to highlight themes from each of the four main speakers, as well as commenting selectively on other areas of the

Report. Oonagh Marron (a community activist from Belfast, and Clár na mBan member) opened by defining most clearly the purpose of the conference:

> As nationalist women and as feminists, we have very often given our support unconditionally to the overthrow of British colonialism in this country. We have often buried our demands for the sake of a common purpose – Brits out. In the past, that has been a way of censoring our demands. The danger is that once again we are going to be asked to bury our demands, this time in the common purpose of achieving peace. I think that it is time to send a message to those negotiating on our behalf that this time around our support will not be unconditional; never again will we collude with the exclusion of people, with the denial of their rights.
>
> (9)

Defiant and poignant words! They reflect the bitterness of so many women's wings of nationalist (and other liberation) movements, who come the Revolution find themselves contained or marginalized (Molyneux, 1985; Thapar, 1993). The reflect, in particular, the painful experience of Irish women after (Southern) Irish independence, who despite their prominent role in the struggle, found themselves written out of the new constitution except as Mothers of the Nation. They illustrate also, in their almost unconscious elision of women and people – both distinguished by exclusion – the historical role of women in such movements as a litmus test for democracy. I will return to the concept of democracy, a recurring theme of the conference.

For now, I want to highlight the way these words reflect a fundamental assumption of Irish republicanism: its sense of an uncomplicated continuity with the Irish nationalists of the early twentieth century. This is reinforced by the Report's Introduction, which sets the context of the conference by reference to heroic women figures from the seventh century onwards, but culminating in the women nationalists of 1914–21. It finishes with a warning to women from Aine Ceannt (widow of one of the martyrs of 1916) which, we are told, is equally relevant today: 'Are we competent to take our proper place in the new Ireland that is dawning for us? Let us see to it that we are worthy successors of Brigid, Maeve and Grainne Mhaol' (6).

These allusions, stretching backwards to the Island of Saints and Scholars and of Celtic myth, are considered more appropriate as a context for the conference than a single reference to the troubled history of Northern Ireland, in the past 25 – or 75 – years. It is as if that history, nightmarish as it has been, especially for Catholics, can now be blotted out. History resumes, after a hiccup, from 1918 (the date of the last All Ireland General

Election, when Sinn Fein won an overall majority in the country, although not in the province of Ulster). That Aine Ceannt does not represent the 'common sense' of conference participants, forged in the stern realities of Northern Irish community activism, goes without saying. But neither is her 'new Ireland' theirs, whether they recognize this or not. One of the things that hinders recognition is the framing of a discussion about the future in the myths of a national past. The only way to ensure that 'this time round our support will not be unconditional' is to step out of the frame.

That such a framework is attractive for (some) Northern Irish feminists, I can understand. There is an acute and unresolved conflict of national identities to be addressed. Nationalism burns bright when fuelled by injustice and exclusion; otherwise it turns toxic. So I fail to understand its resonance for Southern Irish women, such as Carol Coulter, a republican journalist. Her historical account is different in emphasis, reflecting her Southern Irish roots:

> If we look very briefly at the history of Ireland, I think that British and patriarchal, centralised bureaucratic concepts of politics were not entirely shrugged off. They were not seriously shrugged off at all by the nationalist movement which sought the overthrow of British rule in this country. Instead, it was a concept that would allow for the domination of the male elite.

> (11)

Her object is to contrast British, centralized, male political structures, with Irish, open, democratic, community-oriented and — ones. The blank is to be filled by conference participants: I assume from the context (see below) that the appropriate antonym is 'female' rather than feminist. In condemning male forms of political activity, she leaves unscathed its purposes, and the frame within which it is conducted. To describe the history of twentieth-century Southern Ireland as 'male' and 'British' is, paradoxically, to let Irish nationalism off the hook. The point is not to complain about male corruption of worthwhile political purposes, as a woman might, but to engage in a challenge to these purposes, and if necessary a redefinition of them, as a feminist would.

Carol Coulter's heroines are more contemporary and more diverse than Aine Ceannt's: Rosa Luxemburg, Countess Markievicz and the Irish Countrywomen's Association. The latter are favourably mentioned for their campaigns in the post-Independence South, 'for things that actually meant something to peoples' ordinary lives' (12) like rural electrification schemes that would include houses, and not just agricultural machinery. That history lesson takes us up to the Ireland of the 1950s. Whereas Oonagh Marron's significant Other is the history of the Northern Irish state, Carol Coulter's is the history of contemporary Southern Irish feminism. Neither Northern loyalism nor Southern feminism can be addressed by republicans, because they are (or have been) structurally in conflict with Irish nationalism. I would not have expected the conference to provide solutions to such systemic blockages – they form part of the difficult agenda for the future, and it is not solely the responsibility of republican feminists to resolve them. But it does concern me that, in a gathering of like-minded women, they are not even acknowledged – they present themselves instead as symptomatic absences.

Mary Cullen, also from the South, went furthest towards such an acknowledgement. For example she said:

> As a feminist and a historian, I am aware of how much I owe to the women who pioneered feminist movements in Ireland in the nineteenth century, most of them Protestant in religion and in politics supporters of the Union. As a republican with a small 'r', I know how much I owe to the Protestant dissenter contribution in particular.

(9)

She defined feminism and democracy, and argued that feminism has a vital contribution to make to the peace process:

> A shared feminist awareness may be the stepping stone to the broad inclusive democratic debate that is so essential. As citizens and as women each of us will bring different value systems to the debate about justice and peace. Feminist awareness is just one of these. But it is one that women across barriers of political affiliation and class and other divisions share, and could be the basis on which we could build a broad and inclusive debate among women.

(10)

Mary Cullen's speech is as coded as the others; while they are addressed to republican men, hers is addressed to republican women. Under the rubric of feminism, she alludes to the differences between Irish women (and men) which will need to be addressed if the peace process is to get anywhere. I applaud her sentiments, but I wonder whether such differences can be addressed in a productive way if they are not first boldly spelled out. The history of feminism is punctuated with critiques of 'sisterhood' from women who have been marginalized, particularly on grounds of class, race or ethnicity. Autonomous organizations of dissenting and oppressed groups have justified their existence, and continue to do so even when feminists have recognized 'difference'.

Imagine a dialogue between Catholic and Protestant women's groups on the meaning of 'democracy'. Catholic women would be justified in asking whether it includes a state which systematically discriminated against Catholics, excluding them from housing and employment, and letting an armed and sectarian police force loose on them. But would the Protestant women be justified in asking how a democratic agenda for the future can be reconciled with a Protestant unwillingness to accept Irish unity?

The recent Sinn Fein statement at Stormont Castle asserts: 'We believe that the wish of the majority of the Irish people is for Irish unity. We believe that an adherence to democratic principles makes Irish unity inevitable' (*Independent*, 10.12.94). What is the basis for such a belief? Proinsias de Rossa (leader of the Democratic Left Party, currently in the Southern Irish Government) comments: 'Northern nationalists must accept that there is no evidence – either in elections or opinion polls – that the achievement of a united Ireland features high on the list of priorities of the people of the Republic' (*Irish Times*, 3.12.94). Sinn Fein goes on to say:

> The existence (of the six county statelet) lies at the heart of the present conflict. It is our view, therefore, that the British Government should play a crucial and constructive role in persuading the Unionist community to reach a democratic accommodation with the rest of the Irish people.

On that, de Rossa comments: 'the logic of Sinn Fein thinking suggests that the Unionist unwillingness to agree to nationalist demands constitutes a veto, whereas compliance with such demands constitutes consent.' Harsh maybe; there is no love lost between the former comrades-in-arms of the Provisional IRA and of its parent organization the Officials, from which the Democratic Left also sprang. But it does present a challenge to republicans, and particularly to republican feminists who speak in the name of democracy: what kind of democracy is it which would coerce the Unionists into a united Ireland against their will? To rely on the 'persuasive' powers of Britain is utterly cynical: thus Sinn Fein implicitly acknowledges what Britain has made no secret of – its desire to wash its hands of the Union (at least in Northern Ireland). It is war-weariness that Sinn Fein relies on, and not any real attempt to persuade anyone.

Sinn Fein does not have the electoral mandate it had; history has moved on from 1918. The question of democracy, for contemporary republicans, needs careful handling. An open acknowledgement of their minority status (see Hackett, this issue) would provide a more realistic agenda – that of forging alliances with the democratic forces North and South of the border. Interestingly, the statement to the conference from the 'women prisoners of war at Maghaberry Prison' came nearest to broaching that agenda:

> Anti-women legislation certainly exists in all parts of Ireland, and in the New Ireland we hope to see the removal of such repressive laws. The present laws on abortion deny women the right to control their own bodies. No institution, government or church should have the audacity to tell women in which circumstances they will be allowed to seek an abortion. If the rights of women

are to be supported, they must be supported fully and not be addressed in wishy-washy legislation granting the right to travel and to seek information.

(23)

Sinn Fein has not been among the organizations to put such issues on the agenda, and it cannot contribute to the creation of such a 'new Ireland' without learning to work alongside the forces of reform in the South. (It is equally true that the learning must be mutual: many people in the South know little or nothing of life in the North.) However, it is those very forces who are insisting, against Irish nationalism in its constitutional form, on the rights of the Protestant community to be considered as players in the democratic game. Mary Robinson, the Republic's President, is a potent exemplar of such a challenge to republicanism: a feminist lawyer identified with the abortion issue, she has gone out of her way to address the fears of the Protestant community. She was not included in the conference's roll call of Irish heroines.

Bernadette Mc Aliskey's speech, the last in the plenary session, fully dramatized the dangers for Northern republicans of relying on 'ourselves alone' (the literal translation of 'sinn fein'). Like many of the women at the conference, I feel a sense of fragile confidence in the future, which the formidable Mc Aliskey did her best to puncture. She spoke plainly:

> I reject the Hume/Adams agreement, for the simple reason that I have not seen it. I am not buying it until I do. I am not traipsing up and down the Belfast/Dublin road in a yellow jumper until I see what I am traipsing for. John Hume says it's indistinguishable from the Downing Street Declaration. Gerry Adams says its a million light miles away. Far be it from me to say which one of them is telling the truth. My instinct would be Gerry Adams. I have worked with the man for years, and the other man I have worked against for years. But that has nothing to do with it, I am entitled to see it.

(15)

Of course she is right to be suspicious of secret deals done behind closed doors: 'I did not devote the entirety of my adult life to see it reduced to a game of dice by half-a-dozen men' (13). Echoing Carol Coulter, she places an emphasis on the *form* of the peace process: it is not a mechanism for resolving conflict, she says, because it is not democratic and inclusive. Feminism, which she opposes to the present process, 'is not just demands, it's a whole way of working, a whole way of thinking' (16). It would have been interesting, all the same, to hear some of those demands; although, like other speakers she puts community and women's rights at the heart of her agenda, she is curiously vague about what these rights and demands are.

Perhaps the heart of her speech is here:

The first prerequisite of all of this is: who comes to this party? Who is at this discussion? – and that does not include the British Government. Their contribution is how they get off-side. Their contribution is how they get out of here.

(16)

The significant difference with Sinn Fein is that she does not grant the British Government the role of 'persuader' of the Unionists. She is right to be sceptical: she knows (does Gerry Adams?) that the only way the British Government will 'persuade' Unionists is to abandon them. However, she does not say so directly. Nor does she explain why the Downing Street Declaration is 'worthless' (16). It does plainly state Britain's lack of interest in maintaining the link with Northern Ireland; the real problem, however (which she does not mention), may be that it recognizes the Protestant right of veto of a united Ireland. The Declaration illustrates in stark terms that a British intent to withdraw does not in itself guarantee Irish unity. If Gerry Adams accepts that, she is hinting, he should say so. And if he knows anything else that we don't know, he should tell us that too. Otherwise, 'the whole thing is reduced to a lie, and I cannot play it' (16).

What she does not speculate upon is how the loyalists, also in danger of being left to 'ourselves alone' by the Downing Street scenario, must be feeling. Surely they must be at least as suspicious as her – unless some of them, too, have been given assurances that we do not know about? Such uncertainty is frightening, and she is right to highlight it. But the really scary thing, for both communities in the North, is the possibility that the Declaration may contain no hidden messages at all. It may really be as bald as it appears: no British interest in staying, but no Irish unity without consent. The purpose of the peace process, then, would be more complex than some are prepared to accept: to find an interim constitutional framework which would recognize (and help to ease) the structural conflict of identities between Catholic and Protestants in Northern Ireland, but which, necessarily, cannot implement fully either current nationalist, or Unionist, aspirations at the level of the state. Such flexible possibilities as a union of semi-autonomous states, or various forms of federation, must surely be considered among the options.

That this idea has not been fully accepted across the North (and else-where) is clear: Bernadette Mc Aliskey is only one such 'refusenik', easier to sympathize with than her loyalist counterpart, Ian Paisley, or such patrician sceptics in the South as Conor Cruise O'Brien. I hope that she is wrong in her conviction that this process 'will end in tears' (BBC, *Newsnight*, December 1994), by which I assume she means a resumption of violence by those who will realize, sooner or later, that she is right about what is not currently on offer – the fulfilment of republican nationalist aspirations.

She is right in her critique of the process. It is not surprising that some of its aspects are centralized and secretive: military organizations, state-sponsored or otherwise, are not notably democratic in nature. But if constitutional talks were to be accompanied – overtaken even – by the kind of inclusive, wide-ranging and democratic debate that she and others envisage, then a 'new Ireland' might well be possible, beyond the vision of any one group of us. (A working agenda for both parts of the island might include the abolition of structures of discrimination; a secular constitution that guarantees parity for all minorities, not just religious ones; and a redistribution of political power at a central and local level. This agenda might be equally useful for Britain.)

She is right also to affirm, with all the speakers, the important contribution that a feminist agenda, and informal community-based organization, could make to the process. Since the Clár na mBan conference, the group has decided to submit a document to the Ireland Forum for Peace and Conciliation (Hackett, this issue). Thanks to them, and to others on both sides of the border, women's voices *will* be heard this time round, before the next set of constitutional arrangements are set in stone.

Notes

Clara Connolly is a member of Women Against Fundamentalism, and of the Irish Women's Abortion Support Group.

1 Copies of the Conference Report are available from the Bookworm Community Bookshop, 16 Bishop Street, Derry, Tel (01504) 261616. Price £3 per copy; bulk order rates available on request.
2 Clár na mBan means, in English, 'the women's agenda'.

References

CONNOLLY, Clara (1991) 'Communalism: obstacle to social change' *Women: A Cultural Review* 2: 3.

DOWDS, Rae (1984) 'Conference – Irish women in London' *Irish Feminist Review* Dublin: Women's Community Press.

McNAB, Eilish (1984) 'Strip-searching: ex prisoners speak out' *Irish Feminist Review* Dublin: Women's Community Press.

MOLYNEUX, Maxine (1985) 'Family reform in socialist states: the hidden agenda' *Feminist Review* 21, Winter.

THAPAR, Suruchi (1993) 'Women as activists, women as symbols: a study of the Indian Nationalist Movement' *Feminist Review* 44, Nationalisms and National Identities, Summer.

Conflicting Interests

The British and Irish Suffrage Movements

Margaret Ward

FEMINIST REVIEW NO 50, SUMMER 1995, pp. 127–47

Abstract

This article uses a case-study of the relationship between the British suffrage organization, the Women's Social and Political Union, and its equivalent on the Irish side, the Irish Women's Franchise League, in order to illuminate some consequences of the colonial relationship between Britain and Ireland. As political power was located within the British state, and the British feminist movement enjoyed superior resources, the Irish movement was at a disadvantage. This was compounded by serious internal divisions within the Irish movement – a product of the dispute over Ireland's constitutional future – which prevented the Franchise League, sympathetic to the nationalist demand for independence – from establishing a strong presence in the North. The consequences of the British movement organizing in Ireland, in particular their initiation of a militant campaign in the North, are explored in some detail, using evidence provided by letters from the participants.

British intervention was clearly motivated from British-inspired concerns rather than from any solidarity with the situation of women in Ireland, proving to be disastrous for the Irish, accentuating their deep-rooted divisions.

The overall argument is that feminism cannot be viewed in isolation from other political considerations. This case-study isolates the repercussions of Britain's imperial role for both British and Irish movements: ostensibly with a common objective but in reality divided by their differing response to the constitutional arrangement between the two countries. For this reason, historians of Irish feminist movements must give consideration to the importance of the 'national question' and display a more critical attitude towards the role played by Britain in Irish affairs.

Keywords

Irish; revisionism; feminist; suffrage; Ulster; nationalism

FEMINIST REVIEW NO 50, SUMMER 1995

With a tentative peace process underway in Ireland it seems an appropriate time to begin consideration of some of the less obvious consequences of the long years of war. Hostility to the ideology of nationalism, either caricatured in terms of de Valera's Ireland with its priests and 'comely maidens', or otherwise rejected for its emphasis upon the strategy of militarism, has helped to create an intellectual climate where even the expression of a desire to understand what was happening in the North of Ireland was liable to result in accusations of undue sympathy with terrorism. The academic community in Ireland failed in its task of engaging with the issue, so discussion seldom moved on to more fruitful levels. State repression and undisguised censorship was allowed to operate without challenge, while the refusal to accept that what was happening should be of concern to researchers and writers imposed serious distortions upon the ivory towers of Irish academia. The difficulties involved in understanding the complexities of the North of Ireland were solved by the simple device of erecting an intellectual border, shutting off the troublesome six counties from the rest of Ireland. Those living in the North and those committed to the task of developing some understanding of the complexities of the situation were marginalized or ignored. For historians, this practice was legitimized by a revisionist discourse within the discipline which minimized the impact of Britain's colonial role within Ireland. The direct political consequence of this was an implicit assumption that if the British presence in Ireland was less malignant than formerly considered, the struggle of the nationalist minority in the North could be dismissed as an atavistic impulse, to be ignored if not condemned by a progressive new generation. This tendency has echoes within the practice of Irish feminist history. For many Irish feminist historians, the post-nationalist age has arrived and women's struggle for emancipation can now be documented without undue stress being placed upon the age-old story of the British imperial presence in Ireland.[1]

It has often been argued that the Irish struggle for national self-determination is a 'male' question, unconnected with women's fight for citizenship and therefore outside the scope of modern feminist researches. Cliona Murphy, an historian of the Irish suffrage movement, illustrates this approach, contending that: 'the boundaries of nationalism were limited and confined to the interests of certain male groups . . . and . . . was the very antithesis of feminism' (Murphy, 1993: 1009). That ideological view underpins her otherwise invaluable text *The Women's Suffrage Movement And Irish Society In The Early Twentieth Century* (1989), where an 'Irish society' is constituted purely in the image of a twenty-six-county society, with no discussion of the fact that the most militant of all suffrage activities took place in counties Antrim and Down, not in Dublin. Partition is read back into an unpartitioned society and we lose any sense of the reality of the suffrage movement in the North, which was an amalgam of widely differing motivations and aspirations. What is more, by failing to come to terms with events in the North, the reasons why British suffragists chose to establish a presence there is lost, and so too is an opportunity to raise political questions regarding the extent to which feminism can overcome differences when the protagonists are locked into a colonial relationship.

However, if we argue that the movement for national self-determination that existed in Ireland at the turn of the century was as important for women as for men, then the question for feminists becomes one of exploring the extent to which feminist concerns conflicted or were accommodated by nationalists. Instead of dismissing nationalism for its lack of relevance to feminism, one interrogates past nationalist movements for its programmes and examines the extent to which women were able to make an impact. From that process some of the material to forge the basis of a radical agenda for the present might emerge. Feminist historians have valuable skills to offer the society in which they live – and one of those skills is the ability to extract answers to past controversies, providing some guides for those involved in attempts to move the struggle for human emancipation to new heights.

A case study of the relationship between the British and Irish suffrage movements might appear to be far removed from the wider political realities outlined above. However, it is precisely those political realities which determined that relationship. To what extent did the British and Irish suffrage movements support each other in their desire for women's enfranchisement? Did British suffragists, or a section of them, align themselves with the privileged position of their imperial state, assuming that the concerns of those in the metropolitan area were the same for those who existed in what may be described as the periphery? Would any support offered by British suffragists to Irish women have to acknowledge that colonial relationship and be sensitive to the inequalities engendered by it? Did the political repercussions of the Women's Social and Political Union intervention in the North of Ireland exacerbate the sectarian tensions that existed, providing additional information for an assessment of the relationship between feminism and unionism and feminism and nationalism? Providing some answers to these questions creates the space for the development of an informed discussion on present-day concerns and allows for further reflections on the extent to which feminism may be considered as a progressive political force while it remains isolated from other political movements.

The Irishwomen's Franchise League

The Irish Women's Franchise League (IWFL), the militant organization within the wider Irish suffrage movement, was formed in November 1908, five years after the formation of the Women's Social and Political Union (WSPU) in Britain. Although the WSPU was in the process of setting up branches around Britain, including Scotland, Irish women did not consider the possibility of forming an Irish branch of the organization: 'We had no desire to work under English women leaders: we could lead ourselves' (Cousins and Cousins, 1950: 164). What they wanted was: 'a militant suffrage society suitable to the different political situation of Ireland, as between a subject country seeking freedom from England, and England a free country' (164). The League was independent, but it was not anti-nationalist. It hoped to obtain pledges from each Irish Member of Parliament to vote for all women suffrage bills that might be introduced into the House of Commons, while also campaigning for the inclusion of woman suffrage within the terms of Home Rule legislation.

At first, there was a level of co-operation between the two groups that signalled a mutual interdependence. The Imperial Parliament at Westminster had the power to grant citizenship to both British and Irish women, and how the Irish Nationalist Party voted – holding as it did the balance of power between the Liberal and Conservative parties – was as important to British women as it was to Irish women. Christabel Pankhurst visited Ireland in March 1910, to be followed in October by Mrs Pankhurst, who toured the major towns in Ireland as part of a WSPU campaign to build up support for a Conciliation Bill intended to enfranchise a small proportion of women (Cousins and Cousins, 1950: 174). At least eight Irish women were among the 300-strong contingent of women who attempted to petition Parliament on 18 November 1910, an event which became known as 'Black Friday' and four of the Irish women received gaol sentences. Mrs Pankhurst wrote that they were very proud of the Irish women: 'Although the deputation was their first they were always in the very front line of the fight' (Cousins and Cousins, 1950: 200). Between that date and March 1912, thirteen IWFL members would serve prison sentences in England (*Irish Citizen*, 25.5.12).

What motivated those Irish women who responded to Mrs Pankhurst's call to join the WSPU deputation? They did not travel to London simply to add numbers to a deputation of Englishwomen. It was a lobby of Parliament and they had their own Members of Parliament with whom to argue their case. Margaret Cousins was quite clear that they were attending 'in consonance with our Irish political situation', representing Ireland on the deputation because a number of Irish MPs had backed the Conciliation Bill and they wanted to urge those MPs to make representations on their behalf (1950: 175). Each time women from Ireland went over to England they went to great efforts to ensure that their separate identities were preserved. They were exhorted to wear green dresses, they carried Irish flags and sometimes were accompanied by Irish pipers (*Votes for Women*, 10.6.10; 22.7.10; 6.6.11). In Ireland they would not have attempted to appear so self-consciously Irish. There was no necessity for it and their hostility to the parliamentarians of the Irish Party would have ensured that they rejected any implicit identification of themselves with male stage-Irishry. That they insisted upon the creation of such an Irish presence when in London was a recognition of their right to an independent nationhood and symbolic of a deep-rooted ambivalence towards the dominance of the British movement.

Irish militancy

Harmonious relations between British and Irish feminists began to falter once the Home Rule issue began to dominate political life. The undeniable fact that Irish MPs were deliberately blocking attempts to give women the vote because they were determined to keep Asquith and the Liberal Government in office led to Christabel Pankhurst's announcement that the WSPU declared war upon the Irish Party. WSPU strategy now was to declare 'no votes for women – no home rule' (Pankhurst, 1977: 403). It was a tactic which had unfortunate repercussions within Ireland because it could be readily adopted by women who believed in the Unionist cause,

Figure 1   Irish suffrage platform in Hyde Park.

using feminist-inspired arguments as a further tactic to stall Home Rule. The IWFL made no criticism of this change in policy. In a letter to Redmond, the anti-suffragist leader of the Irish Party, they made it quite plain that they regarded the action of the Irish Party in killing the Conciliation Bill to be: 'a distinct act of treachery . . . which we shall neither forget nor forgive'. They warned Redmond to expect: 'the hostility of English women' while they hinted that he would soon have an additional source of anger: 'Whether the Party will have to encounter the hostility of organised Irish women as well depends on your answer to us today' (SS 21: 639). However, their disagreement with the Irish Party did not include rejection of the Home Rule cause.

WSPU anxiety for the IWFL to establish a presence in London revolved around the fact that, for British women, a successful resolution of the Home Rule and female suffrage issue would have benefits for British women also. If women in a Home Rule Ireland were to have the vote then it was obvious the same measure would have to be extended to British women. Annie Kenney wrote to the IWFL in May 1912 to convey Christabel Pankhurst's desire for the IWFL to send one of their most effective workers over to London:

> It would be such a good thing to have one of your representatives with us in London, who could keep in touch with us until the question of the amendment is settled . . . We will do our best to assist you but it is really imperative that someone should be here.

She ended her letter with a short ps to say Christabel was:

> most anxious that the Irish women should begin to agitate and make not only Irish men, but the government, realise that they intend to get the question of votes for Irish women settled in this session. Do as we do in England – simply pester the lives out of cabinet ministers, leaders of the Irish Party, the Labour Party.

(SS 22: 664)

The IWFL agreed to send Hilda Webb to London, but events overtook them. On 13 June Webb was part of the first IWFL window-smashing contingent. It was the militant's protest against the refusal of the Irish Party to consider an appeal from a mass meeting of Irish women which had called for women's suffrage to be included in the Home Rule Bill. The strategy of lobbying politicians in London was no longer relevant to the Irish campaign. Although the different suffrage organizations in Ireland continued to send over lobbyists on each occasion when women's suffrage came before the House of Commons, they were assisted by the London branch of their respective organizations. The Irish lobby remained separate.

As the Irish movement developed in confidence it was no longer content to rely upon *Votes for Women*, the organ of the WSPU, to publicize its activities. Until May 1912, when the *Irish Citizen* first appeared, the Irish suffragists were totally dependent upon either the British journal or upon Irish nationalist publications like *Sinn Fein*, who evaluated the significance of the suffrage issue in terms of the Irish movement for political independence. Frank Sheehy-Skeffington, a freelance journalist for left-wing publications, and husband of a founder of the IWFL, had declared: 'We *must* have a paper of our own to keep the British and Irish suffrage movements distinct and carry on propaganda along our own lines' (Cousins and Cousins, 1950: 203). The Irish movement was small and its supporters did not include the kind of wealthy members of the upper middle class who made large contributions to the WSPU coffers. The Pethick-Lawrences (treasurers of the WSPU and sympathetic to the socialist and pacifist beliefs of the Sheehy-Skeffingtons) were appealed to and they immediately sent over a messenger with £260, the amount asked for. From now on, the Irish women had their own mechanism for ensuring that their separate identity was asserted. The importance of this can be seen once the WSPU decided to continue its campaign in Ireland.

WSPU prisoners in Ireland

In July 1912, three members of the WSPU arrived in Dublin in pursuit of Prime Minister Asquith, who was visiting Ireland in order to reassure the people of his determination to push through the Home Rule Bill. The WSPU women were uninterested in the intricacies of the Irish situation,

Figure 2 Masthead of the *Irish Citizen*.

they were there to continue the WSPU policy of harassing government ministers each time they appeared in public. After a small hatchet was thrown and an attempt made to burn down the Theatre Royal, venue for the Asquith meeting, the women were arrested. Their actions were received with great hostility in Ireland and reactionary organizations like the Ancient Order of Hibernians made this the pretext for verbal and physical assaults on suffragists each time they organized public meetings that summer. Although the IWFL lost members as a result, they did not repudiate the women's actions: 'whatever our private opinion of the timeliness and manner of the act, because we naturally considered the women strictly within their rights' (Sheehy-Skeffington, 1975: 22).

What happened within the confines of the prison walls provides some evidence of the true state of Irish opinion with regards to the British militants. The first eight IWFL prisoners were in Mountjoy Prison at the same time as the British women, although the British women were confined to the prison hospital and unable to have any contact with the others. WSPU organizer Mary Leigh, who had received a punitive five-year sentence, immediately announced her intention of hunger striking to the death unless she was given the vote (GPB Mountjoy Prison 17.8.12). The Irish prison authorities were at a loss as to how to deal with these women but they regarded them in a different light from their Irish counterparts. The governor made a distinction between the English and the Irish women and proposed beginning forcible feeding of the hunger strikers while continuing to delay implementing that threat. One reason for his hesitation was the fact that the initial announcement on forcible feeding had led to an immediate act of solidarity on the part of some of the Irish prisoners. Four of them were almost at the end of their sentence (they were to be released on 19 August) and in response to the governor's declaration of intent they began a hunger strike in sympathy. They were not forcibly fed and presumably that was the reason for the delay in feeding the English women. The prison authorities could not have justified such a discrepancy in treatment. The WSPU made much of the supposed difference in attitudes towards the two groups of women: the one allowed their freedom, the other condemned to endure the horrors of forcible feeding (Pankhurst, 1977: 407). But the contrast was less stark. The four members of the IWFL who undertook the hunger strike were nearly at the end of their sentence and therefore did not require force-feeding. Gladys Evans and Mary Leigh were not forcibly fed until the 20th – the day after the release of the other women – so the authorities had simply waited. What is rarely mentioned in comments concerning this act of feminist solidarity is the fact that there were four other IWFL prisoners in Mountjoy, but they did not hunger strike. They still had four months to serve. Solidarity only went so far.

A petition on the women's behalf, containing 1,400 names, was sent to the Lord Lieutenant by Irish suffragists, but public opinion was hard to mobilize. The hatchet throwing had been a symbolic gesture against the introduction of Home Rule and few people were prepared to tolerate that. Sylvia Pankhurst came over to speak at a public meeting for the women, which was organized by the WSPU, not the IWFL, an indication of IWFL reluctance to initiate a manifestly unpopular demonstration (*Votes for Women*, 6.9.12). She later commented that: 'The meeting in Phoenix Park, so far from being a demonstration of sympathy with the prisoners, was mainly a great roar of hostility' (Pankhurst, 1977: 407). While attempting to lead a march of protest to Mountjoy Prison she found herself inside the gaol, a result of the scuffles that occurred between police and marchers. As she briefly contemplated the prospect of having to stay longer in Ireland than she intended, the thought dawned on her that her 'difficulties would be heightened by (her) nationality' (Pankhurst, 1977: 408). The situation in Ireland was becoming very delicate and Irish suffragists were finding themselves having to tread a difficult path in attempting to keep public support. In itself, the Asquith incident did not signal WSPU determination to pursue its own policy without consultation with their Irish counterparts, but in practice this is what was to occur.

The WSPU in Ireland

WSPU interest in extending their operations increased. Events in Ireland were opening up all sorts of possibilities. The prospect of obtaining an amendment to the Home Rule Bill which would give the vote to some women was not entirely dead and, in the North, the Ulster Unionists were courting the support of women in their efforts to resist incorporation into a Home Rule Ireland. Winning the vote anywhere in Britain or Ireland would be a great victory and the wider political repercussions of such an event happening in Ireland were irrelevant to the WSPU. In an obvious effort to deflect WSPU attention, Hanna Sheehy-Skeffington wrote to Christabel Pankhurst in the summer of 1913. She chose her words carefully:

> We are grateful for any suggestions you could offer as to our present campaign. As you understand and appreciate we want to work on this side on Irish lines and this policy is especially necessary just now . . . but this does not mean that we are not grateful for advice and that we are not entirely with you in every phase of your fight.

> (SS 22: 670)

The hint was not taken. The WSPU announced that it was sending Dorothy Evans to Belfast to set up a branch of the WSPU in Ulster, the purpose

Figure 3 Hanna Sheehy-Skeffington, Irish Women's Franchise League.

being to induce Sir Edward Carson to give votes to women in his proposed
Provisional Government (*Irish Citizen*, 20.10.13). Coincidentally or not,
the day following the WSPU announcement, Dawson Bates, secretary to
the Ulster Unionist Council, wrote to the Ulster Women's Unionist Council
to inform them that the draft articles for the constitution of the provisional
government included votes for women under the local government register.
In addition, before elections were held, it was planned to co-opt members
from the Women's Council on to all the committees in charge of the
arrangements for the Provisional Government (Sawyer, 1993: 78). This

was an enormous breakthrough in the long campaign for women's right to citizenship and the WSPU, to the intense annoyance of Irish feminists, claimed the credit. That month Christabel Pankhurst was able to write to Hanna Sheehy-Skeffington that they were: 'more than satisfied with the response that is being made and we are very glad that we have decided to start a campaign in that part of the world.' WSPU expansionism was not going to stop with Ulster:

> We have come to the conclusion that so far as the WSPU is concerned, there ought not to be a distinction between the English movement and the Irish movement any more than there is a distinction between the English movement and the Scottish movement . . . It is not as though English interests were not at stake in Ireland. They are. Indeed, it may almost be said that the nationalist Members hold the fate of the Suffrage cause for the whole kingdom in their hands.

> (SS 22: 664)

She felt therefore that: 'if only in the interests of English women' they needed to be represented in Ireland. Not only in Ulster but in nationalist Ireland also. The WSPU had decided to send Margaret Edwards to Dublin as organizer: 'with perfect friendliness towards your organisation and with a desire to promote the interests of the movement as a whole.' Pankhurst was confident that the activities of another society would 'have an excellent effect in every way.' She concluded her letter with a bland acknowledgement that there had: 'been some feeling that only Irishwomen can appeal to the Irish' and compounded her lack of sensitivity to Irish affairs by arrogantly declaring that 'it is not nationality but personality that counts' (SS 22: 664).

It hardly needs to be stated that expansive declarations of feminist solidarity are very easy to make when one is the dominant partner, enjoying a superiority of resources and support. Hanna Sheehy-Skeffington's initial response was to write a huge exclamation mark in ink beside the final sentence: 'We are all one in the women's suffrage faith.' Evidently she drew a distinction between British and Irish feminism. Although one would expect that view to find support among present-day historians, schooled to be sensitive to the need to examine the experiences of those without access to political power or influence, those whose personal politics are hostile to nationalism draw conclusions which are equally unsympathetic to the dilemmas of the past. Cliona Murphy's analysis of this exchange of correspondence concludes with the statement that: 'when threatened from without, in true text book style the women's own nationalism was aroused' (Murphy, 1993: 1013). However, Leah Leneman, the historian of the Scottish suffrage movement (which also suffered from the Pankhurst refusal to consider national differences) is much more sympathetic to the

FEMINIST REVIEW NO 50, SUMMER 1995

Irish position: 'The movement in Ireland was quite distinct from that in Great Britain, and given Anglo/Irish relations at the time it is not surprising that Irish suffragists should resent any WSPU attempt to muscle in' (Leneman, 1991: 196). Pankhurst had obviously given the Irish the impression that the Scots had welcomed the imposition of English organizers, as Sheehy-Skeffington also argued that: 'The position in Ireland is very different from that of Scotland – you know that as well as any Irishwomen – therefore your analogy with Scotland does not hold'. Although the Irish hoped to 'continue our friendly relations with the WSPU to whose inspiration we are much indebted', she continued to insist that the Irish remain autonomous:

> Under the circumstances it would have been wiser to have tried to cooperate with the local militant society, as you always have hitherto done most helpfully than to scatter militant forces and dissipate militant energies by the introduction of the English militant organisation.
>
> (SS 24: 134)

Despite Pankhurst's triumphalism, the WSPU was unable to establish any significant presence in Dublin. They also found themselves looked on with suspicion by all the non-militant societies who, by and large, managed to remain on cordial terms with the Franchise League, but who found no compelling reason as to why they should do so with respect to an organization which was both militant and non-Irish. Resentment at this 'interference' in their internal affairs was a common response, leading to an almost complete isolation of WSPU members in the South. They were heavily criticized for not supporting Hanna Sheehy-Skeffington's seven-day hunger strike in December 1913, even though she had been one of those hunger-striking in solidarity with Leigh and Evans (*Irish Citizen*, 6.12.13). The most visible sign of the WSPU presence in Dublin was the group of women who sold the *Suffragette* at a carefully controlled distance from those selling the *Irish Citizen*. The obvious rift caused some amusement in non-suffrage circles: 'Occasionally WSPU ladies invade the territory of their Irish sisters but these very seldom (if ever) make reprisals' (*Evening Telegraph*, 11.8.14).

The WSPU and the North of Ireland

The most enthusiastic converts to the WSPU came from the North, where, up until this time, no militant feminist organization had established itself. While suffrage groups generally had remained deliberately unspecific on the context in which they wanted women to have the vote, the stance of the IWFL in demanding the vote under the terms of the Home Rule settlement did, in some eyes, place them within a particular camp. Hanna Sheehy-Skeffington admitted that in Belfast they were regarded as being 'tainted with nationalism' (Sheehy-Skeffington, 1975: 16) and although she maintained links with Northern women, the IWFL had little presence there. It is difficult to disentangle the complexities behind the motivations of those who now joined the WSPU. Obviously, some were pro-unionist and wanted to ensure that they would have the vote if there was going to be a provisional government that opted out of Home Rule, but there were other women who joined because they saw it as an opportunity to be part of a movement that was more radical than the sedate societies that existed in Ulster. For them, the feminist principle was the only one that mattered.

The Ulster Unionist sudden conversion to suffrage was a great surprise. How to respond to it and yet maintain a unity of ranks was of overriding importance to Irish feminists. Frank Sheehy-Skeffington used his position as editor of the *Irish Citizen* to attempt an assessment of the positive advantages that might eventually emanate from this new twist in the complicated relationship between Irish feminism and the wider world of Irish politics. Suffragists did not want Ulster to opt out of any Home Rule settlement, but underlying this new situation was a feeling that it could not come to that. If women were given the right to full citizenship in Ulster, then surely they would use that opportunity to press for citizenship for their Irish sisters? The expression of such solidarity would therefore be a force for unity, helping to remove some of the political divisions. And as women in the south congratulated the Unionists for their good-will gesture, hostility to their refusal to take part in the Home Rule Parliament would be reduced, along with Unionist distrust of nationalists. Over time it was possible that the power of women could be used to unite the whole of the country – or so was the fervent hope of the idealistic Sheehy-Skeffington (*Irish Citizen*, 17.10.14).

Within the harsher world of Northern politics, some WSPU recruits were pro-nationalist in sympathy, while others were more than happy to contemplate the reality of a separate Ulster state in which they would be full citizens. Given such a mixture of motives, a cautious approach was indicated. However, the English women who came over to Belfast were concerned only with the question of winning the vote. The political opportunism of their strategy entailed a disregard for any political consequences. One of the most obvious of those consequences was the danger that the political divisions would become more acute if the situation was not handled by those who understood how complex the situation had become.

FEMINIST REVIEW NO 50, SUMMER 1995

It soon transpired that the offer of the franchise to women in the North had been a rash promise. And in insisting that the pledge be honoured, the WSPU would find itself implicitly demanding that the Ulster Unionists keep their threat to secede from the union with Britain. Only then could they be in a position to offer the carrot of the vote. But as the problem of Ulster continued to be debated in Westminster, it became clear that the Ulster Unionists were content to stay within the Union if they could be kept out of Home Rule Ireland. Partition of Ireland was being mooted as some interim solution and if that was the case, then the North would remain within the fold of the United Kingdom while the rest of Ireland enjoyed its limited independence. While such possibilities were being raised, the non-militant Northern Committee of the Irishwomen's Suffrage Federation demanded to know what the implications of this were for Ulster women. At the same time Dorothy Evans wrote to Carson to remind him of his 'solemn pledge' to the women of Ulster. Would he now honour the spirit of that pledge by demanding that Ulster women receive the franchise in the Imperial Parliament (*Belfast Newsletter*, 12.2.14)? Carson was forced to state that the pledge was withdrawn and Evans accused him of 'a breach of faith and a betrayal of Ulster women' (*Belfast Newsletter*, 7.3.14). The WSPU responded in predictable fashion. War was declared upon the Ulster Unionists (Rosen, 1974: 229).

Some who now joined the WSPU were close associates of the IWFL and remained so, despite their membership of the British organization. The irony of the contrast between pro-unionist women in the South objecting to the presence of an English organization in Ireland and non-unionist women in the North actually joining that English organization can be explained by two factors: whether or not the individual supported militancy, which was a deciding factor for many, and also the undeniable fact that the North, for historical and geographic reasons, had closer contact with Britain. The latter factor must have had some impact upon Northern political culture and upon the readiness of people to participate in an organization which had its origins across the water. Lilian Metge of Lisburn had remained in the Belfast Women's Suffrage Society (non-party, non-militant) as late as January 1914, when she presided over the organization's annual general meeting (*Belfast Newsletter*, 27.1.14), but by March Metge was writing to Hanna Sheehy-Skeffington of her frustration that the Irish Women's Suffrage Society was 'so weak and wobbly and undecided'. She said that she hoped the militants would go ahead, and she would help. She regretted the fact that the Unionist leader she most wanted to approach was shadowed with an armed guard and could not be touched (SS 22: 265). By April the IWSS had been disbanded, due to the defection of so many of its members and by August Metge was under arrest, for helping in the attempt to blow up Lisburn Cathedral.

On 8 April 1914 Dorothy Evans and Madge Muir became the first to be arrested for WSPU activities in Ireland. They protested against the failure of the authorities to arrest Sir Edward Carson and declared themselves to be: 'the only true Ulster militants' (*Freeman's Journal*, 9.4.14). According to information contained in the prison record sheets, it would seem that most of the imprisoned WSPU activists were British. Few of the Irish women who joined the WSPU actually carried out violent actions. To English eyes, it might have appeared that attacking the property of the Ulster Unionists was no different from attacking government buildings, but in the tense atmosphere of Belfast, which had witnessed many outbreaks of sectarian violence over the years, such actions could have very different connotations.

A united deputation

In early June 1914, while the Belfast WSPU was becoming heavily involved in their attempts to put women's fight for the vote on a par with Ulster Unionist defiance of the British government, suffrage groups throughout Ireland were attempting to find a formula which would enable them to join forces on a united deputation to London. The plan was to meet Asquith and Redmond and put to them their demand for the inclusion of women within the terms of the Home Rule Bill. Government attempts to accommodate Unionist hostility had led to proposals for divisive amendments to the Home Rule legislation, while the knowledge that the Bill was scheduled to come up for Royal Assent in late June lent urgency to the attempt to build an impressive show of unity. But the difficulties facing the deputation's organizers encapsulated the main divisions within the Irish feminist movement. There were two stumbling blocks: was the deputation endorsing the principle of Home Rule by demanding a franchise amendment and would appearing on a united platform compromise those suffragists who were strongly opposed to the militant campaign?

The Irish Women's Suffrage Federation was most reluctant to have anything to do with the deputation. From Britain the United Suffragists did their best to help in achieving some workable compromise, writing confidentially to the IWFL of their difficulty, as an English organization, in persuading the Federation to forgo their reservations over appearing on a platform with militants. They suggested that Hanna Sheehy-Skeffington undertook that task because they believed it to be vital that: 'militant and constitutional bodies are ready to cooperate in a constitutional manner with a view to forwarding the aims and voicing the demands of Irish-women' (SS 22: 665). But militancy was only one of the divisive issues. Dora Mellone, a leading Northern member of the Federation, wrote that she did not want to go to London because she wanted to work in the North: 'the real pressure will come from there, if it comes at all' (SS 22: 665). Significantly, she was also opposed to the Federation taking part in a demonstration about women and Home Rule, which was due to take place in Dublin's Phoenix Park. Many of the members of societies belonging to the Federation (including Mellone herself) were pro-unionist in sympathy and unwilling to participate in anything that appeared to favour national independence. Their publicly voiced desire to maintain a unity of forces concealed fundamental differences. In Belfast, local members of the WSPU were obviously not united on the question of taking part. One member declared: 'local society doesn't think the occasion important enough to send delegates' (SS 22: 665). Lilian Metge, who had taken part in the WSPU's unsuccessful deputation to the King on 21 May, sent a short note of regrets to Hanna Sheehy-Skeffington: 'Can't go over again so soon. Wish you all good luck. Excuse pc am knocked up again – but quite happy!' (SS 22: 665). The symbolism of petitioning the British monarchy would have been quite unacceptable to many Irish women, certainly to all the members of the IWFL. Margaret McCoubrey, originally from Scotland and now married to a Belfast trade unionist, eventually went to London on behalf of the WSPU, but she was not representative of the majority of that organization (SS 22: 665).

The WSPU in England was not involved in arrangements for the deputation. There is no evidence of any offers of help from that particular quarter. Those who lent their support to the Irish women were those who combined the demand for suffrage with some understanding of the need for wider reforms in society. Emmeline Pethick-Lawrence, expelled from the WSPU and now an active member of the United Suffragists, gave beds to women in her London flat while the Women's Freedom League was at pains to state that they would nominate one of their Irish members to speak and they would put a notice in *The Vote*, urging all their London-Irish members to take part. In the end Redmond and Asquith refused to meet the deputation and although many were pleased that militants and non-militants had managed to share a platform it is debatable whether the experience did much to draw the organizations closer. Political and strategic differences remained.

WSPU withdrawal

Two months later, the final blow came with the announcement that the British government had declared war upon Germany. British feminist ranks disintegrated as the Pankhursts declared their support for the war effort. The militant campaign was immediately called off and the order given that all local branches were to close down at once. Those imprisoned in Belfast gaol were visited and prevailed upon to abandon militancy for the duration (Chief Secretary's Office, GPB, 12.8.14).

Margaret McCoubrey was in despair at the prospect of the entire Northern suffrage movement collapsing at a time when the future of Ulster remained in considerable doubt, and just when a strong presence was vital in order to keep women's claims to the fore. The *Irish Citizen* had immediately produced a poster which defiantly declared 'Votes for Women Now! Damn Your War!' and McCoubrey hoped that a branch of the IWFL could be formed in Belfast, to fill the vacuum left by the departure of the WSPU. She initiated a close correspondence with Hanna Sheehy-Skeffington, whose 'accumulated wisdom' she greatly valued (SS 24: 133). This lengthy exchange provides an invaluable insight into political life in the North of Ireland during this period. McCoubrey was determined 'never again to have a society run on lines of WSPU', a clear reference to its notorious lack of any internal democracy.

The WSPU would not lease their building to the struggling IWFL, although Dorothy Evans herself was not unfriendly. As she explained in a letter to Sheehy-Skeffington: 'Can't sublet WSPU Belfast office – HQ says that must be for municipal body' (SS 22: 667). Premises a few doors down from the old WSPU office were eventually found. McCoubrey worried over the wisdom of this proximity but concluded:

> We will just live and that's all. Suffrage in the north has some way been strangled. But in the future it may be of service to the suffrage movement here in Ireland to have even a feeble off-spring of the IWFL here.

Dorothy Evans did not sever her ties with Ulster but remained in close contact with many of the Irish activists for years to come. Soon after the war began, Lilian Metge had let it slip that Christabel Pankhurst was considering the position of Ireland: 'and that the moment there is the least call for militancy in Ireland they will be here whether the work in England is taken up or not' (SS 24: 133). McCoubrey believed that this scenario was what Evans was hoping for. However, in what circumstances would the WSPU have returned? Given the thrust of their campaign in Ulster, could they have contemplated the possibility of calling for women's suffrage in the context of an independent Ireland? As this was not on their agenda before 1914, it is unlikely that they would have suddenly turned around to welcome such an event. And given the existence of the Irish suffrage groups, their efforts would only have duplicated work already undertaken. As they were staunchly pro-British all the evidence suggests that a

Sing "Biff! Bang! Bash!!"
With a right good smash.
Heave ho, with a one, two, three.
A big stone dash
Through a window crash!
Then, hurrah for liberty!

Figure 4   Cartoon: *The History of the Irish Suffrage Movement 1876–1922: 'Did your Granny have a hammer? (1985)', The Lepracaun,* **1913.**

partitioned Ulster linked to Britain continued to meet with favour in the inner circle of the WSPU.

Few of the former Belfast WSPU members expressed any enthusiasm for a branch of the IWFL. Mabel Small, who had been one of the WSPU prisoners, at first offered to go on the new committee, but McCoubrey confided that: 'being an Englishwoman I don't think she actually grasps the Irish point of view'. Before long Small was wearing a Union Jack in her lapel, considering resignation from the committee and talking about the inadvisability of suffrage work. Some ex-members became involved in the anti-war movement or the co-operative movement, but sectarian differences also re-emerged. When McCoubrey tried to get a delegation of experienced activists to visit Sir Edward Carson, those who supported the Unionist cause refused to go. One told her: 'the Franchise League savours so much of nationalism'. Some vowed a: 'Dublin society will never do here' and went to great lengths to ensure that no items of WSPU office equipment went to the struggling new group. Those who hoped that the WSPU would return appear to have been those most hostile to the IWFL influence, a fact which would indicate that when it came down to basics, they supported the Ulster Unionist cause.

From the nationalist side in Belfast there was no hostility and even a certain amount of good will, but tangible support was no greater. Women were putting their energies into Cumann na mBan, the nationalist women's organization, and therefore found themselves unable to take a prominent part in a suffrage organization which accepted the right of Westminster to legislate for Ireland. But feminist considerations were still important. Home Rule had been passed, only to be shelved for the duration of the war, and women's claims were still being ignored by politicians of all parties. Only the struggling Belfast labour movement could give the group any support and McCoubrey concluded sadly that her 'dreams of united womanhood' were vanishing, while anarchism or syndicalism now appeared as more attractive propositions. By spring 1915 the attempt to establish a branch of the IWFL in Belfast had come to an end. After the Easter Rising of 1916 the acute political divisions in the North did not allow for any feminist presence.

Historical lessons

History and the search for a constitutional solution to the problems of Ireland are inextricably linked. Revisionist historians who dismiss the impact of Britain's imperialist role in Ireland are consciously attempting to influence the political current in a particular direction. Why argue for a united Ireland if Britain has been a benign, modernizing influence? Those of us who favour a different direction need to be clear on what it is we wish to do. If the argument is that Britain should no longer intervene in Irish affairs, then historical evidence to support this is an important contribution to the wider debate. The evidence presented in this case-study of the relationship between the Irish Women's Franchise League and the Women's Social and Political Union is that British intervention in Irish affairs was motivated purely from British-inspired concerns and proved to be disastrous for the Irish, accentuating divisions which Irish women had hoped to modify. The only principled and constructive response for historians is to subject to scrutiny those factors which have contributed to the present situation in order to help in the quest of finding a solution to the divisions which have held back progressive movements for centuries. Ignoring sectarianism, resistance and British intervention by means of some intellectual *cordon sanitaire* leaves the past misunderstood and the future in great doubt.

Notes

Margaret Ward grew up in Belfast. She now teaches Irish history at Bath College of Higher Education. She is editing *In Their Own Voice: Women and Irish*

FEMINIST REVIEW NO 50, SUMMER 1995

Nationalism (Attic Press), as a contribution to women's efforts to be included in the all-male peace dialogue. She is also writing a biography of Hanna Sheehy-Skeffington – Irish suffragist and Sinn Feiner.

1 There are exceptions to the general tendency to isolate considerations of nationalism from other concerns of feminist history. Cullen (1985) is a brief, dispassionate assessment of the extent of radicalism within both feminism and nationalism, although it too omits consideration of the North. For discussions of the state of women's history in Ireland, see Ward (1991), Cullen (1991) and Luddy (1992).

References

Archival material

The papers of Hanna and Francis Sheehy-Skeffington (SS followed by manuscript number in text) in the National Library of Ireland are an indispensable source for the study of the Irish suffrage movement.

The National Archives in Dublin contain the papers of the General Prisons Board (GPB in text), three (unsorted) boxes of which concern the imprisonment of Irish suffragists.

Irish Citizen 1912–15
Votes for Women 1908–13

Publications

The following references include some works not cited in the text, but which are important contributions to the development of feminist history in Ireland.

COUSINS, J.H. and COUSINS, M.E. (1950) *We Two Together* Madras: Ganesh.
CULLEN, Mary (1985) 'How radical was Irish feminism between 1860 and 1920?' in Corish, P.J. (1985) *Radicals, Rebels and Establishments* Belfast: Appletree Press.
—— (1991) 'Women's history in Ireland' in Offen, Karen, Roach, Ruth and Rendall, Jane (1991) editors, *Writing Women's History: International Perspectives* London: Macmillan.
CULLEN OWENS, Rosemary (1984) *Smashing Times* Dublin: Attic Press.
—— (1985) *Did Your Granny Have a Hammer?* Dublin: Attic Press.
HEARN, Dana (1992) 'The Irish Citizen 1914–1916' *Canadian Journal of Irish Studies* Vol. 18, No. 1: 1–14.
LENEMAN, Leah (1991) *'A Guid Cause': The Women's Suffrage Movement in Scotland* Aberdeen: Aberdeen University Press.
LUDDY, Maria (1992) 'An agenda for women's history: 1800–1900' *Irish Historical Studies* Vol. XXVIII, No. 109: 19–37.

MULVIHILL, Margaret (1989) *Charlotte Despard* London: Pandora Press.

MURPHY, Cliona (1989) *The Women's Suffrage Movement and Irish Society in the Early Twentieth Century* London: Harvester.

—— (1993) 'Suffragists and nationalism in early twentieth-century Ireland' *History of European Ideas* Vol. 16, No. 4: 1009–15.

PANKHURST, Sylvia (1977) *The Suffragette Movement* London: Virago.

PETHICK-LAWRENCE, Emmeline (1938) *My Part in a Changing World* London: Victor Gollancz.

ROSEN, Andrew (1974) *Rise Up Women* London: Routledge.

SAWYER, Roger (1993) *We Are But Women* London: Routledge.

SHEEHY-SKEFFINGTON, Hanna (1975) 'Reminiscences of an Irish suffragette' in Sheehy-Skeffington, A.D. and Owens, R. *Votes for Women: Irishwomen's Struggle for the Vote* Dublin.

WARD, Margaret (1983) *Unmanageable Revolutionaries: Women and Irish Nationalism* London: Pluto.

—— (1991) *The Missing Sex: Putting Women into Irish History* Dublin: Attic Press.

Women Disarmed

The Militarization of Politics in Ireland 1913–23

Sarah Benton

FEMINIST REVIEW NO 50, SUMMER 1995, pp. 148–72

Abstract

The movement for 'military preparedness' in America and Britain gained tremendous momentum at the turn of the century. It assimilated the cult of manliness – the key public virtue, which allowed a person to claim possession of himself and a nation to reclaim possession of itself. An army was the means of marshalling a mass of people for regeneration. The symbol of a nation's preparedness to take control of its own soul was the readiness to bear arms.

Although this movement originated in the middle-class, Protestant cultures of the USA and England, its core ideas were adopted by many political movements. Affected by these ideas, as well as the formation of the Protestant Ulster Volunteers in 1913, a movement to reclaim Irish independence through the mass bearing of arms began in South and West Ireland in autumn 1914. Women were excluded from these Volunteer companies, but set up their own organization, Cumann na mBan, as an auxiliary to the men's. The Easter Rising in 1916 owed as much to older ideas of the *coup d'état* as new ideas of mass mobilization, but subsequent history recreated that Rising as the 'founding' moment of the Irish republic.

It was not until mass conscription was threatened two years later that the mass of people were absorbed into the idea of an armed campaign against British rule. From 1919 to 1923, the reality of guerrilla-style war pressed people into a frame demanding discipline, secrecy, loyalty and a readiness to act as the prime nationalist virtues. The ideal form of relationship in war is the brotherhood, both as actuality and potent myth. The mythology of brotherhood creates its own myths of women (as not being there, and men not needing them) as well as creating the fear and the myth that rape is the inevitable expression of brotherhoods in action. Despite explicit anxiety at the time about the rape of Irish women by British soldiers, no evidence was found of mass rape, and that fear has disappeared into oblivion, throwing up important questions as to when rape is a weapon of war.

The decade of war worsened the relationship of women to the political realm. Despite active involvement as 'auxiliaries' women's political status was permanently damaged by their exclusion as warriors and brothers, so much so that they disappear into the status of wives and mothers in the 1937 Irish Constitution.

Keywords

brotherhood; founding; Ireland; military; rape; women

Introduction

From wherever you start in feminist politics or history, you are drawn ineluctably to the question of war as the defining experience for a nation's political arrangements. From whatever point you start in Irish history and politics, it is hard not to be drawn back to its 'founding moment' in 1916; that is, to the few days in Easter week 1916 when the combined forces of the Irish Volunteers, the Irish Citizen Army, the youthful Fianna Eireann, the women's Cumann na mBan, the Irish Republican Brotherhood and supporters, tried to mount an insurrection. The subsequent execution of fifteen insurgents came to be part of that founding moment.

All nations have a myth of origin, but not all have a myth of foundation by human act. The myth of foundation is extraordinarily important for women. It is in that myth that women are often deleted from history and the peculiar 'warrior' qualities of men are elevated to heroic status. The myth of foundation tells us who are the founding fathers or the 'authors' of the nation, and thus defines what acts and styles are 'authentic' and whose voices have authority. It is in this telling of national myth that the political authority of women has so often been expunged.

This is the notion of foundation which, I think, is defined by J.G.A. Pocock as the event and document which found 'a "tradition" or a transmissible "style" of politics' (Ball and Pocock, 1988: 56). The power of the Rising over the imagination has stretched long and wide. The event and document of founding is widely taken to be Patrick Pearse's reading of the Declaration of Independence on Easter Morning 1916. For instance, the influential analyst of imperialism, Edward Said, accepts this 'proclamation' as having 'founded the Irish Republic' (Said, 1994: 285) though legally this might rather be the 1919 Dáil's 'Declaration of Independence', the Treaty instituting partition and ratified by Dáil Eireann in 1922, or the new Constitution, ratified in 1937.

A vital thread of this foundation tradition, or myth, was that there was a distinct 'Gaelic character' and this was essentially military; that armed

FEMINIST REVIEW NO 50, SUMMER 1995

Irishmen had risen in insurrections against the British in 1798, 1803 and 1867, and that these insurrections had failed through inadequate preparation or betrayals. No civic innovations in, for instance, local government, formed part of the tradition.

Between 1913 and 1923, from the founding of the armed Ulster Volunteers through the formation of the Irish Volunteers, through the First World War, the Rising, the war with the Black and Tans (1919–21), and the civil war of 1922–3, war thrust its way through Irish life. In that decade, the military ethos became the dominant ethos. That meant the values of manliness, of brotherhood, of tactical necessity and of unity were dominant. Unity meant, not universal agreement, but the laying aside of those ideas and desires which did not further the paramount cause, the establishment of an independent Ireland.

This history, on which all accounts of contemporary Irish politics touch down at some point, excludes women as people and feminism as a body of ideas and a movement. There is nothing inevitable about the supremacy of this history, and perhaps from the 1990s that history will have no contemporary purpose, and will recede into forgetfulness. It has been sustained not as the foundation of independent Ireland, but as the frayed binding of politics, North and South and the gap in between. It was a solace for defeat of the ideal of a united, egalitarian republic.

Two consequences of the settlements made by the war decade were the partition of Ireland and the political subjugation of women. Today's revisionist history must engage with that decade if only to understand that women's political subordination is not natural. It is made by defeats, by military necessity, by the settlements men arrive at to finish wars.

This, then, is a survey of that militarization of politics and culture, and the implications for women. My argument hinges on these principal points:

- Once a movement becomes militarized, the consequent military ethos and command structure subjugate or even annihilate other values and civic organizations.

- This, on its own, does not explain the subsequent place of women. Some nationalist wars entail a war against women, as the reproducers of the nation or as the bearers of the nation's honour (for instance, in the 'Rape of Nanking' in 1937, in Bangladesh in 1971 or Bosnia in 1992–3). There is a contemporary assumption that the rape of women is inevitable in war, and British and American investigations in 1920 into the Black and Tan atrocities certainly expected to find evidence of rape.

My argument is that mass rape and sexual terrorism are not inevitable in nationalist wars, and I cannot find the evidence that this took place in Ireland. Whether or not it does is a complicated question, depending on the type of war, how far the aggressors' male culture is eroticized, and whether or not the war is between 'neighbours' where overlapping identities is a salient point of contention making sexual terrorism far more common.

- War creates, in actuality and in myth, potent forces for defining and enforcing gender divisions. The 'manliness' cult, *c.* 1880s–1915, prepared the way for war and in turn was organized as a military virtue. As myth, both brotherhood and rape are concerned with whether or not women matter, indeed have a material existence at all. In actuality, rape tests the authority of the soldiers' commanding officer to control or unleash male violation of the sacred.

- One impelling idea of the state is as a protectorate. The ideology of protectorate was especially resonant in colonies where imperial power was justified as the power that would protect the chosen (colonized) country from the depredations of enemies and competitors. The protective state will take care of those who offer it their first loyalty.

This is one reason why the political place of women is always contested – for surely women owe first loyalty to husband and family, not the state? Can they then ever be full citizens? In Ireland, the dilemma of women's loyalty and status was resolved through a tacit 'lay-off' between republicans and Catholic Church, in which women were left inside the domestic zone under the protective patronage of the Church. The weaker the protective patronage of a religion over the 'domestic sphere', the more vulnerable women are as targets of military aggression.

Before the wars

The culture of military preparedness and upstanding manhood emerged at least two decades before the war years. From its beginning in military defeats and conquests (the Franco-Prussian War, the American-Spanish War, the Boer War) and escalating public concern about the breakdown of hygiene and the laws of sexual and class propriety in cities, military preparedness was offered as a solution. (For this, and the 'martial chorus', see Pearlman, 1984 and Ferraro, 1933.) It stiffened the backbone of many a Protestant chap and inspired countless movements for camping out, parading in uniform and practising military drill with broomsticks.

FEMINIST REVIEW NO 50, SUMMER 1995

Although it was a more powerful phenomenon in Protestant countries than Catholic, such was the anxiety about decadence and such was the versatility of military preparedness, that hardly an organization with an aim of redeeming society did not make use of military forms and language.

The two most influential popularizers of military manliness in Protestant culture, Britain's Lord Baden-Powell and America's Teddy Roosevelt, clearly affected Irish nationalism, as objects of derision and emulation. (The Irish Republican Brotherhood's paper, *Irish Freedom*, quoted at length from Roosevelt's rambling lecture, 'Manhood', extolling the virtues of honesty, decency, cleanliness, and the 'courage, resolution, the power to make yourself felt as a man . . .' in December 1910, and again on the responsibilities of manhood being 'the refuge of the nation' in May 1911.)

There is much dispute today over how influential the Irish Republican Brotherhood (IRB) was in shaping Irish history. There is no doubt that it, more than any other organization, took the *Zeitgeist* of military manliness and adapted it to its own end. It turned the general summons for clean, disciplined manliness into specific summons for men to realize themselves and Ireland's destiny through bearing arms. ('[A]nd behold, arms turned them into men, and made them realise they were Irishmen', as *Irish Freedom* (December 1910), a new monthly edited by IRB member Bulmer Hobson, said of the 1790s, as it said in every issue of every past episode in which Irishmen had formed any sort of rudimentary army.)

As part of the preparation, Hobson had written his own *Defensive Warfare: A Handbook for Irish Nationalists* (Townshend, 1983: 240–3). The IRB was alone because, in those pre-war years, the military manhood school was waging a war against, in their eyes, inertia, defeat and resignation and, in the eyes of others, the freedom to pursue pleasure and the propriety of politics.

Before 1910, culture, language and politics were the means by which the Irish would regain possession of themselves. (The themes of sovereignty and self-possession are central to the evolution of nationalism, and have profound implications for women.) The Gaelic League stood for cultural revival; the parliamentary party for the propriety of politics. (Sinn Fein, founded in 1906 as an anti-violent, non-republican league, did not stand for militant Irish nationalism until 1918.)

The change is most apparent in the Gaelic Athletic Association, which for twenty-five years had been seen as part of the cultural revival of Irishness. After about 1910 its leaders saw it as a forerunner of the essential qualities of brotherhood and manliness, set up to counter the alien sports taken up by 'degenerate dandies' of the day; for 'when a race is declining in martial spirit' national games are neglected by the men 'whose reason is unhinged' who 'deck themselves in gaudy frippery and fading flowers, thereby demonstrating that the throne of man's dignity is uncrowned' (*Irish Freedom*, January and February 1911). The hurley stick was reborn as the symbol of man's throne, and of his gun in drills.

From culture to militarism

The decisive shift from culture and politics to manliness and militarism reflected the escalating militarism of the times, in which Clausewitz's *On War* (1832/1968) can be seen as a founding document of the modern age.

While civil associations had been cultural or agrarian up to the first decade of the twentieth century, after that point they were military, labour or feminist. There is, of course, no clean break. Possibility as well as ideology gave mass, military organization more power than cultural revival, the romance of secret societies and the *attentat*.

By 1923, the military form and language were dominant. The republican movement's own 'boy scouts', founded in 1909 by Countess Markievicz and Bulmer Hobson (the man who did most to revive the pre-war moribund IRB) and named Fianna Eireann in honour of legendary Irish warriors, was the first para-military organization of the time. The Irish Citizen Army came four years later, formed in 1913 during the transport workers' lock-out. Roger Casement sent an immediate telegram of support, saying he hoped 'it may begin a widespread national movement to organise drilled and disciplined Irish Volunteers to assert Irish manhood and uphold the national cause' (quoted in Fox, 1943, 43). The ICA would defend workers against police violence, transform the incoherent mass of selfish individuals into a single force with common purpose, and, by its distinguishing marks of red-hand badges, uniforms and arm-bands, separate the true soldiers from the rest. 'Who fears to wear the blood-red badge/Upon his manly breast?' exhorted a poem in the labour press in 1913. In fact, and uniquely, the ICA admitted women from the start and spoke a distinct language of sexual equality, a tribute as much to founder James Connolly as to the labour movement of the time.

The idea of a disciplined mass army as *the* agent for change was compelling, from around the 1880s to the First World War, in the USA, Japan and much of Western Europe. For those who welcomed mass democracy and those who feared it, the idea of the mass army became the dominant idea of marshalling masses of people. (Serious critics of army uniformity only emerged after the First World War.) The imagery and structure of an army are evoked over and over again by those advocating workers' political parties, urban regeneration movements, and nationalist uprisings against imperialism. Suffragettes adopted the imagery, though more hesitantly.

For revolutionaries, the idea was an implicit, sometimes explicit, rejection of secretive acts of violence favoured by, among others, anarchists such as Emma Goldman and those enamoured of, in Maud Gonne's words, 'the romance of secret societies' (Gonne MacBride, 1938: 314).

The overwhelming claim of the mass army was that it would transform the members in it as much as the society around them. How did such an idea become so powerful? It owed something to the prevailing military theory of the time and much to the hope that military organization would effect 'the amalgamation of certain elements in two classes of men opposed to each other in every respect save [their] quality of manhood' (General Leonard Wood, leader of the movement for universal military conscription in America, quoted in Pearlman, 1984). It owed something to the awe-inspiring power of capitalism to transform society by marshalling the incoherent mass into a uniform machine, and something to an anti-imperialist reclaiming of military virtues.

In the *Irish Worker*,

> there had been many articles glorifying the stand made by Tone and Emmet, uncompromising fighters for National Independence. The men of the tenements were urged to regard themselves as the rightful successors to those earlier fighters.
>
> (Fox, 1943, 4)

The event in Ireland which galvanized the embrace of mass militarism was the formation of the Ulster Volunteer Force in 1913. Throughout 1911 Orange Lodges had been drilling in preparation for resistance to Home Rule, and their success in bringing together men across the class divide gave them confidence. 'As a body the men were magnificent, hardy toilers from shipyard and factory marching shoulder to shoulder with clergy, doctors, lawyers, business men and clerks', breathes Edward Carson's biographer admiringly, in language indistinguishable from that of the Americans whose eyes grew moist at the thought of rough and refined men going on camp together (Hyde, 1974: 341).

In 1912, the Ulster Unionist Council had organized a mass male signing of a 'Solemn League and Covenant' (with a separate pledge from women). The militarization of Ulster politics paralysed the British government while it inspired the Nationalists. Publicly, they determined to see it as a sign that all Irish people could be mobilized for self-possession, rather than as a sign of enmity towards fellow, but Catholic, Irish people.

In November 1913, the Irish Volunteers were founded at a mass meeting in Dublin. With resounding speeches from the platform about the reclamation of manliness, heckling from the ICA who spied bosses' friends in the ranks of the Nationalists, and with the women secluded in the gallery, this founding offered a republican ideal of how change could be brought about.

It was a crucial moment in Irish republicanism, a pivot in the move from civic republicanism to the military brothers' republicanism. The civic republican argument from the eighteenth century was that the readiness to bear arms for the state was the qualification *par excellence* for citizenship. It assumed the republic had already been made. Bearing arms was an ordinary civic duty for ordinary, domestic men. Military republicanism prepared men to make the republic.

The new martial ethos signalled by the formation of the Volunteers proposed that military training or sport would inculcate the civic virtues necessary to combat the effeminacy of the age. Only those men who would put the nation before all else would be eligible. Military republicanism assumed the nation had to be remade through a violent severance with the status quo. By *action*, by discipline, by a readiness to bear arms, the men of Ireland would awaken the sleeping spirit of the nation, and regain possession of itself. The Volunteers' meeting was the pivot because it made possible the shift from the first concept to the second without apparently breaking the link. One link was virility. In either argument, virility is *the* civic virtue.

In contrast with this Protestant ethic of republican virility, the Irish stress on martyrdom and blood sacrifice might seem to belong to the Catholic heritage of tales of the martyrdom of tortured saints. In one of his most quoted phrases, Patrick Pearse (legendary hero of the Rising, executed 3 May 1916) extolled the arming of Irishmen because 'bloodshed is a cleansing and a sanctifying thing and the nation which regards it as the final horror has lost its manhood' (in an article in *An Claidheamh Soluis* in November 1913; quoted in Edwards, 1977).

In fact the idea that men prove themselves brothers and create new life through the spilling of their sacred bodily fluids is common to many nationalist discourses. The distinctive Catholicism of Ireland's military decade is more apparent in the role of the clergy and the Catholic hierarchy than in ideological differences.

New world disorder and manliness

'Manliness' was a protean quality, which would rescue nations from degeneracy, but also awake them from sleep. The 'degeneracy' which haunted Germany, Britain and the USA from around the 1880s to 'world war' was a hotchpotch of miscegenation, immigration, trans-national powers and conspiracies, effeminacy and brute criminality. Stirring up this farrago of terrors was the impact of imperialism; like its more flexible friend, the global capitalism of today, it precipitated the break-down of the old order, a break-down completed by the First World War. (Two years of the restructuring required by total war was 'the real point at which the old European order succumbed.' This explains the timing of the 1916 Rising, *not* the instigating role of the IRB, argues Charles Townshend (1983: 278).)

Manliness was the cure-all. Capitalism had destroyed virility by creating a class of idle, 'effeminate' youth and another of illiterate good-for-nothings. The demanning artifices of class would be overcome by the practice of brotherhood in leisure time. The archetypal man was a soldier, the ideal community a platoon of soldiers. Brotherhood would teach men common purpose, loyalty and unselfishness, the nucleus of nationhood. Hardship would teach them self-possession, so they could snatch back their souls from the seductions of urban life. Or, in the case of Ireland, from the blandishments of England, which had corrupted the souls of the Irish parliamentary party by offering its MPs positions and stuffing their mouths with an alien tongue.

Awakenings

The impact of the First World War on this volatile mood was different in England and Ireland. In Ireland, it quickly destroyed the already crumbling authority of the parliamentary party. War also radically changed Britain's ability to govern Ireland. And war opened new imaginable possibilities for Irish independence. Here the second curative power of 'manliness' could seize the imaginative lead: the power of awakening the nation from sleep. 'Awake! awake!' cry speeches, pamphlets, articles in Ireland in the 1910s.

The imagery of a dormant nation is a commonplace in revolutionary rhetoric. It allows the belief that the silent community is still there, intact. It may come to life in the 'spontaneous awakening' of an 'intifada' (Abdo, 1994) or through the igniting spark of the revolutionary leadership. As a self-conscious revolutionary and maker of the modern age, Richard Wagner studded his Ring cycle with awakenings, like Brynhilde's in *Siegfried* ('Hail bright sunlight!/. . . Who is the man/wakes me to life?').

A sugar and spice version of the sexual kiss which wakes women from passivity is Sleeping Beauty. The notion of a people being woken from enchantment, 'sighing deeply, it rubbed its eyes as if waking up', was used by Tom Nairn of the British people waking from the monarchist spell (*Observer*, 3.7.94). Sleep, as a myth of life in death, is found in the Feast of

Dormition, or the Falling Asleep of the Virgin Mary (Warner, 1976: 87–9). Sleep, for all proselyters of hope, explains the absence of the life that must be present in order to substantiate hope.

Perhaps the men who call for awakenings are claiming that death can be vanquished and they themselves have the power to create life. From 'the blood of patriots spring armed men' said *Irish Freedom* in 1910, anticipating the sacrifice of the Fianna youth. (Their foresight was realized. In 1922, *Poblacht na hEireann* (4.7.22), then the War News bulletin, said 'The Republic is founded on the blood of boys used by the very men who climbed to office over the bleeding sacrifices of these boys.' In one of the many echoes of this theme, Patrick Pearse told a graveside crowd in August 1915 that:

> [our foes cannot destroy the] miracles of God who ripens in the hearts of young men the seeds sown by the young men of a former generation. And the seeds sown by the young men of '65 and '67 are coming to their miraculous ripening today. . . . Life springs from death; and from the graves of patriot men and women spring living nations.

> (Patrick Pearse's oration for O'Donovan Rossa, Edwards, 1977: 236)

The speeches in which men call out for the awakening portray a state of depression, in which the body is inert until galvanized by the great energizing emotions of hope and anger. The men named these feelings 'Will'. It is these emotions that the call to manhood evoked. Real men, unlike slaves or women who were naturally passive, would be angry about British rule. Real men would have hope, because they would have faith in their own strength. Real men would *act*, unlike ineffectual intellectuals.

In their actions lay the potency of manliness. They had to fight against the 'danger that inertia and inactivity would sap its [Irish manhood's] virility' wrote Florence O'Donoghue, spinning the foundation tradition (1952: 41). Not all men were men, of course. The gentlemen would lie abed (and later curse the day they were not there). And even the women with the best claim as awakeners, like Maud Gonne and Constance Markievicz, were transmuted in this myth into mere totems for the men.

For Irish revolutionaries, in whom the mythology of insurrections betrayed by informers was ingrained, the paramount quality of manliness was utter loyalty to the nation, and to a brotherhood as surrogate for the nation. Brotherhood treats women, insofar as it acknowledges them, as its greatest threat, for women embody the mythology of betrayal. At best women offer absolute loyalty to 'their' man. Only a primary allegiance to the selfless cause fitted people to be citizens.

Despite the precedent of the mixed-sex ICA, the Volunteers were only ever seen as a manifestation of the manliness that made up the core of civic virtue. The helter-skelter towards European war consolidated these currents of mass, military, manly mobilization.

Rising, and conscription

The Rising was planned by the highly secret Military Council of the Irish Republican Brotherhood, despite their 1873 Constitution which bound the IRB *not* to initiate military action on its own, but to await the 'fit hour', to be decided by the 'Irish nation, as expressed by a majority of the Irish people' (Broin, 1976: 7).

The Volunteers split in 1914, the majority going, as the National Volunteers, with John Redmond, the leader of the parliamentary party, who had called in 1914 for the Irish to support the British war effort. Since then, there had been pressure from the remaining Irish Volunteers to make use of their refusal to go to war and cleanse it from any taint of cowardice. James Connolly had been urging an insurrection during England's hour of weakness on the Western Front. War seems to have gone to his head, persuading him that a putsch would topple the British and rouse the people. Or at least that, if they didn't go for it now, Ireland's humiliation would be insupportable. The IRB militants feared his ICA might instigate an 'insurrection' on its own. In this rivalrous jostle of anxiety for action, the IRB dare not squander its leading role.

By January 1916, the IRB Military Council settled on a date for the Rising. Popular response to the rising was hostile or indifferent. The extraordinary creation of 'the triumph of failure' (the phrase was used by Desmond Ryan, participant in the Rising and literary executor of Patrick Pearse) is commonly said to begin with the executions of the Rising leaders and the internment of scores of others, their bloody death being the seed that brought the nation to life.

But it is doubtful that even this slew of martyrs would have been enough to make of 1916 a 'founding moment'. The Volunteers, who had become an especial target for 'popular contumely' after the Rising, did not begin to revive until 1918 (Fitzpatrick, 1977: 115). Despite the mass welcomes for the return from Britain of imprisoned insurrectionists in 1917, the few had a hard time keeping 'the flame alive' between such celebratory moments.

What brought new life to Irish nationalism was the threat of mass conscription. In April 1918, after years of indecision, the British Parliament finally passed a Military Service Bill, threatening conscription in Ireland. This transformed the mass politics of Ireland. Unlike the Rising, it touched all adults including women, among whom Cumann na mBan (see page 206) organized a pledge that they would never take men's work. It catapulted Sinn Fein, which resolutely opposed conscription, into the leading political position. It brought in the hierarchy of the Roman Catholic Church who condemned conscription as 'inhuman'. It threw men back into military mode, which, after the dismal failure of the armed Rising had fallen into disfavour.

Recruitment to the Irish Volunteers soared. From the threat of conscription, the militarized section of the nationalist movement became more and more dominant, until all other political activity became subservient to the needs and priorities of the Volunteers.

War with Britain and civil war

By 1919 the armed nation of Volunteers was becoming the Volunteers of the Irish Republican Army, whose will, expressed through action, had become the surrogate for the will of the people, and whose readiness to act, by dying if need be, embodied the people's will to realize themselves through nationhood. The shift from mass to minority was made by the drift into active war with the British, 1919–21. The further move from a minority of citizen soldiers to soldiers contemptuous of politics was consolidated by the years of civil war, 1922–3.

In the general election of 1918 Sinn Fein candidates won virtually every seat in Ireland outside Ulster and established their own, unofficial Dáil Éireann and government ministries. This act of defiance against British rule shifted the idea of citizenship from being Irish 'by birth or descent' to proving allegiance to the Republic, meaning its own institutions. The British, of course, did not recognize these, and further, 'proclaimed', or banned, Sinn Fein in 1919.

War with the British (the infamous Black and Tans) evolved from the sporadic raids by Volunteers on British military and police stations to acquire arms. By the middle of 1919, the best proof of loyalty to the Republic was less the oaths of allegiance demanded than the readiness to fight and die. The guerrilla warfare of 1919–21 owed nothing to the republican ideal of the ordinary citizen bearing arms. It was fought by secretive, single men on the run. Or 'men who go around in small bands, but those appear to spend their whole time in attempting to avoid capture' as a British intelligence report sneered (Weekly Intelligence Summary, 17.5.21 of the Sixth Division, O'Donoghue, 1954: 118).

The war with Britain created a new leadership imbued with military virtue. The 1922 peace treaty (which recognized an Irish Free State but at the price of partition and allegiance to the British monarch as nominal head of state) split that leadership. The majority, led by Michael Collins, accepted the treaty as the best they could get. The minority determined that *this* time the fight for independence would be pursued to the end; it would be done because it *could* be done; because they had their own army. This time there would be no betrayal by loose-lip informers. Republicanism would be immune to seduction. The maintenance of arms, of military action and of the forms and values of fraternity would see to this.

So much was this so, that for many Volunteer/IRA leaders the very *purpose* of military action was to keep the band of brothers together. Because they had become involved in the 1918 election, wrote one, 'many had ceased to be soldiers and had become politicians.' There was a danger of disintegration, a danger which had been growing since the threat of conscription disappeared a few months earlier. 'I was convinced that some sort of action was absolutely necessary' (Dan Breen in *My Fight for Irish Freedom*, 1924, quoted in Townshend, 1975: 16). 'However much pains may be taken to combine the soldier and the citizen in one and the same individual' Clausewitz had written, those who are engaged in war 'will always look upon themselves as a kind of guild, in the regulation, laws and customs in which the "Spirit of War" by preference finds its expression . . . The crystals of military virtue have a greater affinity for the spirit of a corporate body than for anything else' (Clausewitz, 1832/1968: 255). From 1920, the fighting men of action resisted any attempts to subject them to political discipline, and spurned any movement which put political change first.

Civil war broke out in January 1922. The IRA lost its central role as the 'guardian' of the Republic. Civil war broke any organic connection to a political tradition of civic republicanism. (The IRA was declared illegal in Eire in 1936.) This trajectory is different from that of the anti-colonial armies which merge with the new state, providing much of the state's initial personnel and organizing capacity and, in one-party states, reproduce the army's ethos of unified command.

Civil war froze 1916 as the unique and unifying foundation. The men who died fighting British rule did become the legendary heroes; but their legend was only honoured in practice as the protectors of vulnerable Catholics in Northern Ireland – a role largely created by the desultory and fearful practice of British government in Northern Ireland. The IRA's own heritage of mystical manliness, of fear of betrayal, its overruling concern with secrecy and its single tactic of military action prevented it taking a hegemonic role as the protector of the nation, or as the embryo of universal republican virtues.

Woman remade as 'bereaved mother'

The defeat of the possibility of an all-Ireland, all-adult secular republic entailed the defeat of women as political citizens. Like the Boers, whose war against the mighty British Empire had a profound effect on Irish nationalism,[1] women survive in legend as the suffering and bereaved mothers. It was not the sexual partners of men who were dispossessed by the British, but the mothers; not the wives who made the sacrifice of losing their beloved men, but the mothers. Sinn Fein's 1918 election pamphlet appealed for women's vote with 'Save Ireland by voting as Mrs Pearse will vote', Mrs Pearse being the now sacred mother of Patrick and William Pearse, both brothers executed after the Rising. Women's claim is thus, in legend, to be protected and revered as mothers; not to be making the nation in their own right.

The warriors, however, did not sacrifice themselves as the protectors of mothers, but as the defenders of the nation. The distinguishing mark of citizenship is whether a person 'belongs' to state – or to family. Much of the ideological energy of nationalist republicanism in any country goes into consolidating the argument that the nation properly belongs to the people, and the people to it. How this becomes an argument that the nation-state belongs to the men, and the men to it, is one of the most important questions for feminism. For the shift from the nation of all people to the state of men undoubtedly takes place in many new states, dispossessing women of their claim to equal citizenship.

From nation in arms to élite of brothers

Much depends on the type of war that is fought – its form, its aims, its ideology, its relation to the non-combatant people. In Ireland, the shift between 1913 and 1923 of military volunteers from being the people in arms to being a secretive élite of young male warriors on the run is the lever which ejects women from their fragile place in public life.

The republican ethic that all citizens should bear arms had, in Britain, France, Germany and the USA become an argument that the nation *was* the citizens in arms (though for Black soldiers in the American Civil War, and indigenous regiments in the Indian army, it was an ethic of loyalty to the governing state, not of being the nation-state.) As an ethic it still excluded women from the arms-bearing citizenry, and placed them as members of the private household which the male citizen must protect. The difference is that the armed citizen of, say, an American militia is an ordinary domestic man, rooted in private home. The guerrilla is a special man with particular military skills whose loyalty is to his comrades, not his home.

Young men on the run in 1922 did not have wives and children. Or at least, according to *Poblacht na hEireann* and many women activists in the Irish National Aid Fund they didn't. They sent their dying messages to their mothers; their sisters kept vigil and bore them food in prison. The IRA ideal was closer to that of an armed priesthood than Tom Paine's domestic man who must arm himself because his 'life and children are destitute of a bed to lie on' (Paine, 1775: 85). When Cathal Brugha (IRA Chief of Staff 1917–19 and Minister of Defence 1919–22) was killed in the first weeks of the civil war, *Poblacht na hEireann* (7.7.22) wrote reverently that he had prepared twenty years for the rising, 'as a priest for ordination'. Like priests, the men who bore arms were special, and should not encumber their idealism with home lives. (It was one of the biblical 'laws of war' – Deuteronomy 20 – that a man with a new house, vineyard or betrothed should not be called as a soldier.)

The myth of brotherhood

'Brotherhood' is both myth and reality. In reality, it is an effective form of organization, stressing unity, selflessness, loyalty and secrecy. Where brotherhood rules, it shapes other social relations. For instance, when men are brothers on the run, women become the invisible bearers of messages and the ones who keep the home fires burning. It also separates an élite of brothers from ordinary men. The older men, who had exercised paternal authority, are displaced.

The myth of brotherhood is a myth of male independence of women, it is a myth of human society with no women and no children, a myth of human life where death is always a chosen act of self-sacrifice for the common good. It is a myth about men who are free of base desires, of which the most base and the most possessing is sexual desire for women.

But such brotherhoods are sterile and perhaps this explains the pervasive imagery of men generating new life through their bodily fluids. And is it because they are the bearers of death, or because they are bound by homoerotic desire, that the brotherhood myth also throws up, again and again, the image of cleansing, a washing away of foul bodily fluids as well as an erotic dwelling on the naked male body? Brotherhoods embody the libidinal links between men, denying their tie to family home (For the 'libidinal' ties of men in armies, see Freud, 1985: 119–28; for the homo-erotic imagery of soldiers bathing, see Mosse, 1985: 117–18.)

Brotherhood embodies ideals of unselfishness and loyalty inside the gang in contrast to the mass outside. Brotherhoods are not an embryo of the whole people, but of the leadership of the people. They become dominant only when the mass of people are asleep but none the less are understood to have given their consent to the brotherhood's alert militancy. The dormant people must be seen to accept the brotherhood's own self-glorification as the kernel of the whole nation. The ideal nation is remade in their idealized image.

When a myth of brotherhood becomes dominant it expunges the reality of women and of men's relation to them.

The myth of rape

The myth of brotherhood excites veneration – and instils fear in non-brothers. The most common fear is of mass rape, and there is an assumption that the rape of women is inevitable in war. It is strange to discover that this is now forgotten, though it was a vital question about Ireland in 1921–2.

Fraternal, or gang, rape does happen in some wars; but not all. The 'common sense' that it is inevitable is the myth of rape. A myth, said Levi-Strauss, must tell a story which resolves a contradiction, and one contradiction it resolves is between women as vital to the life of the nation, and women as having no real existence. If women are raped, they are real, and of sufficient worth to be the first target for destruction. The myth of rape counters the myth of brotherhood which deletes women from real life. The myth of rape proposes that the end of all male activity is the destruction of women as self-possessed individuals.

The presumption of rape is a presumption that men, freed from the constraints of civilization, will always go on the sexual rampage. If there is then no outcry, this is because 'the subject was so taboo that the victims were unwilling to give evidence' (as Diana Norman avers in her biography of Constance Markievicz, Norman, 1987).

Several inquiries into the 'atrocities' of 1919-20 were held at the time.[2] Rape was a pressing question because of the above assumptions, because of publicity for German sexual 'atrocities' against Belgian nuns and rumours of sexual offences by American troops in 1917–19. Rape had not been specified as a war crime in the 1907 Hague Convention, although later war crimes tribunals have taken it to be a crime under point 11 of the 4th Convention specifying that 'family honour and rights' must be respected (Friedman, 1985).

The 1921 interim report of the American Commission on Conditions in Ireland said:

> The testimony shows that women and girls have been searched by members of the Imperial British forces, the privacy of their bedrooms has been invaded in the

FEMINIST REVIEW NO 50, SUMMER 1995

dead of night, and their hair cut off; but in no case has the crime of rape been specifically charged by Irish witnesses before us against the Imperial troops. The fact that for four years and a half an army of at least 78,000 British has been occupying Ireland without provoking charges of major sensual offences against Irish women is remarkable. It would seem to us the one bright spot in the darkness of war.

(American Commission, 1921: 86)

It attributed this bright spot to a readiness by British officers to control their men on this one issue alone.

There is no doubt that 'forces of the Crown' subjected women to acts of sexual humiliation 1920–1, or that women found it difficult to speak of this. Labour's 1920 Commission to Ireland reported: 'Unfortunately, in their work of hunting down people, the agents of the British Government often act in a way which is terrifying to women' and:

This rough and brutal treatment of women is by no means the worst that is to be said against men in the service of the British Crown. It is, however, extremely difficult to obtain direct evidence of incidents affecting females, for the women of Ireland are reticent on such subjects.

(*Report of the Labour Commission to Ireland.* There were no women members on the Commission.)

The catalogue of the terrorism of the forces of the Crown is still shocking to read today, even after seventy years in which accounts of the behaviour of invading soldiers has made such events commonplace. The Labour Commission found the same evidence of 'Sinn Fein' women having their hair cut off, people made destitute by arson commonly used to destroy private homes and, with particular ferocity, the co-operative creameries. In none of the inquiries, nor the Dáil's own 'Weekly Summary of Acts of Aggression Committed in Ireland by Military and Police of the Usurping Government', are acts of rape recorded.

The peculiar sexual modesty of Irishwomen was taken as an article of faith by every branch of opinion. Sinn Fein leader Arthur Griffith had famously declared, 'All of us know that Irish women are the most virtuous women in the world.' Socialist James Connolly asserted 'the innate morality of womanhood, and the superiority of the morals of the women of the real people' over the divorce-ridden bourgeoisie. When Nationalists attacked a suffrage meeting in 1912 the Sinn Fein National Council chided them as 'un-Irish and unmanly' and appealed 'to all Irishmen to sustain the reputation of Ireland as a country that has always held women in honour and respect' (decision of the weekly National Council meeting on 25.7.12, reported in *Irish Citizen*, 3.8.12). Irish suffragettes themselves referred sardonically to the 'Isle of Chastity' (*Irish Citizen*, 28.12.12).

However, the taboo on overt sexual discussion had been breached by the Suffragettes' vigorous denunciations of the White Slave Traffic (1912–14). Constance Markievicz seems to have been describing child sexual abuse in 1923 when she describes as 'painful and revolting' the 'horrible evidence' given by three small girls, in an article in *Irish Citizen* appealing for women magistrates (Marreco, 1969: 246).

It is undoubtedly true that the wartime rape of women is frequently unspoken, especially where rape is a shame that cannot be endured; but suggestions of rape, even in the most 'honour'-bound countries such as southern Italy in 1944 and Bangladesh in 1971, do leak into the public domain where the men need to portray the aggressors as being outside the pale of civilization.

The terrorist act of gang rape has several effects. It bonds the rapists' brotherhood (a peculiarly gross mingling of their bodily fluids). It 'pollutes' the group whose claim to sovereignty rests on their ethnic integrity. It deprives women of their self-possession. It undermines the men whose claim to statehood is as the protectors of women and children. 'Neighbourhood' wars, where ethnic entitlement to land and statehood is the salient issue, may make rape as an act of war more likely. Wartime rape may also depend on the way in which men's culture has been sexualized. Life in barracks imbues men's discourse with a violent and imperious sexuality. Or, as the American Commission suggested, men may only commit group rape at the implicit or explicit command of senior men.

This does not mean that no soldier ever raped an Irish woman during either the war against the British or the civil war. But for rape to be a *weapon* of war it must have a mass intimidatory effect and thus must be publicized. If rape was not used as a weapon of war then its absence helps define the sort of wars that were fought in Ireland. At the least, the absence tells us the fighters honoured rules and a sort of decorum which the British in India neither respected nor expected, an honour which subsequent British mythology about Ireland has denied to the Irish.

In 1921, the British forces wanted to crush insurgents, not lay claim to being the native authority. The hastily assembled rag-bag of Black and Tans had no interest in establishing their own protectorate. The British Government wanted to crush the 'wild men' so that, through the propriety of politics, it could reach a settlement.

The Republicans *did* want to establish their protectorate. In the war against the British, this meant destroying the authority of, and expelling, the alien British. Protestants in the pale of Ulster were tacitly left inside the British protectorate. The subsequent civil war did not entail a threat to desecrate the womanhood of the other side. It did not embroil whole communities in a dispute about ethnic 'belonging'. Rape was not an issue. Above all, throughout the war decade women remained within the Church's powerful protectorate. Despite their brief claim to total hegemony, Sinn Fein accepted a separation of powers with the Church. When the men were at war, the sexual control of women could be entrusted to the priesthood as the de-sexualized guards of the homes of absent men.

Respectability and the defeat of women

The defeat of women was barely intimated in 1919 when the first Dáil Éireann was held. It was thoroughly established by 1937 when the Dáil ratified Ireland's Constitution.

Once Countess Markievicz lost her post in the 1919 Dáil Cabinet, women as people were wholly missing from the Republican leadership (Gardiner, 1993). None of the political issues which women had tried to push into the nationalist mainstream before the world war survived for long afterwards. As David Fitzpatrick writes in his generally sour account:

> After the Treaty the search for respectability displaced revolutionary enthusiasm; imitation drove out imagination; the solemn trappings of familiar institutions enveloped and began to stifle the iconoclasts.
>
> (Fitzpatrick, 1977: 232)

Women were not the only losers; but as de Valera's 'unmanageable revolutionaries', their loss was the most enduring.

In January 1919, the first Dáil adopted a Democratic Programme. This programme was still resonant with the democratic and socialist voices of the pre-war period. It asserted that the nation's sovereignty extends 'to all men and women of the nation' as well as to its material wealth, that the country should be ruled according to the principles of 'Liberty, Equality and Justice for All', that 'every man and woman' had a duty to give allegiance to the commonwealth, that 'every citizen' had a right to 'an adequate share' of the produce of the nation's labour, that the 'first duty' of the Republic was to provide for the well-being of the children, that it must substitute a native scheme for 'the care of the nation's aged and infirm' and it was a duty of the Republic to 'safeguard the health of the people' (Berresford Ellis, 1972: 244).

The 1937 Constitution did not abandon the rhetoric of Ireland belonging to the people, but it institutionalized the Church's protectorate by naming the Roman Catholic Church as the particular guardian of the people's faith, made the equality of citizens conditional on 'due regard' for sexual differences, gave the state the role of ensuring women should not have to neglect their proper role in the home, and prohibited divorce. Divorce legislation had been prohibited by the Free State in 1925, shortly before the foundation of Fianna Fail in 1926. Fianna Fail went on to become the nation's dominant party, standing for an Ireland 'whose countryside would be bright with cosy homesteads, whose fields and villages would be joyous with the sounds of industry, the romping of sturdy children, the contests of athletic youths, the laughter of comely maidens' (de Valera's 1943 St Patrick's Day broadcast, quoted in Norman, 1987: 249).

Was there no women's movement?

How did this come about? Was there no women's movement in pre-Treaty Ireland? Was the Catholicism of Ireland so inimical to a republic of free citizens? Was industrial Ireland too small to sustain a civic culture? Or was the mystique of a selfless band of brothers simply overwhelming?

Many voices spoke for a radical republic in the pre-war days when to be wild and unrespectable was to manifest the spirit of Ireland. Several voices came from women. There was the nationalist Inghinidhe na hEireann (Daughters of Ireland), started by Maud Gonne in 1900, with its own paper, *Bean na hEireann* 1908–11; and the Irishwomen's Franchise League, founded in 1908, which effectively had its own paper in *Irish Citizen*; the Irish Women's Suffrage Federation, founded in 1911; and the Irish Women Workers' Union, also founded in 1911 by James Larkin and his sister, Delia.

The suffrage organizations presented an argument for citizenship that was different from the nationalists'. As in England, this was more about the composition of the electorate than the vote as an individual right, and a citizenry that did not represent feminine virtues was lacking in essential civic virtues. But it barely survived the war years, which crushed all civic virtues under the press of military necessity. A deputation from the Irishwomen's Franchise League to president Arthur Griffith, to demand that women over twenty-one should have the right to vote in any plebiscite on the Treaty, was rebuffed with the argument that this was a ploy to destroy the Treaty as this was the first time in the history of the Dáil they had raised the issue (Ward, 1983: 175–6).

The argument for women's right to vote is raised by the IRA – but as rhetoric to serve the military cause. It justified its war against the Irish Free State by arguing that the new state had no mandate, as the election had been fought on a rotten register which disfranchised most of the young men 'and all the young women' (*Poblacht na hEireann*, 30.6.22).

FEMINIST REVIEW NO 50, SUMMER 1995

The organization that did survive (to this day) was Cumann na mBan (Irish Women's Association) founded in 1914 explicitly as an auxiliary to the (all-male) Volunteers, where it stayed. (The link between military preparedness and women's franchise was made in Britain in 1909 with the formation of the nursing auxiliary service. See Summers, 1988.)

It hovered on asserting autonomy in 1921 but the Convention which discussed and dismissed this did decide members must take an oath of loyalty because some IRA commanders had been reluctant to trust the girls with their secrets (Ward, 1983: 160–1). Their loathing of treacherous women spilled out in this attack on the Women's Battalion of the Free State, employed to 'spy upon and hand over to Death Courts their Republican neighbours.' We hope, they said, citizens like the idea of entrusting their lives to 'the jealousies, spites and personal vendettas of the class of women who will act in this Battalion' (*Poblacht na hEireann*, 3.10.22). Cumann na mBan had been so thoroughly transformed into a military auxiliary by 1923 that its connexion to a movement for women's citizenship and interests had withered.

The Church as protector

Until legend establishes the founding fathers, a new nation-state may be fatherless unless a paternal authority is left in place throughout the tumult and unseatings of revolution. In Ireland, the paternal authority of the Church over women and domestic life was hardly threatened by republicanism. The Catholic hierarchy excommunicated some, denounced socialism (as anti-family and private property), bearing arms and taking oaths. Their attitude changed with the threat of mass conscription, the evident decline of British authority and the growing role of priests in establishing a new authority.

The IRB's pre-war response was not to denounce the Church but to argue that bearing arms and taking oaths were justified in Catholic doctrine when the aim was to overthrow an unjust regime. The mass of Irish people, they explained, found in Roman Catholicism the Church which showed most sympathy for 'the weak, wronged and defenceless'. It was hardly surprising that a semi-ignorant but 'manly people' should follow the 'manly lead' offered in early times by the priests (*Irish Freedom*, July 1911).

Ironically, the Roman Catholic Church found it easier to assimilate armed struggle than did the women, and it emerged from the wars in a much stronger position than the women. Republican imagery assimilated the familiar cadences of Catholicism, a language rich in reminders of suffering and self-sacrifice. De Valera's friend and later Fianna Fail propagandist,

Aodh de Blacam, thought Irish republicanism was a unique union between Roman Catholic religion and Irish people, when 'a manhood will arise among whom Colmcille might walk as he walked with his companions of old' (de Blacam, 1921, 247). In stark contrast to the Protestant ethic, whose hierarchy of values were the authority of the father, work, and individual independence, Irish nationalist values subordinated the republican ethic to Leo XIII's famous Social Encyclical: 'To suffer and to endure, therefore, is the lot of humanity, let them strive as they may' (quoted approvingly by de Blacam, 1921: 238).

From the moment of martyrdom after the Rising, the priesthood led the Church into the nationalist struggle. It was priests who attended condemned men's executions, heard their confessions, carried their last messages to their mothers, held masses for them. (It was reported with pleasure that all but one of the fifteen executed after the Rising turned to the Roman Catholic Church and made confession before their deaths. The exception was not James Conolly, but old republican Tom Clarke.) The women of Cumann na mBan raised money for the Irish Dependants' Aid Fund outside churches after Sunday Mass.

The first issue of *Poblacht na hEireann* (the IRA's war bulletin) reported that at the outbreak of civil war hostilities, the 'boys'' first act was to kneel and recite the rosary, in Irish, 'placing themselves and their cause under the protection of the Blessed Virgin and all the patriot martyrs of the Irish Republic' (28.6.22).

As community leaders and as the message-bearers and comforters of the dying, the clergy could not remain immune to the militarization of political life. Different as they were, priests and women shared an auxiliary role in war. Because neither belonged wholly to the armed struggle, their allegiance was suspect, but they could also act as go-betweens. Both provided an essential fringe of flexibility in the rigidities of oath-bound loyalties. Both served the cause by serving the men. By not killing, both preserved the ethic of respect for human life, and a promise of a life more fruitful than that which bands of brothers could provide. They cleansed the men, literally and spiritually, of the sin of violence.

Militarism, like nationalism, can assimilate or subjugate all other movements. This hegemonic power strips other movements of their autonomy and defines their aims, and activists, as disloyal or selfish – unless it accepts a separation of powers, as it did with the Church. The abandonment of women's interests is the price women had to pay for the right to belong. Unlike other movements, militarism not only claims a unique power for regenerating and directing society, but can also claim the dictates of necessity. Nothing can stand against the driving rule of military need.

FEMINIST REVIEW NO 50, SUMMER 1995

Once the Irish struggle had become both militarized and Catholicized, placing women firmly in the roles of auxiliaries, grievers, and those who kept the home fires burning while the men were on the run, women's own embryonic notion of an egalitarian republic was quashed.

Notes

I would like to thank Ros Carne and James Wood without whose help I could not have written this article.

Sarah Benton works as a researcher, journalist, and a lecturer for, among others, Birkbeck College and the *Guardian*.

1 See the account, in particular, of the 1913 Women's Monument in Bloemfontein, in Gaitskell and Unterhalter (1989). Women could also belong directly as daughters of the nation. Roy Foster says that Maud Gonne founded 'Daughters of Erin', Inghinidhe na hEireann, 'in the ferment of the anti-Boer movement' (Foster, 1988: 450), although in Margaret Ward's account, the spur is the women's Patriotic Treat Committee, which organized an alternative children's treat on the occasion of Queen Victoria's Jubilee visit to Ireland (Ward, 1983: 47). Maud Gonne does not say in her own autobiography (Gonne MacBride, 1938), although she leaves no doubt that the rebellion of the Boers was an inspiration to Irish Nationalists, just as organizing against the Boer War brought some women into national and international prominence.

2 The fact-finding missions were organized by the Labour Party (for which feminists Maud Gonne and Charlotte Despard, President of the Women's Freedom League, garnered information), the Women's International League of Peace and Freedom, the Society of Friends and the American Commission. The Commission was drawn from a 'Committee of One Hundred', in fact 150 people, of the great and the good. It included 21 women (including feminist Jane Addams), 15 bishops, a Cardinal and various other religious leaders, and a few of the most established Black leaders, including W.E.B. Du Bois and James Weldon Johnson of the NAACP. Its interpretation of the 'bright spot' owes much to its belief that British officers were conniving in the atrocities of their men, and could have controlled them if they wanted to. The American Commission had a lasting effect on American attitudes towards British imperialism and towards Ireland.

References

Newspapers and reports

THE AMERICAN COMMISSION ON CONDITIONS IN IRELAND (1921) Washington.
REPORT OF THE LABOUR COMMISSION TO IRELAND (no date) Chairman Arthur Henderson. Published by the Labour Party.

Poblacht na hEireann from 1922.
Irish Citizen from 1913.
Irish Freedom from 1910.

Books

ABDO, Nahla (1994) 'Nationalism and feminism: Palestinian women and the *Intifada* – no going back?' in Moghadam, Valentine M. (1994) editor, *Gender and National Identity* London: Zed Books for the United Nations University.

BALL, Terence and POCOCK, J.G.A. (1988) editors, *Conceptual Change and the Constitution* University Press of Kansas.

BERRESFORD ELLIS, P. (1972) *A History of the Irish Working Class* Letchworth: The Garden City Press.

BROIN, Leon O. (1976) *Revolutionary Underground* Dublin: Gill & Macmillan.

CLAUSEWITZ, Carl von (1968) *On War* Rapoport, Anatol editor, first published 1832, Harmondsworth: Penguin.

CONNOLLY, James (1954) *Labour Nationality and Religion* New Books Publications; first published 1910.

DE BLACAM (1921) *What Sinn Fein Stands For* Dublin: Mellifont Press.

EDWARDS, Ruth Dudley (1977) *Patrick Pearse. The Triumph of Failure* London: Victor Gollancz.

FERRARO, Guglielmo (1933) *Peace and War* London: Macmillan.

FITZPATRICK, David (1977) *Politics and Irish Life, 1912–21: Provincial Experiences of War and Revolution* Dublin: Gill & Macmillan.

FOSTER, Roy (1988) *Modern Ireland 1600–1972* London: Allen Lane.

FOX, R.M. (1943) *The History of the Irish Citizen Army* Dublin: James Duffy & Co.

FREUD, Sigmund (1985) 'Group psychology', 1st English publication 1922, in Pelican Freud Library, Vol. 12, Harmondsworth: Penguin.

FRIEDMANN, Leon (1985) editor, *The Law of War: A Documentary History* two volumes, New York: Random House.

GAITSKELL, Deborah and UNTERHALTER, Elaine (1989) 'Mothers of the Nation' in YUVAL-DAVIS and ANTHIAS (1989).

GARDINER, Frances (1993) 'Political interest and participation of Irish women 1922–1992: the unfinished revolution' in SMYTH, Ailbhe (1993) editor, *Irish Women's Studies Reader*, Dublin: Attic Press.

GONNE MACBRIDE, Maud (1938) *A Servant of the Queen*; republished 1983 by Boydell & Brewer, Suffolk.

HYDE, H. Montgomery (1974) *Carson: The Life of Sir Edward Carson* London: Constable, first edition 1953.

MARRECO, Anne (1969) *The Rebel Countess* London: Corgi, first published 1967 by Weidenfeld & Nicholson.

MOSSE, George L. (1985) *Nationalism and Sexuality: Respectability and Abnormal Sexuality in Modern Europe* New York: Howard Fertig.

NORMAN, Diana (1987) *Terrible Beauty* London: Hodder & Stoughton.

O'DONOGHUE, Florence (1954) *No Other Law* Dublin: Irish Press.

PAINE, Thomas (1775) 'Common sense', in *The Thomas Paine Reader* Harmondsworth: Penguin, 1987.

PEARLMAN, Michael (1984) *To Make Democracy Safe for America* Chicago: University of Illinois Press.

SAID, Edward (1994) *Culture and Imperialism* London: Vintage.

SUMMERS, Anne (1988) *Angels and Citizens* London: Routledge & Kegan Paul.

TOWNSHEND, Charles (1975) *The British Campaign in Ireland 1919–21* Oxford: Oxford University Press.

—— (1983) *Political Violence in Ireland* Oxford: Oxford University Press.

WARD, Margaret (1983) *Unmanageable Revolutionaries* London: Pluto Press.

WARNER, Marina (1976) *Alone of All her Sex* New York: Alfred A. Knopf.

YUVAL-DAVIS, Nira and ANTHIAS, Floya (1989) editors, *Woman-Nation-State* London: Macmillan.

'Women are trouble, did you know that Fergus?'

Neil Jordan's *The Crying Game*

Sarah Edge

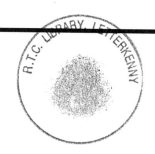

FEMINIST REVIEW NO 50, SUMMER 1995, pp. 173–86

Abstract

The subject of this article is Neil Jordan's film *The Crying Game*. Released in 1992, it was widely received as a film that challenged stereotypes in relation to both the IRA and questions of race, sexuality and desire. This article calls into question such a radical reading by analysing the way in which Jude the IRA woman is represented. Through a feminist deconstruction, the article proposes that the character of Jude can be seen to represent both national and international anxieties concerning contemporary masculine and feminine subject positions. The article plots this by investigating how the film deals with the specifics of gender and Irish nationalism. It then moves on to consider how these specifics can be seen to articulate international postmodern concerns about contemporary gender identities.

Keywords

Nationalism; Irish Republican Army; masculinity; femininity; sexuality; representation

The political crisis in Northern Ireland has featured in over a hundred dramas for both television and the cinema. Many of these have used the 'troubles' merely as a backdrop for more universalizing stories in which the specifics of the political crisis in Northern Ireland are almost insignificant. Others attempted to deal with elements of the 'troubles' themselves. The subject of this article is Neil Jordan's film *The Crying Game*, and I would argue that it can be seen to fit within both types of drama. Clearly, Northern Ireland and the political crisis is seen as a backdrop to put across an (international) universalizing message about love and humanity. However it would be a mistake not to consider the specific representation of the IRA and the IRA man (national) within this film, coming as it did amid a flurry of international media interest in Northern Ireland initiated by the peace process.

However, what I wish to consider is how these two messages, which I have loosely designated as international and national, come together, inform and interact with one another. Furthermore, to additionally problematize this relationship I also wish to consider the place of gender within the film.

The Crying Game was released in 1992. It tells the story of the IRA capture of a Black British soldier, Jody, who is held hostage. The first section of the film focuses on the developing relationship between the Black soldier and an IRA man, Fergus. When Fergus is ordered to shoot Jody, he is unable to do it. However, during the army ambush of the hostage site Jody is run over and killed by an army Saracen. Fergus flees to London where he carries out Jody's last wish, that he find his girlfriend, a hairdresser, Dil. Fergus falls in love with her only to find out that she is a transvestite man. The IRA track Fergus down in London and Jude, an IRA woman, informs him that they want him to carry out the killing of a judge. When Fergus does not turn up and Maguire, another IRA man, is killed carrying out the assassination, Jude seeks him out. She is then shot and killed by Dil. Fergus takes the blame for Jude's murder and is sent to prison. The film closes with Dil, dressed as a woman, visiting Fergus in prison.

The narrative is initially set in Northern Ireland, and opens with the kidnapping of the Black British soldier Jody (Forest Whitaker), by the IRA unit made up of Fergus (Stephen Rea), Jude (Miranda Richardson) and Maguire (Adrian Dunbar). On its initial release, *The Crying Game* was heralded as a film that broke new ground on many counts. It was, therefore, with great interest that I went along to see the movie, and cannot deny that I was impressed. On a surface viewing the film did appear to be breaking new ground in a number of ways – firstly in relation to dominant traditions of representing the IRA man as a violent psychotic and secondly through the film's apparent consideration of race, sexuality and desire. It was also reviewed in these terms. In the film magazine *Variety* it was welcomed as 'A fearlessly penetrating examination of politics, race, sexuality and human nature' (14.9.92: 47). Other reviewers proclaimed that 'it leaves stereotypes in shreds', or 'There's never been anything quite like it' (*Premier*, December 1992: 36). However, in relation to such a radical interpretation, what many of the critics and spectators of the film failed to identify was the clearly problematic representation of the only 'real' woman in the film, Jude. Contrary to the general reception of the film as 'challenging stereotypes' the way that the character Jude is represented can be seen to fit firmly into traditional, mythological, representations of women in a number of ways. What I propose to do in this article is to demonstrate how the representation of the character Jude can be unpacked to reveal the different meanings she carries and the way in which these meanings interact to produce a number of complex messages. In this sense some signifiers attached to the character are revealed as a mechanism for establishing a 'national' difference – Irishness – more specifically the politically contested meanings surrounding representations of the IRA. This could be seen as a question of a 'national' representation, that of the psychopathic, IRA, woman, killer: 'the woman more evil than evil itself'. This dominant representation of the IRA woman has recently been recirculated within a number of contemporary film and drama productions, for instance the IRA woman in the Hollywood blockbuster *Patriot Games* (1992) or the untrustworthy and betraying Leyla in Ronan Bennet's recent television drama *Love Lies Bleeding*. These representations of the IRA woman can also be seen to operate within news and documentary coverage, the signifiers of 'truth'. In this context, the IRA woman can be seen to carry quite specific meanings. However the IRA woman and cultural representations of her can also be interpreted more generally in relation to how a woman who kills is perceived within dominant culture. As Beatrix Campbell has identified:

> The woman who kills is exactly what she is supposed *not* to be. Her act is deemed not only unnatural but impossible in a real woman; so she is 'unwomaned' by her violence and seen as a classic aberration, exiled from her community and her gender.
>
> (Jones, 1991: xi)

Clearly, then, the IRA woman confronts a number of dominant ideologies surrounding gender – specific qualities and modes of acceptable feminine behaviour and the 'trouble' that this creates is articulated within these different cultural representations.

As an Irish writer and producer, Neil Jordan also poses a number of interesting questions surrounding the concept of an 'indigenous' culture, the representation of Irishness and authenticity. This is not a straightforward relationship. I would argue that the perceptions of an essential 'Irish' experience, which can be transparently represented, belies the powerful and pervasive workings of dominant ideology. In 1987 film theorist John Hill proposed that in a number of contemporary Irish films the 'representations of the Irish characteristically associated with sources outside of Ireland have now, apparently, become so 'natural' and 'normal' that they are providing a framework for certain sections of Irish film-making as well' (Hill, 1987: 178).

In this context the question must be 'how free is Neil Jordan's film of traditional representations of both the Irish and the IRA? His conscious desire to 'tell the truth, that's all, and to look at the thing accurately' (Burke, 1993: 17) has little to do with it. For as John Hill's observation indicated, dominant 'ideas' about the Irish and the IRA have now been so widely dispersed they have entered into the popular consciousness of the Irish themselves. Like the working of all successful ideologies they have now become normal, natural and internalized.

Correspondingly in considering a feminist deconstruction of the film the question could also be posed, how free is Neil Jordan's text from dominant representations of women? In relation to his defence against criticisms of the film as misogynistic (Burke, 1993: 17), again his conscious desires have very little to do with it.

That national/cultural identity struggles in the 'real' Northern Ireland have traditionally had problems with women's involvement in them has been examined by a number of feminist film-makers within Northern Ireland, for instance Anne Crilly's courageous and revealing documentary *Mother Ireland* produced for Channel 4 in 1988, or Pat Murphy's film *Maeve* (1981). In this sense women's involvement within the political crisis in Northern Ireland, and the popular cultural representations of the IRA woman I have briefly mapped out above, can be seen to have a direct relationship. Women's involvement and interest in national identity struggles, I would propose, causes a problem because it disrupts traditional and dominant ideologies surrounding femininity on a number of levels. Women who are involved in violence disrupt dominant ideologies of the feminine as passive and peace-loving. Similarly, women's involvement in the public world of politics disrupts ideologies surrounding women's space in the private world of home and family. In nationalist/cultural identity struggles, women's demand for a national/cultural identity dislocates the place and right of patriarchal authority to define such an identity for her. I would argue that on one level the way that Jude is represented in *The Crying Game* is a consequence of the coming together of these currently incompatible signifiers surrounding cultural/national identity and gender identity. Furthermore, I hope to reveal that this problematic relationship can be seen to operate not only in relation to the peripheral concern of a national/cultural identity, 'Irishness', but also in relation to a current global concern with the rethinking and reworking of gender identities. In this sense, I wish to proceed by revealing that Jude can be deconstructed to reveal both her local and international meanings and their historical significance.

The opening shots and accompanying music of the film begin a kind of misogynistic undercurrent that carries on throughout the movie 'When a man loves a woman' introduces us to a funfair/carnival scene. Initially it operates as an accompanying sound track but enters into the narrative of the movie proper as the camera swings on to the loud speaker blurting the song out. The camera pans down to reveal Jude and Jody, the Black British soldier, arm in arm. Jude at this stage is represented in slightly dated, feminine, ordinary clothes, perhaps what could be coded to read as slightly tarty and cheap: blond hair, big earrings, denim jacket and short skirt. The song lyrics tell us, 'If she is bad he can't see it', 'she can bring him such misery'; as Jude entices Jody away to an isolated spot, another rock song screams out 'baby baby what you doing to me'. Jody is now ambushed and captured by three IRA men. Jude in this context has been seen to use her 'natural' female sexuality in an 'unnatural' way, to capture and betray Jody. In view of the song playing overhead, love of women brings misery and pain which indeed, it could be argued, it has done for Jody. The beginning of the film makes it clear that women, and in particular women who initiate sexual activity – a now well-established signifier for the 'liberated' woman, are not to be trusted.

Thus, the way that the character of Jude is represented from the film's opening scene can already be seen to disrupt traditional and stable gender identities. Jude is therefore clearly a problem for all the male characters, who cannot 'meet' Jude within the traditional boundaries of acceptable male/female behaviour. This representation of Jude as transgressive is strengthened as the narrative progresses until by the end of the film she has become a monstrous opposite of how dominant patriarchal culture perceives traditional femininity. Jude's threat, as such, to the dominant and stable gender identities of the patriarchal order, is clearly depicted throughout the film.

In the first section of the film narrative, located within Northern Ireland, Jude is treated in a hateful manner by all the male characters. This oscillates between the traditional representation of IRA women as helpers and supporters of the 'cause' by, of course, making tea and sandwiches, to the sheer hatred of her abnormality represented in the way in which Maguire the 'true'[1] IRA man speaks to her, 'shut up, or shut the fuck up Jude'. (Interestingly, it should be noted that this appears to shift once the narrative moves to London. Jude is then represented as having the 'upper hand' with Maguire.) The difference between Jude as a soldier and as a woman is also expressed, when her male 'comrades', alongside Jody, are unable to understand how she may feel about what she has done, or rather what Jody has done to her in order for his capture to take place.

While a form of respect develops between Jody and Fergus, as different types of soldiers, Jude's use of her feminine sexuality to capture Jody is regarded as unforgivable and incomprehensible. In a scene which refers to the initiating sexual capture, Jody jumps on Jude screaming, 'you fucking bitch, you fucking whore'. Jude rushes out and is depicted frantically brushing her body down; she states to Fergus, 'Fucking animal . . . I had him all over me'. The use of this term by Jude can be seen to play on dominant racist ideologies surrounding bestial Black male sexuality, thus further alienating Jude from any radical feminist/race alliance, but significantly initiating the coming together of Jody and Fergus against Jude. It was this developing relationship that was perceived as important by both the film's critics and Neil Jordan himself. It does not, on the surface, appear to include Jude; it was, rather, the relationship between two male characters (soldiers), Fergus the IRA man and Jody the Black British soldier. As one reviewer put it, 'Fergus is a sensitive recruit who develops an intense rapport with the good natured, emotionally open Jody' (*Variety*, 14.9.92: 47). This moment in the film, and the representation of Fergus within it, was perceived by many critics and viewers of the film as a more modern, progressive and compassionate representation of the IRA man, 'Despite their political differences, Fergus and Jody develop a solidarity of souls' (*Premier*, December 1992: 36). However, contrary to this belief, there has actually been a long tradition (Hill, 1987) of representations of two types of masculinity in films that portray the IRA man; the cold and emotionless IRA killer as represented in *The Crying Game* by the character of Maguire, and the fundamentally decent IRA man who has doubts about his violent deeds. Fergus is, of course, this man, and Stephen Rea's physical characteristics fit such a reading well: his big, brown eyes, soft sensitive face and apparently quiet and thoughtful disposition. The bonding between these two male characters was recognized as a significant moment in the narrative by both critic and writer, not quite however, I would maintain, for the reasons they seem to consciously propose. Instead, I would argue that, as Jody and Fergus bond, we begin to see emerging one of the underlying concerns of this film: that of male power, status and unity.

In this initial section of the film an exchange takes place between Jody and Fergus that is highly significant in relation to a feminist interrogation of the film's hidden meanings and concerns. However, this exchange can also be seen to play rather dangerously with dominant racist ideologies about the Irish and the violent conflict within Northern Ireland. A number of theorists have revealed how, historically, the Irish have been constructed, within different discourses, as an inherently violent, uncivilized and uncontrollable race of people (Hill, 1987; Curtis, 1984; Curtis, 1971). This construction of a supposed Irish nature or temperament has been ideologically mobilized to offer an explanation for both the historical and contemporary use of violence by the Irish. In the scene where Fergus is holding Jody captive, Jody tells Fergus that he knows he won't be set free by the IRA even if the government accepts their demands. When Fergus asks him why they wouldn't, Jody tells him, because it's 'not in your nature', to which Fergus replies, 'what do you know about my nature?'

'I am talking about your people, not you,' states Jody. 'What the fuck do you know about my people?' replies Fergus. 'Only', screams Jody, 'that you're all tough undeluded motherfuckers. And it's not in your nature to let me go.' Once again the Irish are depicted as an inherently violent people by nature. That they are supposedly an uncivilized people in a modern world is also later established when Jody tells Fergus he joined the army to get a job and was 'sent to the only place in the world they call you nigger to your face'. However, as the narrative progresses, Fergus by rejecting/questioning his Irishness, his 'difference', is now offered a way out by accepting a civilizing humanity based on good and bad people as opposed to racial, sexual and class difference.

This leads into the story-telling, male-myth-making exchange in which Jody reveals the truth about life to Fergus. That truth is, that there are in fact only two types of people – those who give and those who take. The kind frog and the evil scorpion. In this context social, political, racial and sexual differences are not a consequence of inequality, oppression and exploitation but basic human differences between good and bad people, a human essence, natural, unchanging, and outside history. Fergus as we are about to see (when he removes the sack from Jody's head), is a good person, caring, sensitive and humanitarian – a frog. However, Jude, who interrupts this male-bonding scene, is without compassion, hard, tough and untrustworthy – she is the scorpion. Her opposition to traditional essentialist notions of the feminine is articulated when Jody now screams at her, 'You've got no feelings woman.' In the film's only display of physical violence that we see by her, Jude smashes the gun into Jody's face, Fergus is disgusted. He lifts the hood and wipes the blood away, Fergus and Jody bond further against Jude. 'Women are trouble, did you know that?' Jody asks Fergus. 'I didn't,' is his reply. 'Some kinds of women are,' says Jody. 'She can't help it,' states Fergus. In this context the implication is clear: she can't help it because it's in her nature. In opposition to the traditional ideologies of femininity as naturally, sensitive, caring, humanitarian and passive, Jude's character, in respect of her republicanism and feminism (at this stage in the film represented by her 'active' sexuality) can only stand as its opposite, an aberration of the feminine. While Fergus and Jody become more 'feminine', Jude becomes the opposite; she is, because of this, 'naturally' bad. While Fergus and Jody's masculinity shifts and they are represented as taking on some of the traditional qualities of the feminine, Jude becomes the opposite to the socially constructed qualities of the feminine, that is not masculine but rather something 'other' than feminine.

In her text *The Powers of Horror: An essay on Abjection* (Kristeva, 1982), Julia Kristeva uses psychoanalytic theory to argue that, for the individual to become a fully formed subject by entering patriarchal culture, a series of expulsions must take place of 'things' deemed 'improper and unclean'. That which is expelled is constituted as abject, in this sense, the powerful mother of the pre-symbolic mother/child dyad, must be expelled so that the dyad can be split, and a social 'individual' can be formed through the taking up of 'traditional' masculine or feminine subject positions. For Kristeva that which has been abject still exists on the other side of an imaginary border which separates the subject from all that threatens its existence. It worries and troubles the subject from its position on the other side of an imaginary border. The representation of Jude as something other than traditional femininity threatens the stability and normality of dominant masculine and feminine subject positions within the paternal signifying system. In Kristeva's terms, Jude does not respect the 'borders positions and rules' of patriarchal culture and therefore she disturbs 'identity, systems, order'. Thus Jude threatens the naturalized order of patriarchal culture through her refusal to be firmly situated within the symbolic order. Within this film it may be possible to see an analogy between Jude as a member of the IRA who threatens boundaries in relation to 'colonial' power, and national/cultural identity and Jude as a transgressive woman who also threatens the imaginary border between what Kristeva describes 'the paternal law' of the father and the place of 'maternal authority'. In this sense it is possible to read the character of Jude as threatening two borders that separate order from disorder – where the stable and dominant definitions operate to legitimize the existing orders of society.

Fergus in the concluding section of this part of the film is now ordered by Maguire to kill Jody. However, as I have argued, Fergus now signifies another (new) type of caring, humanitarian masculinity and cannot do this. Jody is now, somewhat ironically, run over by a British army Saracen.

The film now shifts its location to London and we are introduced to a more traditional representation of femininity, Dil (Jaye Davidson). Unlike Jude, Dil is constructed in relation to the traditional signifiers of the feminine: she is beautiful and sexy. She prides herself on her looks, is narcissistic and preens and presents herself for Fergus (who has changed his name to Jimmy). She also works in a beauty parlour. When Fergus/Jimmy develops a relationship with Dil, it is represented as romantic and loving, old-fashioned and traditional with restaurants and flowers. He protects Dil through his masculine strength (violence). When Dil visits Fergus/Jimmy at the building site all the full-blooded men shout and whistle at her. Thus Dil is represented, in the film, as a more desirable woman than Jude. But, of course, Dil is not a woman – she is a man, as the castration and castrating anxiety ridden scene reveals. In a scene that is shot from a childlike point of view in order to structurally recall the moment of recognition of difference, the camera slowly moves down from Dil's (the Mother's) face along her body to her penis. This is the castration moment in reverse. Our shock as spectators, along with Fergus/Jimmy, is not that she doesn't have a penis but rather that she does. In this sense everything seems to be thrown into disorder. The anxiety over castration, in this case, is not however directed at the absent 'Father' but rather at Jude, the monstrous feminine – the phallic mother who has the potential to rob Fergus (and all men) of his 'power'. Jude can be seen to represent such a danger in a number of complex ways. First, she does so through her nationalism and feminism, represented through her rejection of traditional 'feminine' signifiers, and her threat as a disruption to the patriarchal symbolic order. This is reinforced through her use of phallic signifiers such as her gun and the silver car in which she hunts Fergus/Jimmy down, and even her authoritative relationship to Maguire the 'true' IRA man.

Moreover, because the film's narrative is now situated in London, the city as opposed to the rural setting of Ireland, Jude's appearance can now make this threat more apparent. She is now visually coded to recall her cinematic predecessor – the evil spider woman, the return of the *femme fatal* of film noir.[2] Jude and Maguire have by now traced Fergus/Jimmy to London. In the scene when Jude and Fergus/Jimmy meet again, Jude confronts him in his bed sit. In this scene the lighting is dark and doom-laden; she comes out from the shadows, evil and menacing; the light from the blinds cuts across her face signifying in the noir tradition her duplicitous and untrustworthy nature. Her black gloves, harsh black hair and black phallic gun recall the iconography of her cinematic predecessor. Her active and perverse sexuality is represented as she grabs Fergus/Jimmy by the bollocks and says, 'fuck me Fergus'. However, what is also significant about this scene is that Jude is now visually coded to connect with a much more recent cinematic representation of a woman. The bad, feminist, career woman, power-dressing: padded shoulders, suits, harsh make-up and hairstyles. 'I was sick of being a blonde, I needed a tougher look', Jude tells Fergus/Jimmy. Jude can also, now, be seen to represent another type of modernity, the modernity of feminism and all that it appeared to be demanding in opposition to tradition (the relationship between Fergus and Dil is posted as old-fashioned and traditional, flowers and romance, wined and dined; he protects Dil through his masculine strength – violence – symbolic of the desire for a myth, the good old days before feminism when 'everyone' knew where they stood). In this sense the character of Jude in the later section of the film can be seen to recall, perhaps, the now most infamous contemporary representation of the feminist, career woman Alex Forrest/ Glenn Close from the 1987 film *Fatal Attraction* (Faludi, 1991; Holmlund,

1991). This brings me to the central point raised by such a rereading of the film. On the one hand, this movie, as an 'indigenous' Irish movie, may well be interpreted as being involved in the construction of ideologies around Irishness and republicanism. Moreover, as I have already indicated, the film can be seen to have major difficulties in combining such ideologies with the dominant meanings attached to women and traditional femininity. On the other, this film can also be seen to be concerning itself with a more international problem. The film can also be situated within what has been identified, by a number of feminist critics, as a current international concern with stable gender identities and relationships of power in a postmodern world. The re-emergence of the feminist movement in the 1960s has been sited as just one of a number of discourses and movements that challenged the authority of Western male thought and its legitimacy. This has created a cultural climate of uncertainty where old forms of power, identities, histories and legitimacy have been called into question, what has been termed the complex destructuring, disintegration of the founding structures in the West (Creed, 1987), Man, Truth, History (Lyotard, 1984). This crisis has thrown into question the naturalized status of the sexual divisions of patriarchal society, and a number of feminist texts have since proposed that such a crisis has resulted in a re-imagining and re-conceptualization of both masculinity and femininity. Film critic Barbara Creed points to the function film has played within this re-imagining of gender identities. In North America, she noticed that the 'putting into discourse of "woman" or the feminine as problematic – seems to exist here only at the level of representation. It has been externalised and thematized rather than practised' (Creed, 1987: 49).

This re-conceptualization of woman she identifies as taking place predominantly within the arena of popular film production. I would propose that *The Crying Game* can be viewed as just such a film. In this sense, what I am arguing is that the representation of the character Jude within the film has a double transgressive signification: First, nationally, as IRA women; and, second, internationally, as a liberated/feminist woman. It would seem that Jude is a Judas on more counts than one. It is because of this that her fate within the narrative is doomed from the beginning of the film. Within a traditional narrative structure the very role and function of the trans-gressing woman is to make sure that she is seen to be punished for her challenge to the patriarchal order. For narrative resolution and order to be regained she must either be restored to correct femininity through marriage or destroyed and punished through death – usually a violent and spec-tacular death. This is, of course, the fate of Jude in *The Crying Game*, when she is symbolically shot in the throat and thus silenced forever. Moreover, in this film Jody, Fergus and Dil can also be seen to represent 'otherness' in relation to traditional masculinity. Fergus in relation to national and republican identity as an outsider, having chosen to question the republican movement and its use of violence; Dil and Jody also represent 'otherness' in terms of their sexuality and race. However I would propose that through their male bonding, based on a new-found individuality, compassion, sensitivity and love, they also represent 'sameness'. For they are all of course, still 'men'. One reviewer put this clearly, stating that the film, 'questions the basis of all human "differences", be they sexual, national or racial and in doing so posit an essential humanity common to all, a humanity expressed through love and compassion' (Flynn, 1992: 60).

Unfortunately for Jude as representative of female, independence, power and control, such an expression of humanity, love and compassion does not include her.[3]

Ultimately, a feminist deconstruction of this film reveals it to be caught up in two very dominant forms of representation, first in relation to Irish stereotypes, perceptions and understandings of the IRA, and second in relation to a new reworking of an old stereotype, the transgressing (feminist) woman and her subsequent punishment. As an independent production and an 'indigenous' Irish film, *The Crying Game* does not exist in a void removed from the concerns, anxieties and fears voiced in international productions. It is possible that the international reception of *The Crying Game* has more to do with its representation of a new, caring, loving, type of masculinity than with its representation of Irishness and the political crisis in Northern Ireland. This new consideration and alliance between men is developed by a narrative that excludes women, in which the film's resolution is ultimately based on their expulsion and punishment for daring to challenge the naturalized status of patriarchal power and culture. In this respect, *The Crying Game* has more in common with some of the lavish Hollywood productions that we have recently seen in cinemas. From the punishment of transgressing women in movies like *Fatal Attraction* and *Basic Instinct* (1992) to a new-found masculine identity, based on compassion, respect and love between men, negotiated across films like *Parenthood* (1989), *Hook* (1991) and *Terminator II: Judgment Day* (1991). Stephen Rea as Fergus has more in common with Arnold Schwarzenegger than might first meet the eye. As film critic Susan Jeffords has observed in relation to the action movie, 'What Hollywood Culture is offering, in place of the bold spectacle of male muscularity and/as violence, is a self-effacing man, one who now, instead of learning to fight, learns to love' (Cohan and Hark, 1991: 245). What is being constructed is a bond between men that crosses racial, national and sexual differences: the 'new man' who now can find himself through his ability to love, the good man

FEMINIST REVIEW NO 50, SUMMER 1995

versus the bad man, or rather, in the context of *The Crying Game*, the good man versus the bad woman; the frog and the scorpion. In the film's concluding scene Fergus, who is now in prison, is visited by Dil. Fergus brings him into the 'brotherhood' by the telling of universalizing myths, stories and truths. The narrative closure of the movie is cemented by the lyrics of the Lyle Lovett cover version of 'Stand by Your Man', intended consciously as ironic, but unconsciously, I would propose, revealing one of the main concerns of this film. In many ways it is surprising how close Neil Jordan comes to consciously articulating the 'hidden' problematic of the movie, as he states, 'I think that what women find threatening about this movie is that men make choices that exclude them' (Burke, 1993: 19); and on the destruction of Jude: 'Yeah, of course she gets killed. What's wrong with that? I don't understand this argument you know, I really don't. It puzzles me. I wrote her quite consciously as a monster, a monstrous part, because all the men who survive make female choices and the women make male choices. It's very consciously done' (Burke, 1993: 18).[4]

Notes

Sarah Edge is a full-time lecturer in Media Studies at the University of Ulster in Coleraine. Previous to that, she was a curator at Rochdale Art Gallery, and a member of the editorial collective of FAN: Feminist Art News. She is also a practising artist, working in the media of photography and performance art.

This article is based on a paper originally given at the 'Imagining Ireland' Irish Film Institute's Conference in 1993.

1 Maguire can be seen to fit clearly into the traditional representation of the 'cold emotionless but positively pathological IRA killer' (Hill, 1987: 166). His difference to Fergus is expressed particularly in the scene in London when he leans over and sadistically stubs out his cigarette on Fergus' hand in the back of the car.

2 Film noir refers to a type of film (thriller) produced between the 1940s and 1950s. The *femme fatale* in these films has been identified as symbolically representing the fears and threat of the 'new woman' in the 1940s (see Kaplan, 1978). It is also clear that a number of contemporary films which deal with the feminist/career woman recall the iconography of the 1940s *femme fatale* imagery.

3 This fluidity of 'differences' between men, and their 'sameness' as men set against the static sign 'woman', can only be seen as a fleeting alliance. Jody could be seen to represent the 'good' Black man, the myth of the loyal (army) and submissive Blackman. Dil also operates as a symbol to recognize but alleviate the problems of male bonding between men from different races. Symbolically Dil can represent the fear of 'contagion' through interracial sexual relations – the removal

of racial difference (see Young, 1990). However, in the 'real', this is halted by the visual symbols of 'her' masculinity – the penis. Thus bonding between different 'types' of men, which is also threatening, is contained.

4 This alliance between different types of 'men', offers certain problems and disruptions for traditional masculinity. Within the film's narrative these alliances are not permanent. Fergus and Dil's 'relationship' cannot continue as Fergus is now in prison. The bonding between men of different races which confronts white male supremacist ideologies is also problematic for the film. However, by the end of the film Jody is dead and Dil is also possibly dying from a blood condition (AIDS?). It is also possible to see a rather stereotypical representation of gay male sexuality. Jody is quite willing to go with Jude, and shouts at her later, 'I thought you liked me'. Dil asks Jude in the film's concluding scenes if she 'used those tits and that ass to get him [Jody]'. Jody, in this context, is represented as being unable to resist a 'real' woman. Also reaffirming that women's active sexuality is to blame for Jody's destruction.

References

BURKE, Marina (1993) *Film Ireland* No. 34 (April/May): 16–21.

COHAN, Steven and HARK, Ina Rae (1993) *Screening the Male – Exploring Masculinity in Hollywood Cinema* London and New York: Routledge.

CREED, Barbara (1987) *From Here To Modernity: Feminism and Postmodernism, Screen* Vol. 28, No. 2: 47–67.

———— (1993) *The Monstrous Feminine. Film Feminism and Psychoanalysis* London and New York: Routledge.

CURTIS, Liz (1984) *Nothing But The Same Old Story: The Roots of Anti-Irish Racism* London: Information on Ireland.

CURTIS, L.P. (1971) *Apes and Angles: The Irishman in Victorian Caricature* Newton Abbot: David & Charles.

FALUDI, Susan (1991) *Backlash. The Undeclared War Against Women* London: Chatto & Windus.

FLYNN, Roddy (1992) *CIRCA* No. 63 (Spring) 1993: 60–1.

HILL, John (1987) 'Images of violence' in Rocket, Gibbons and Hill (1987) *Cinema and Ireland* London: Routledge.

HOLMLUND, C. (1991) 'Reading character with a vengeance: the *Fatal Attraction* phenomenon' *Velvet Light Trap* Vol. 27 (Spring): 26–36.

JAMESON, F. (1983) 'Postmodernism and consumer society' in Foster, H. (1983) editor, *The Anti-Aesthetic: Essays in Post Modern Culture* Port Townsend, Washington: Bay Press.

JEFFORDS, Susan (1993) *Can Masculinity Be Terminated?* in COHAN and HARK (1993).

JONES, Ann (1991) *Women Who Kill* London: Victor Gollancz.

KAPLAN, E.A. (1978) *Women In Film Noir* London: B.F.I. Publishing.

———— (1993) *Motherhood and Representation. The Mother in Popular Culture and Melodrama* London and New York: Routledge.

FEMINIST REVIEW NO 50, SUMMER 1995

————(1994) 'Sex work and motherhood subjectivity in recent visual culture' in Bassin, Honey and Mahrer (1994) editors, *Representations of Motherhood* Yale: Yale University Press.

KRISTEVA, Julia (1982) *Powers of Horror: An Essay on Abjection* Trans. Roudiez, L., New York: Columbia University Press.

LYOTARD, J.F. (1984) 'The Post-modern condition; a report on knowledge' in *Theory and History of Literature*, Vol. 10, Manchester: Manchester University Press.

MODLESKI, Tania (1991) *Feminism Without Women. Culture and Criticism in a Post Feminist Age* London: Routledge.

RAY, Robert (1985) *A Certain Tendency of the Hollywood Cinema 1930–1980* Princeton, NJ: Princeton University Press.

RUTHERFORD, J. (1990) *Community, Culture Difference* London: Lawrence & Wishart.

YOUNG, Lola (1990) 'A nasty piece of work: a psychoanalytical study of sexual and racial difference in *Mona Lisa*' in RUTHERFORD (1990).

Noticeboard

Conference

Desperately Seeking Sisterhood: Still Challenging and Building

The eighth Women's Studies Network (UK) Conference will be held at University of Stirling, Scotland, 23–25 June 1995. Focus will be on questions such as: Who are the sisters? Who is seeking whom? Where are the meanings in contemporary sisterhood? Are we really desperate? There will be an equal emphasis on Theory, Practice and Campaigning. Workshops: Women's Identities; Images of Ourselves and Each Other; The Politics of Thinking/Doing Research; Relationships; Women and Technologies; plus an Open Stream. Information: Millsom Henry, Dept. of Applied Social Science, University of Stirling, Stirling FK9 4LA, Scotland. Tel: 01786 467703. E-mail: ctisoc@stirling.ac.uk.

Calls for papers

Feminism and the Aesthetics of Difference

There will be a one-day conference in September 1995 organized by The Institute of Romance Studies and Falmouth College of Arts. Papers on any aspect are invited, the following broad categories are offered as general indicators, but contributions that deal with the intersections of race (including whiteness) and gender are particularly welcome. Binarism, Reaction and Containment; Race, Gender and Diversity; Aesthetic Experience and the Social; Women, Aesthetics and Money; Identification, (Self) Definition and Reading/Interpretation/Looking; Dress, the Body and Surface-Depth; Contextual Approaches to Aesthetics; Methodologies. Organizer: Dr Penny Florence, Reader in Cultural Theory and Feminism, Falmouth College of Arts, Falmouth, Cornwall TR11 4RA, England. Tel: 0326 211077. Fax: 0326 211205.

Praxis ♀ Nexus Feminist Methodology, Theory, Community

The conference will be held at the University of Victoria, BC, Canada, 18–20 January 1996. The deadline for proposals for papers is 25 August 1995.

FEMINIST REVIEW NO 50, SUMMER 1995

Suggested topics: Being in the community as a scholar/Being in the academy as an activist; Successful projects/Failed attempts; Theoretical implications of a changing feminist praxis; Methodological frontiers and cautions; Solidarity in praxis/Divisions in practice; Legitimation of subjugated knowledges; Research design; Epistemological advances and the implications for praxis. Contact: Pamela Moss, Dept. of Geography, University of Victoria, PO Box 3050, BC, Canada V8N 3P5. Tel: 604 721 7347. Fax: 604 721 6216. E-mail: moss@uvic.uvvm.ca.

Middle Eastern Exiled, Refugee and Immigrant Women

Call for submissions of writings by and about exiled, refugee and immigrant women from the Middle East and different diasporic locations for inclusion in an anthology. The purpose of the collection is to create an alternative discursive site where an understanding of Middle Eastern immigrant women's experience of racism, sexism and multiple forms of political exclusionary practices can emerge. Abstracts by 30 June 1995 to the editors: Parvin Abyaneh, Assistant Professor, Ethnic and Women's Studies, 3801 West Temple Ave., California Polytechnic State University, Pamona, Ca 91768, USA. E-mail Pabyaneh@CSUPomona.Edu and Minoo Moallem, Beatrice M. Bain Research Group, Univ. of California, Berkeley, 2539 Channing Way, Room 21, Berkeley, Ca 94720-2050, USA. Fax: 510 643 7288.

Announcements

NGO Forum 95 Fourth World Conference on Women

Women's International League for Peace and Freedom are organizing a Peace Train from Helsinki to Beijing to the Conference. On the journey there will be stops to visit women's projects, historical and cultural sights and to meet with local politicians. Dates: 7–29 August 1995. Contact: WILPF, 1 rue de Varembé, 1211 Geneva 20, Switzerland. Fax: 41 22 740 10 63.

Women Working Worldwide

Women Working Worldwide have started to compile an ongoing catalogue of periodicals and books published by women's organizations and activists in the South. Their aim is to give worldwide publicity to existing publications and to encourage direct sales or exchanges. If you have a publication you wish to be included, or you would like a copy of the catalogue, contact: WWW, c/o LVSRC, 356 Holloway Road, London N7 6PA, England. Fax: c/o 44 181 691 1969. E-mail: g.reardon@geo2. poptel.org.uk.

Older Feminists Network

OFN aim to counter negative stereotypes of older women in society and to provide a framework for mutual support and contacts. They publish a bi-monthly newsletter and meet on the second Saturday of each month from 11.30 a.m. to 5 p.m. at Millman Street Community Centre, 34–36 Alleyway, London WC1. Information: OFN, c/o 54 Gordon Road, London N3 1EP, England.

Glasgow Women's Library

The Library moved to city centre premises in 1994 and provides a unique resource for women in Scotland. The library can be used for reference or for lending (to members) and also acts as a social space for women and as an information centre. Glasgow Women's Library, 109 Trongate, Glasgow G1 5HD. Tel: 0141 552 8345.

Gays and Lesbians in Academe: an ethnographic study seeks respondents

Toni A.H. McNaron, Professor of English and Women's Studies at the University of Minnesota, seeks gay and lesbian faculty to participate in an ethnographic study of American universities and colleges in relation to the lesbian and gay people who work in them. This study will interweave personal narratives of lesbian and gay faculty with quantitative data and theoretical analyses of historical and cultural contexts for lesbian and gay issues in higher education. One goal is to delineate the complexities of individual actions and consciousness within socially and historically defined circumstances.

Respondents should be academic professionals who have worked in colleges and universities for at least fifteen years. Closeted gay and lesbian faculty are especially encouraged to participate. Anonymity will be strictly maintained.

For more information or to request a questionnaire, write to Toni A.H. McNaron, Department of English, University of Minnesota, 207 Church St. SE, Minneapolis, MN 55455. E-mail: mcnar001@maroon.tc.umn.edu.

FEMINIST REVIEW NO 50, SUMMER 1995

1 Women and Revolution in South Yemen, **Molyneux**. Feminist Art Practice, **Davis & Goodal**. Equal Pay and Sex Discrimination, **Snell**. Female Sexuality in Fascist Ideology, *Macciocchi*. Charlotte Brontë's *Shirley*, **Taylor**. Christine Delphy, **Barrett & McIntosh**. OUT OF PRINT.

2 Summer Reading, **O'Rourke**. Disaggregation, **Campaign for Legal & Financial Independence** and **Rights of Women**. The Hayward Annual 1978, **Pollock**. Women and the Cuban Revolution, **Murray**. Matriarchy Study Group Papers, **Lee**. Nurseries in the Second World War, **Riley**.

3 English as a Second Language, **Naish**. Women as a Reserve Army of Labour, **Bruegel**. Chantal Akerman's films, **Martin**. Femininity in the 1950s, **Birmingham Feminist History Group**. On Patriarchy, **Beechway**. Board School Reading Books, **Davin**.

4 Protective Legislation, **Coyle**. Legislation in Israel, **Yuval-Davis**. On 'Beyond the Fragments', **Wilson**. Queen Elizabeth I, **Heisch**. Abortion Politics: a dossier. Materialist Feminism, **Delphy**.

5 Feminist Sexual Politics, **Campbell**. Iranian Women, **Tabari**. Women and Power, **Stacey & Price**. Women's Novels, **Coward**. Abortion, **Himmelweit**. Gender and Education, **Nava**. Sybillaa Aleramo, **Caesar**. On 'Beyond the Fragments', **Margolis**.

6 'The Tidy House', **Steedman**. Writings on Housework, **Kaluzynska**. The Family Wage, **Land**. Sex and Skill, **Phillips & Taylor**. Fresh Horizons, **Lovell**. Cartoons, **Hay**.

7 Protective Legislation, **Humphries**. Feminists Must Face the Future, **Coultas**. Abortion in Italy, **Caldwell**. Women's Trade Union Conferences, **Breitenbach**. Women's Employment in the Third World, **Elson & Pearson**

8 Socialist Societies Old and New, **Molyneux**. Feminism and the Italian Trade Unions, **Froggett & Torchi**. Feminist Approach to Housing in Britain, **Austerberry & Watson**. Psychoanalysis, **Wilson**. Women in the Soviety Union, **Buckley**. The Struggle within the Struggle, **Kimble**.

9 Position of Women in Family Law, **Brophy & Smart**. Slags or Drags, **Cowie & Lees**. The Ripper and Male Sexuality, **Hollway**. The Material of Male Power, **Cockburn**. Freud's *Dora*, **Moi**. Women in an Iranian Village, **Afshar**. New Office Technology and Women, **Morgall**.

10 Towards a Wages Strategy for Women, **Weir & McIntosh**. Irish Suffrage Movement, **Ward**. A Girls' Project and Some Responses to Lesbianism, **Nava**. The Case for Women's Studies, **Evans**. Equal Pay and Sex Discrimination, **Gregory**. Psychoanalysis and Personal Politics, **Sayers**.

11 **Sexuality issue**
Sexual Violence and Sexuality, **Coward**. Interview with Andrea Dworkin, **Wilson**. The Dyke, the Feminist and the Devil, **Clark**. Talking Sex, **English, Hollibaugh & Rubin**. Jealousy and Sexual Difference, **Moi**. Ideological Politics 1969–72, **O'Sullivan**. Womanslaughter in the Criminal Law, **Radford**. OUT OF PRINT.

12 ANC Women's Struggles, **Kimble & Unterhalter**. Women's Strike in Holland 1981, **de Bruijn & Henkes**. Politics of Feminist Research, **McRobbie**. Khomeini's Teachings on Women, **Afshar**. Women in the Labour Party 1906–1920, **Rowan**. Documents from the Indian Women's Movement, **Gothoskar & Patel**.

13 Feminist Perspectives on Sport, **Graydon**. Patriarchal Criticism and Henry James, **Kappeler**. The Barnard Conference on Sexuality, **Wilson**. Danger and Pleasure in Nineteenth Century Feminist Sexual Thought, **Gordon & Du Bois**. Anti-Porn: Soft Issue, Hard World, **Rich**. Feminist Identity and Poetic Tradition, **Montefiore**.

14 Femininity and its Discontents, **Rose**. Inside and Outside Marriage, **Gittins**. The Pro-family Left in the United States, **Epstein & Ellis**. Women's Language and Literature, **McCluskie**. The Inevitability of Theory, **Fildes**. The 150 Hours in Italy, **Caldwell**. Teaching Film, **Clayton**.

15 Women's Employment, **Beechey**. Women and Trade Unions, **Charles**. Lesbianism and Women's Studies, **Adamson**. Teaching Women's Studies at Secondary School, **Kirton**. Gender, Ethnic and Class Divisions, **Anthias & Yuval-Davis**. Women Studying or Studying Women, **Kelly & Pearson**. Girls, Jobs and Glamour, **Sherratt**. Contradictions in Teaching Women's Studies, **Phillips & Hurstfield**.

16 Romance Fiction, Female Sexuality and Class, **Light**. The White Brothel, **Kappeler**. Sadomasochism and Feminism, **France**. Trade Unions and Socialist Feminism, **Cockburn**. Women's Movement and the Labour Party, **Interview with Labour Party Feminists**. Feminism and 'The Family', **Caldwell**.

17 Many voices, one chant: black feminist perspectives

Challenging Imperial feminism, **Amos & Parmar**. Black Women, the Economic Crisis and the British State, **Mama**. Asian Women in the Making of History, **Trivedi**. Black Lesbian Discussions, **Carmen, Gail, Shaila & Pratibha**. Poetry. Black women Organizing Autonomously: a collection.

18 Cultural politics

Writing with Women. A Metaphorical Journey, **Lomax**. Karen Alexander: Video Worker, **Nava**. Poetry by **Riley, Whiteson** and **Davies**. Women's Films, **Montgomery**. 'Correct Distance' a photo-text, **Tabrizian**. Julia Kristeva on Femininity, **Jones**. Feminism and the Theatre, **Wandor**. Alexis Hunter, **Osborne**. Format Photographers, Dear Linda, **Kuhn**.

19

The Female Nude in the work of Suzanne Valadon, **Betterton**. Refuges for Battered Women, **Pahl**. This is the Feminist Issue, **Diamond**. New Portraits for Old, **Martin & Spence**.

20

Prisonhouses, **Steedman**. Ethocentrism and Socialist Feminism, **Barrett & McIntosh**. What Do Women Want? **Rowbotham**. Women's Equality and the European Community, **Hoskyns**. Feminism and the Popular Novel of the 1890s, **Clarke**.

21

Going Private: The Implications of Privatization for Women's Work, **Coyle**. A Girl Needs to Get Street-wise: Magazines for the 1980s, **Winship**. Family Reform in Socialist States: The Hidden Agenda, **Molyneux**. Sexual Segregation in the Pottery Industry, **Sarsby**.

22

Interior Portraits: Women, Physiology and the Male Artist, **Pointon**. The Control of Women's Labour: The Case of Homeworking, **Allen & Wolkowitz**. Homeworking: Time for Change, **Cockpit Gallery & Londonwide Homeworking Group**. Feminism and Ideology: The Terms of Women's Stereotypes, **Seiter**. Feedback: Feminism and Racism, **Ramazanoglu, Kazi, Lees, Safia Mirza**.

23 Socialist-feminism: out of the blue

Feminism and Class Politics: A Round-Table Discussion, **Barrett, Campbell, Philips, Weir & Wilson**. Upsetting an Applecart: Difference, Desire and Lesbian Sadomasochism, **Ardill & O'Sullivan**. Armagh and Feminist Strategy, **Loughran**. Transforming Socialist-Feminism: The Challenge of Racism, **Bhavnani & Coulson**. Socialist-Feminists and Greenham, **Finch & Hackney Greenham Groups**. Socialist-Feminism and the Labour Party: Some Experiences from Leeds, **Perrigo**. Some Political Implications of Women's Involvement in the Miners' Strike 1984–85, **Rowbotham & McCrindle**. Sisterhood: Political Solidarity Between Women, **Hooks**. European Forum of Socialist-Feminists, **Lees & McIntosh**. Report from Nairobi, **Hendessi**.

24 Women Workers in New Industries in Britain, **Glucksmann**. The Relationship of Women to Pornography, **Bower**. The Sex Discrimination Act 1975, **Atkins**. The Star Persona of Katharine Hepburn, **Thumim**.

25 Difference: A Special Third World Women Issue, **Minh-ha**. Melanie Klein, Psychoanalysis and Feminism, **Sayers**. Rethinking Feminist Attitudes Towards Mothering, **Gieve**. EEOC v. Sears, Roebuck and Company: A Personal Account, **Kessler-Harris**. Poems, **Wood**. Academic Feminism and the Process of De-radicalization, **Currie & Kazi**. A Lover's Distance: A Photoessay, **Boffin**.

26 Resisting Amnesia: Feminism, Painting and Post-Modernism, **Lee**. The Concept of Difference, **Barrett**. The Weary Sons of Freud, **Clément**. Short Story, **Cole**. Taking the Lid Off: Socialist Feminism in Oxford, **Collette**. For and Against the European Left: Socialist Feminists Get Organized, **Benn**. Women and the State: A Conference of Feminist Activists, **Weir**.

27 **Women, feminism and the third term:** Women and Income Maintenance, **Lister**. Women in the Public Sector, **Phillips**. Can Feminism Survive a Third Term?, **Loach**. Sex in Schools, **Wolpe**. Carers and the Careless, **Doyal**. Interview with Diane Abbott, **Segal**. The Problem With No Name: Re-reading Friedan, **Bowlby**. Second Thoughts on the Second Wave, **Rosenfelt & Stacey**. Nazi Feminists?, **Gordon**.

28 **Family secrets: child sexual abuse:** Introduction to an Issue: Family Secrets as Public Drama, **McIntosh**. Challenging the Orthodoxy: Towards a Feminist Theory and Practice, **MacLeod & Saraga**. The Politics of Child Sexual Abuse: Notes from American History, **Gordon**. What's in a Name?: Defining Child Sexual Abuse, **Kelly**. A Case, **Anon**. Defending Innocence: Ideologies of Childhood, **Kitzinger**. Feminism and the Seductiveness of the 'Real Event', **Scott**. Cleveland and the Press: Outrage and Anxiety in the Reporting of Child Sexual Abuse, **Nava**. Child Sexual Abuse and the Law, **Woodcraft**. Poem, **Betcher**. Brixton Black Women's Centre: Organizing on Child Sexual Abuse, **Bogle**. Bridging the Gap: Glasgow Women's Support Project, **Bell & MacLeod**. Claiming Our Status as Experts: Community Organizing, **Norwich Consultants on Sexual Violence**. Islington Social Services: Developing a Policy on Child Sexual Abuse, **Boushel & Noakes**. Developing a Feminist School Policy on Child Sexual Abuse, **O'Hara**. 'Putting Ideas into their Heads': Advising the Young, **Mills**. Child Sexual Abuse Crisis Lines: Advice for Our British Readers.

29 **Abortion: the international agenda:** Whatever Happened to 'A Woman's Right to Choose'?, **Berer**. More than 'A Woman's Right to Choose'?, **Himmelweit**. Abortion in the Republic of Ireland, **Barry**. Across the Water, **Irish Women's Abortion Support Group**. Spanish Women and the Alton Bill, **Spanish Women's Abortion Support Group**. The Politics of Abortion in Australia: Freedom, Church and State, **Coleman**. Abortion in Hungary, **Szalai**. Women and Population Control in China: Issues of Sexuality, Power and Control, **Hillier**. The Politics of Abortion in Nicaragua: Revolutionary Pragmatism – or Feminism in the realm of necessity?, **Molyneux**. Who Will Sing for Theresa?, **Bernstein**. She's Gotta Have It: The Representation of Black Female Sexuality on Film, **Simmonds**. Poems, **Gallagher**. Dyketactics for Difficult Times: A Review of the 'Homosexuality, Which Homosexuality?' Conference, **Franklin & Stacey**.

30 **Capital, gender and skill:** Women Homeworkers in Rural Spain, **Lever**. Fact and Fiction: George Egerton and Nellie Shaw, **Butler**. Feminist Political Organization in Iceland: Some Reflections on the Experience of Kwenna Frambothid, **Dominelli & Jonsdottir**. Under Western Eyes: Feminist Scholarship and Colonial Discourses, **Talpade Mohanty**. Bedroom Horror: The Fatal Attraction of *Intercourse,* **Merck**. AIDS: Lessons from the Gay Community, **Patton**. Poems, **Agbabi**.

31 **The past before us: 20 years of feminism:** Slow Change or No Change?: Feminism, Socialism and the Problem of Men, **Segal**. There's No Place Like Home: On the Place of Identity in Feminist Politics, **Adams**. New Alliances: Socialist-Feminism in the Eighties, **Harriss**. Other Kinds of Dreams, **Parmar**. Complexity, Activism, Optimism: Interview with **Angela Y. Davis**. To Be or Not To Be: The Dilemmas of Mothering, **Rowbotham**. Seizing Time and Making New: Feminist Criticism, Politics and Contemporary Feminist Fiction, **Lauret**. Lessons from the Women's Movement in Europe, **Haug**. Women in Management, **Coyle**. Sex in the Summer of '88, **Ardill & O'Sullivan**. Younger Women and Feminism, **Hobsbawm & Macpherson**. Older Women and Feminism, **Stacey; Curtis; Summerskill**.

32 'Those Who Die for Life Cannot Be Called Dead': Women and Human Rights Protest in Latin America, **Schirmer**. Violence Against Black Women: Gender, Race and State Responses, **Mama**. Sex and Race in the Labour Market, **Breugel**. The 'Dark Continent': Africa as Female Body in Haggard's Adventure Fiction, **Stott**. Gender, Class and the Welfare State: the Case of Income Security in Australia, **Shaver**. Ethnic Feminism: Beyond the Pseudo-Pluralists, **Gorelick**.

33 Restructuring the Woman Question: *Perestroika* and Prostitution, **Waters**. Contemporary Indian Feminism, **Kumar**. 'A Bit On the Side'?: Gender Struggles in South Africa, **Beall, Hassim and Todes**. 'Young Bess': Historical Novels and Growing Up, **Light**. Madeline Pelletier (1874–1939): The Politics of Sexual Oppression, **Mitchell**.

34 **Perverse politics: lesbian issues**
Pat Parker: A tribute, **Brimstone**. International Lesbianism: Letter from São Paulo, **Rodrigues**; Israel, **Pittsburgh**, Italy, **Fiocchetto**. The De-eroticization of Women's Liberation: Social Purity Movements and the Revolutionary Feminism of Sheila Jeffreys, **Hunt**. Talking About It: Homophobia in the Black Community, **Gomez & Smith**. Lesbianism and the Labour Party, **Tobin**. Skirting the Issue: Lesbian fashion for the 1990s, **Blackman & Perry**. Butch/Femme Obsessions, **Ardill & O'Sullivan**. Archives: The Will to Remember, **Nestle**; International Archives, **Read**. Audre Lorde: Vignettes and Mental Conversations, **Lewis**. Lesbian Tradition, **Field**. Mapping: Lesbians, AIDS and Sexuality: An interview with Cindy Patton,

O'Sullivan. Significant Others: Lesbians and Psychoanalytic Theory, **Hamer.** The Pleasure Threshold: Looking at Lesbian Pornography on Film, **Smyth.** Cartoon, **Charlesworth.** Voyages of the Valkyries: Recent Lesbian Pornographic Writing, **Dunn.**

35 Campaign Against Pornography, **Norden.** The Mothers' Manifesto and Disputes over 'Mutterlichkeit', **Chamberlayne.** Multiple Mediations: Feminist Scholarship in the Age of Multi-National Reception, **Mani.** Cagney and Lacey Revisited, **Alcock & Robson.** Cutting a Dash: The Dress of Radclyffe Hall and Una Troubridge, **Rolley.** Deviant Dress, **Wilson.** The House that Jill Built: Lesbian Feminist Organizing in Toronto, 1976–1980, **Ross.** Women in Professional Engineering: the Interaction of Gendered Structures and Values, **Carter & Kirkup.** Identity Politics and the Hierarchy of Oppression, **Briskin.** Poetry: **Bufkin, Zumwalt.**

36 'The Trouble Is It's Ahistorical': The Problem of the Unconscious in Modern Feminist Theory, **Minsky.** Feminism and Pornography, **Ellis, O'Dair Tallmer.** Who Watches the Watchwomen? Feminists Against Censorship, **Rodgerson & Semple.** Pornography and Violence: What the 'Experts' Really Say, **Segal.** The Woman In My Life: Photography of Women, **Nava.** Splintered Sisterhood: Anti-racism in a Young Women's Project, **Connolly.** Woman, Native, Other, **Parmar** interviews **Trinh T. Minh-ha.** Out But Not Down: Lesbians' Experience of Housing, **Edgerton.** Poems: **Evans Davies, Toth, Weinbaum.** Oxford Twenty Years On: Where Are We Now?, **Gamman & O'Neill.** The Embodiment of Ugliness and the Logic of Love: The Danish Redstockings Movement, **Walter.**

37 Theme issue: Women, religion and dissent
Black Women, Sexism and Racism: Black or Antiracist Feminism?, **Tang Nain.** Nursing Histories: Reviving Life in Abandoned Selves, **McMahon.** The Quest for National Identity: Women, Islam and the State of Bangladesh, **Kabeer.** Born Again Moon: Fundamentalism in Christianity and the Feminist Spirituality Movement, **McCrickard.** Washing our Linen: One Year of Women Against Fundamentalism, **Connolly. Siddiqui** on *Letter to Christendom*, **Bard** on *Generations of Memories*, **Patel** on *Women Living Under Muslim Laws Dossiers 1–6*, Poem, **Kay.** More Cagney and Lacey, **Gamman.**

38 The Modernist Style of Susan Sontag, **McRobbie.** Tantalizing Glimpses of Stolen Glances: Lesbians Take Photographs, **Fraser and Boffin.** Reflections on the Women's Movement in Trinidad, **Mohammed.** Fashion, Representation and Femininity, **Evans & Thornton.** The European Women's Lobby, **Hoskyns. Hendessi** on *Law of Desire: Temporary Marriage in Iran*, **Kaveney** on *Mercy*.

39 Shifting territories: feminism & Europe
Between Hope and Helplessness: Women in the GDR, **Dolling.** Where Have All the Women Gone? Women and the Women's Movement in East Central Europe, **Einborn.** The End of Socialism in Europe – A New Challenge For Socialist Feminism?, **Haug.** The Second 'No': Women in Hungary, **Kiss.** The Citizenship Debate: Women, the State and Ethnic Processes, **Yuval-Davis.** Fortress Europe and

Migrant Women, **Morokvasíc**. Racial Equality and 1992, **Dummett**. Questioning *Perestroika*: A Socialist Feminist Interrogation, **Pearson**. Postmodernism and its Discontents, **Soper**. Feminists and Socialism: After the Cold War, **Kaldor**. Socialism Out of the Common Pots, **Mitter**. 1989 and All That, **Campbell**. In Listening Mode, **Cockburn**. **Women in Action: Country by Country:** The Soviet Union; Yugoslavia; Czechoslovakia; Hungary; Poland. **Reports:** International Gay and Lesbian Association: Black Women and Europe 1992.

40 Fleurs du Mal or Second-Hand Roses?: Nathalie Barney, Romaine Brooks, and the 'Originality of the Avant-Garde', **Elliott & Wallace**. Poem, **Tyler-Bennett**. Feminism and Motherhood: An American 'Reading', **Snitow**. Qualitative Research, Appropriation of the 'Other' and Empowerment, **Opie**. Disabled Women and the Feminist Agenda, **Begum**. Postcard From the Edge: Thoughts on the 'Feminist Theory: An International Debate' Conference at Glasgow University, July 1991, **Radstone**. Review Essay, **Munt**.

41 Editorial. The Selling of HRT: Playing on the Fear Factor, **Worcester & Whatley**. The Cancer Drawings of Catherine Arthur, **Sebastyen**. Ten years of Women's Health 1982–92, **James**. AIDS Activism: Women and AIDS activism in Victoria, Australia, **Mitchell**. A Woman's Subject, **Friedli**. HIV and the Invisibility of Women: Is there a Need to Redefine AIDS?, **Scharf & Toole**. Lesbians Evolving Health Care: Cancer and AIDS, **Winnow**. Now is the Time for Feminist Criticism: A Review of *Asinimali!*, **Steinberg**. Ibu or the Beast?: Gender Interests in Two Indonesian Women's Organizations, **Wieringa**. Reports on Motherlands: Symposium on African, Carribean and Asian Women's Writing, **Smart**. The European Forum of Socialist Feminists, **Bruegel**. Review Essay, **Gamman**.

42 **Feminist fictions:** Editorial. Angela Carter's *The Bloody Chamber* and the Decolonization of Feminine Sexuality, **Makinen**. Feminist Writing: Working with Women's Experience, **Haug**. Three Aspects of Sex in Marge Piercy's *Fly Away Home*, **Hauser**. Are They Reading Us? Feminist Teenage Fiction, **Bard**. Sexuality in Lesbian Romance Fiction, **Hermes**. A Psychoanalytic Account for Lesbianism, **Castendyk**. Mary Wollstonecraft and the Problematic of Slavery, **Ferguson**. Reviews.

43 **Issues for feminism:** Family, Motherhood and Zulu Nationalism: The Politics of the Inkatha Women's Brigade, **Hassim**. Postcolonial Feminism and the Veil: Thinking the Difference, **Abu Odeh**. Feminism, the Menopause and Hormone Replacement Therapy, **Lewis**. Feminism and Disability, **Morris**. 'What is Pornography?': An Analysis of the Policy Statement of the Campaign Against Pornography and Censorship, **Smith**. Reviews.

44 **Nationalisms and national identities:** Women, Nationalism and islam in Contemporary Political Discourse in Iran, **Yeganeh**. Feminism, Citizenship and National Identity, **Curthoys**. Remapping and Renaming: New Cartographies of Identity, Gender and Landscape in Ireland, **Nash**. Rap Poem: Easter 1991, **Medbh**. Family Feuds: Gender, Nationalism and the Family, **McClintock**. Women as Activists; Women as Symbols: A Study of the Indian Nationalist Movement, **Thapar**.

Gender, Nationalisms and National Identities: Bellagio Symposium Report, **Hall**. Culture or Citizenship? Notes from the Gender and Colonialism Conference, Galway, Ireland, May 1992, **Connolly**. Reviews.

45 Thinking through ethnicities

Audre Lorde: Reflections. Re-framing Europe: Engendered Racisms, Ethnicities and Nationalisms in Contemporary Western Europe, **Brah**. Towards a Multicultural Europe? 'Race' Nation and Identity in 1992 and Beyond, **Bhavnani**. Another View: Photo Essay, **Pollard**. Growing Up White: Feminism, Racism and the Social Geography of Childhood, **Frankenberg**. Poem, **Kay**. Looking Beyond the Violent Break-up of Yugoslavia, **Coulson**. Personal Reactions of a Bosnian Woman to the War in Bosnia, **Harper**. Serbian Nationalism: Nationalism of My Own People, **Korac**. Belgrade Feminists 1992: Separation, Guilt and Identity Crisis, **Mladjenovic**. Litricin. Report on a Council of Europe Minority Youth Committee Seminar on Sexism and Racism in Western Europe, **Walker**. Reviews.

46 Sexualities: challenge and change

Chips, Coke and Rock-'n-Roll: Children's Mediation of an Invitation to a First Dance Party, **Rossiter**. Power and Desire: The Embodiment of Female Sexuality, **Holland, Ramazanoglu, Sharpe, Thomson**. Two Poems, **Janzen**. A Girton Girl on the Throne: Queen Christina and Versions of Lesbianism 1906–1933. Changing Interpretations of the Sexuality of Queen Christina of Sweden, **Waters**. The Pervert's Progress: An Analysis of 'The Story of O' and The Beauty Trilogy, **Ziv**. Dis-Graceful Images: Della Grace and Lesbian Sadomasochism, **Lewis**. Reviews.

47

Virgin Territories and Motherlands: Colonial and Nationalist Representations of Africa, **Innes**. The Impact of the Islamic Movement in Egypt, **Shukrallah**. Mothering on the Lam: Politics, Gender Fantasies and Maternal Thinking in Women Associated with Armed, Clandestine Organizations in the US, **Zwerman**. Treading the Traces of Discarded History: Photo-Essay, **Marchant**. The Feminist Production of Knowledge: Is Deconstruction a Practice for Women?, **Nash**. 'Divided We Stand': Sex, Gender and Sexual Difference, **Moore**. Reviews.

48 Sex and the state

Editorial. Not Just (Any) *Body* Can be a Citizen: The Politics of Law, Sexuality and Postcoloniality in Trinidad and Tobago and the Bahamas, **Alexander**. State, Family and Personal Responsibility: The Changing Balance for Lone Mothers in the United Kingdom, **Millar**. Moral Rhetoric and Public Health Pragmatism: The Recent Politics of Sex Education, **Thomson**. Through the Parliamentary Looking Glass: 'Real' and 'Pretend' Families in Contemporary British Politics, **Reinhold**. In Search of Gender Justice: Sexual Assault and the Criminal Justice System, **Gregory and Lees**. God's Bullies: Attacks on Abortion, **Hadley**. Sex Work, HIV and the State: an Interview with Nel Druce, **Overs**. Reviews.

49 Feminist politics – Colonial/postcolonial worlds

Women on the March: Right-Wing Mobilization in Contemporary India, **Mazumdar**. Colonial Encounters in Late-Victorian England: Pandita Ramabai at

Cheltenham and Wantage, **Burton**. Subversive Intent: A Social Theory of Gender, **Maharaj**. My Discourse/My Self: Therapy as Possibility (for women who eat compulsively), **Hopwood**. Poems, **Donohue**. Review Essays. Reviews.

Feminist Review was founded in 1979. Since that time it has established itself as one of the UK's leading feminist journals.

● Why not subscribe?
Make sure of your copy

All subscriptions run in calendar years. The issues for 1995 are Nos. 49, 50 and 51. You will save over £5 pa on the single copy price.

● Subscription rates, 1995 (3 issues)

Individual Subscriptions

UK/EEC	£24
Overseas	£30
North America	$42

A number of reduced cost (£15.50 per year: UK only) subscriptions are available for readers experiencing financial hardship, e.g. unemployed, student, low-paid. If you'd like to be considered for a reduced subscription, please write to the Collective, c/o the Feminist Review office, 52 Featherstone Street, London EC1Y 8RT.

Institutional Subscriptions		Single Issues	
UK	£68	UK	£8.99
Overseas	£74	North America	$12.95
North America	$110		

☐ Please send me one year's subscription to **Feminist Review**

☐ Please send me _____ copies of back issue no. _____

METHOD OF PAYMENT

☐ I enclose a cheque/international money order to the value of _____
made payable to Routledge Journals

☐ Please charge my Access/Visa/American Express/Diners Club account

Account no. ☐☐☐☐☐☐☐☐☐☐☐☐☐☐☐☐

Expiry date _____ Signature _____

If the address below is different from the registered address of your credit card, please give your registered address separately.

PLEASE USE BLOCK CAPITALS

Name _____

Address_____

_____

_____ Postcode _____

☐ Please send me a Routledge Journals Catalogue

☐ Please send me a Routledge Gender and Women's Studies Catalogue

Please return this form with payment to:

Routledge Subscriptions Department, Cheriton House, North Way, Andover, Hants SP10 5BE

Marina Tsvetaeva
The Double Beat of Heaven
and Hell
Lily Feiler

"Lily Feiler's startling insights into
Tsvetaeva's life and poetry are enriched
by her reading of Alice Miller, Lacan
and Winnicott. . . it is the great
strength of this remarkable and
scholarly biography to show how
Tsvetaeva's "poetry of proper names"
. . . rises above the limits of ordinary
life and love to widen our experience
of both."—Cathy Porter,
Independent on Sunday
392 pp, 15 b&w photos, £32.95 hb

The First Woman in the Republic
A Cultural Biography of
Lydia Maria Child
Carolyn L. Karcher

"This is a magnificent book. Child's
character emerges as a model for what
a woman can be . . . With Child in the
foreground, the American nineteenth
century stands revealed anew—in all
its idealism, violence, ugliness, and
splendor. Truly, a work of great
love."—Jane Tompkins, author of
West of Everything 928 pp, 10 b&w
photographs, large format, £35.95 hb

Representing Women
Law, Literature, and Feminism
**Susan Sage Heinzelman and
Zipporah Batshaw Wiseman,
editors**

Beginning with an exploration of the
ways in which women are represented
—how they either tell or have their
stories told in literature, in the law, in
a courtroom—this collection
demonstrates the interrelatedness of
the legal and the literary.
416 pp, 16 illus., £18.95 pb

Fat Art, Thin Art
Eve Kosofsky Sedgwick

Eve Kosofsky Sedgwick's first volume
of poetry opens up another dimension
of her continuing project of crossing
and recrossing the electrified
boundaries between theory, lyric,
and narrative. 184 pp, £14.95 pb

Materialist Feminism
**Toril Moi and Janice Radway,
editors**

Along with the lively "conversation"
between Juliet Mitchell and Toril Moi,
the essays gathered here remind us that
the debate—among feminists themselves
—is as feisty as ever.
A Special Issue of SAQ
200 pp, £9.50 pb

Negotiating Performance
Gender, Sexuality, and Theatricality
in Latin/o America
**Diana Taylor and
Juan Villegas, editors**

By redefining performance to include
such events as Mayan and AIDS
theatre, the Mothers of the Plaza de
Mayo, and Argentine drag culture, this
energentic volume discusses the
dynamics of Latino/a identity politics
and the sometimes discordant
intersections of gender, sexuality, and
nationalism. 400 pp, 36 b&w photos,
£17.95 pb, £52.50 hb

Half Sisters of History
Southern Women and the
American Past
Catherine Clinton, editor

A comprehensive and much-needed
tribute to southern women's history,
this book brings together the most
important work in this field over the
past twenty years. 256 pp, £14.95 pb

DUKE UNIVERSITY PRESS, AUPG, 1 Gower St., London WC1E 6HA